Hacking
BlackBerry®

Hacking
BlackBerry®

Glenn Bachmann

Wiley Publishing, Inc.

Hacking BlackBerry®

Published by
Wiley Publishing, Inc.
10475 Crosspoint Boulevard
Indianapolis, IN 46256
www.wiley.com

Copyright © 2007 by Wiley Publishing, Inc., Indianapolis, Indiana

Published simultaneously in Canada

ISBN-13: 978-0-471-79304-5
ISBN-10: 0-471-79304-3

Manufactured in the United States of America

10 9 8 7 6 5 4 3 2 1

for Nick, Julianne, and Courtney

About the Author

Glenn Bachmann is president and founder of Bachmann Software, a privately held company that has grown to become a leading provider of mobile and wireless software products and services. Founded in 1994, Bachmann Software (www.bachmannsoftware.com) develops and markets PrintBoy, a wireless printing solution for Palm OS, Windows Mobile, BlackBerry, and Symbian handhelds and smartphones, and FilePoint, a solution providing remote wireless access to documents and other files on desktop computers and networks.

Mr. Bachmann also runs Bachmann Handheld Solutions, a division of Bachmann Software dedicated to providing enterprise, startup, and mobile software companies and other clients with a team of expert software developers to help design, program, and complete critical mobile computing projects. Bachmann Handheld Solutions can be found on the Web at www.bachmannhandheldsolutions.com.

In addition to heading Bachmann Software, Mr. Bachmann is the noted author of a number of books on programming for handheld devices, including *Palm OS Programming* and *Professional Palm OS Programming*.

Credits

Executive Editor
Chris Webb

Development Editor
Kelly Talbot

Technical Editors
Craig Johnston
Edward Lineberry

Copy Editor
Nancy Rapoport

Editorial Manager
Mary Beth Wakefield

Production Manager
Tim Tate

**Vice President and
Executive Group Publisher**
Richard Swadley

Vice President and Executive Publisher
Joseph B. Wikert

Compositor
Kate Kaminski,
Happenstance Type-O-Rama

Proofreader
Jen Larsen, Word One

Indexer
Melanie Belkin

Anniversary Logo Design
Richard Pacifico

Cover Design
Anthony Bunyan

Contents at a Glance

Contents

Part I: Customizing the BlackBerry with Tweaks, Secret Codes, Hidden Keys, and Add-On Applications

Chapter 10: Beyond BrickBreaker: Fun, Games, and Entertainment . . . 147

Part II: Advanced BlackBerry Hacks: Put Your BlackBerry to Fun and Wacky Uses with Creative Software Projects

Chapter 11: Developing Your Own BlackBerry Applications 169

Acknowledgments

"Impossible is really just someone's opinion."

Somewhere in the middle of writing this book, I was attending a pre-race dinner for the San Diego Rock and Roll Marathon and was fortunate to hear this quote, which has been stuck in my mind ever since. The idea of having enough commitment, dedication, stubbornness, and desire to make the seemingly impossible happen is a fascinating one to me. At my company, Bachmann Software, our engineers are challenged regularly to create software products that perform magical tasks on the tiniest handheld computers. Indeed, the BlackBerry phenomenon, and the wireless industry overall, is now providing the world with instant access to people, data, and information, anytime, anywhere — a capability that not very many years ago surely must have sounded like science fiction. I must thank all of those who through their efforts make the wireless world the ever-changing, fast-moving, and innovating industry that makes me look forward to coming to work every day.

On a more personal level, in the past year I've been privileged to work with an organization known as Team In Training, part of the Leukemia and Lymphoma Society (www.teamintraining.org). This wonderful organization is dedicated to helping fight leukemia and other cancers. I've come to know the stories of the courageous individuals who fight the ultimate battle, one in which they are fighting for their very lives. I've also come to know many of the most giving people I have ever met. These children, men, and women challenge the notion of the word "impossible" with every single passing day and are a daily inspiration to me. Thank you!

Finally, the very fact that you are reading this book places you firmly in the camp of those who have insatiable curiosity, who are driven to push the envelope, who pick up a product and inevitably find themselves itching to find more ways to do more things with it than what is listed in the owner's manual. I love to see this kind of spirit, and it is for you that I wrote this book.

So, to all of you who continually prove that "impossible is really just someone's opinion": I thank you.

I'd also like to extend heartfelt thanks to Chris Webb and Kelly Talbot at Wiley, who helped guide and support me through the writing of this book and who always managed to push me just a bit harder than I would have pushed myself. You guys are great!

As you might expect, many BlackBerry tips and tricks can be found around the Web, posted by enthusiastic users eager to help other BlackBerry owners by sharing the information they have found themselves, either through experimentation or word-of-mouth. In fact, there are now several websites that are devoted to the idea of providing an online community where BlackBerry owners can meet and swap experiences, questions, and answers. There are far too many to mention here by name, but I'd like to thank the many BlackBerry enthusiasts who actively participate in BlackBerryForums.com, BlackBerryCool.com, and PDAStreet.com for sharing what they've learned.

Last, of course, I must thank the company responsible for the BlackBerry itself, Research In Motion. Very few products manage to change the rules and become ingrained in our daily lives as has BlackBerry, although countless products have tried to do so and failed. Research In Motion and the BlackBerry are a fascinating success story, one that continues to unfold before us.

Introduction

The BlackBerry is the fastest growing, most popular wireless e-mail device ever sold. Dubbed the "CrackBerry" as a tribute to how obsessively BlackBerry users will check their e-mails, the BlackBerry is best known for its unique and well-executed "push e-mail" functionality. This feature makes it a favorite of mobile professionals who need to be connected while on the go.

This book is all about how to do different, weird, fun, and amazing things with your BlackBerry. Before you start changing how your BlackBerry works, however, you need to understand what kind of product you are starting out with. Because the BlackBerry is a recent phenomenon, very little has been written about it, and most people — regardless of whether they own a BlackBerry — have only a very limited view of what the device is all about.

This section introduces the BlackBerry device, explains some of the reasons why it produces a fanatical devotion in its users, and provides a short history of the device, which has grown from a single-purpose text-messaging utility to a fully capable wireless e-mail device, personal digital assistant (PDA), and general-purpose mobile application platform.

I also provide an overview of the range of devices available on the market today, and survey the built-in capabilities of the BlackBerry hardware, as well as the included operating system and application software.

If you already own a BlackBerry, this introduction will give you a greater perspective and understanding of the device before you set about changing it. If you are thumbing through this book because you are curious about the BlackBerry phenomenon, and perhaps are considering obtaining one for yourself, this introduction will give you a sense for why you see devices everywhere and why people are so attached to them.

What Is the BlackBerry?

The BlackBerry is a handheld device whose most notable feature is its wireless electronic messaging capability. With a BlackBerry handheld, millions of people who rely on e-mail communications to stay in touch with customers, clients, co-workers, friends, and family can now access, read, write, and send e-mail messages anytime, anywhere.

The BlackBerry is also a general-purpose computing device complete with a processor, memory, storage, and an operating system. Like your desktop computer, your BlackBerry can be outfitted with additional application software programs that provide functionality not found on the basic product. In addition, the BlackBerry has other features associated with desktop or laptop computers, including basic PIM (address book, calendar, to-do, and memo) functionality and basic web browsing.

There are programs that can add all kinds of features to your BlackBerry, including getting weather updates, using word processing capabilities, storing your travel itinerary, connecting to RSS feeds, accessing enterprise systems, and much more. BlackBerry programs are available for purchase or can even be found for free. You can get more information on how to find and install these programs in Chapter 2.

If you know how to write your own software programs or work with web content, you can even create your own BlackBerry applications and web services. As you can imagine, this book exploits this aspect of the BlackBerry device quite extensively! See Chapters 11 through 15 for more ideas.

Modern BlackBerrys also double as cell phones, allowing you to use your device as both a phone and an e-mail messaging center.

What Makes the BlackBerry Special

Although all its cool features certainly make the BlackBerry popular among those in the technology industry, people who own a BlackBerry are not all computer geeks on the cutting edge of technology. Look around you in any airport or commuter train and you are sure to spot people from all walks of life staring intently at their BlackBerry screens. They are catching up on e-mail, pecking out messages on the tiny keyboards with their thumbs, or consulting their calendars.

Why has this tiny piece of technology become such a magical product for so many?

BlackBerry and E-mail: Great Partners

Like other brands that have passed into usage as generic names for a broad class of products (think Xerox, Palm, iPod, and TiVo), BlackBerry has become a synonym for "mobile e-mail device." E-mail is the number-one computing application in the world and the electronic equivalent of the telephone in terms of its impact on our ability to communicate with one another. The BlackBerry's design makes it perfectly suited to extend the concept to the point where your e-mail access is always with you.

Think about that concept for a moment: Your e-mail is always with you. Messages can be sent to you wherever you are, and you receive them almost instantaneously, with no work required on your part. This represents a major breakthrough in how we communicate with one another. For better or worse, it also is a major factor behind a changing view of how accessible you are to those who need to communicate with you. Indeed, many people now assume that you have 24/7 e-mail access, and they expect you to read and respond to e-mail within hours or even minutes, not days.

A key factor in the BlackBerry's success is its specific approach to the problem of mobile e-mail. Many mobile handheld products allow you to access your e-mail, but the BlackBerry early on grew a reputation for being the only device that could effortlessly deliver, or "push," your e-mail to you in real time, without needing to perform menu commands or wait for your messages to download. When you pick up your BlackBerry, your latest e-mail is already retrieved and waiting for you. Although "push e-mail" is a seemingly simple concept, the BlackBerry is the only device to date that has been able to successfully deliver this capability inside a well-executed wireless handheld computer.

As though the e-mail capability were not enough, all modern BlackBerrys double as cell phones. Instead of carrying a cell phone and a BlackBerry with you, all you need is a BlackBerry hooked up to your wireless voice and data service. For the millions of people who use a cell phone every day, the BlackBerry offers a simple but powerful way to add mobile e-mail while retaining the ability to place and receive calls.

In addition, many believe that the BlackBerry has become so popular because it is so well-designed for the purpose it was intended for. In particular, BlackBerry users by far have enjoyed the best implementation of a QWERTY keyboard found on any mobile device, which is very important considering that composing and responding to e-mail messages is a primary BlackBerry feature. Furthermore, BlackBerrys have an outstanding battery life, lasting many days on a single charge, an extraordinary feat given that competing devices generally require a charge at the end of every day.

The BlackBerry Difference

A little research reveals that many products are now available that combine a traditional cell phone with wireless e-mail capability. Aside from the most basic cell phone models, most phones on the market allow some form of messaging or e-mail. So why is the BlackBerry so different?

As with many well-designed products, the BlackBerry difference is not found in a feature list or on a spec sheet. It doesn't have the fastest processor, the biggest screen, or the most memory. Instead, the BlackBerry difference is all about the experience of using one. If you don't already own a BlackBerry, talk to someone who does or, better yet, get one yourself and start using it. As your e-mail arrives effortlessly and you are able to quickly type out messages to people without needing to reach for the phone, you will find yourself increasingly thinking of yourself as much more connected to work and family — and they will think the same of you. Perhaps this cuts to the core of why the BlackBerry is different. Rather than giving you a complicated mobile gadget, the BlackBerry truly changes the way you think about your connectedness to the world.

The BlackBerry achieves this experience in part by providing excellent integration with corporate e-mail servers and public Internet pop3 e-mail services.

Tip The BlackBerry is designed to be simple to use yet powerful. For example, the trackwheel enables one-handed access to your list of e-mails, making it quick and easy to read your e-mail on the go. When you need to compose an e-mail, the small but remarkably easy-to-use built-in QWERTY keyboard gives you the ability to compose and send e-mails. To understand how important it is that the trackwheel and keyboard enable one-handed operation, just try checking your e-mail and responding to an urgent message while running through an airport carrying baggage! Very few products would make this acrobatic feat even possible, but BlackBerry does.

The Importance of Being Wireless

No wireless product is going to succeed if you cannot connect. BlackBerry is widely available from multiple wireless carriers, assuring owners that they will be able to access their e-mail from virtually anywhere. Given the inevitable tradeoffs of producing a handheld computer, Research In Motion (RIM), the designer of the BlackBerry, has made excellent choices in designing a device that doesn't necessarily do everything well, but is fantastic at the most important tasks.

The BlackBerry's competitors are primarily PDAs, which have gained wireless e-mail and phone capabilities. A good example of this kind of product is Palm's Treo smartphone. In addition, Nokia, Motorola, and other manufacturers normally associated with the cell phone now offer devices that sport tiny keyboards reminiscent of the one on the BlackBerry, along with wireless e-mail and other basic calendaring and address book features. While many of these are fine products, none of them seem to have hit upon the magic formula that the BlackBerry has succeeded with for many years now.

Why Hacking Your BlackBerry Is Fun

So what makes the BlackBerry such an interesting device to hack?

First, because the BlackBerry is based on the Java platform, it is programmable. Although the BlackBerry does not run a full Java implementation like the one on your desktop computer, the device does run a slimmed-down version of the Java environment called Mobile Information Device Profile (MIDP); anyone with enough programming knowledge and desire can write her own software programs to do lots of interesting things on the device. Chapter 11 covers how you would actually go about creating your own software applications. Whether you write your programs or download them from the Internet, you can make your BlackBerry do useful, fun, and interesting things that extend its functionality.

Second, the built-in capabilities on the BlackBerry itself are applicable to solving a wide range of problems, with little or no programming knowledge required. E-mail itself can be used to creatively solve many real-world problems and, with a little planning and some additional tools on your desktop computer, the basic e-mail capability of your BlackBerry can be made to do all sorts of interesting things, such as retrieving documents, weather forecasts, or even web information lookups, as you will see in several of the chapters in Part I. Additionally, because most modern BlackBerrys can access web pages on the Internet, anyone with a basic ability to create and work with web pages can create a mobile web solution or service that is accessible from a BlackBerry.

Third, a BlackBerry has a screen, keyboard input, menu system, wireless, processor, memory storage, as well as programming interfaces to access all of these things. Because a BlackBerry contains all the same basic ingredients that a normal desktop computer has, it is very much open to being extended in a variety of ways, such as a drawing tool, information retrieval device, word processor, and more, as you will learn in this book

This book shows you these and many more fun and useful tricks and features that can be added to the BlackBerry handheld device itself. And when you take advantage of the built-in wireless data capabilities, your opportunities for extending the BlackBerry are even greater because wireless connectivity means that you can, in theory, interact with and even control other computers, which can be reached over a network such as the Internet.

History of the BlackBerry

Research In Motion (RIM), founded in 1984 and based in Waterloo, Ontario, originally produced wireless components for other companies. By 1997, the Internet was clearly here to stay
and e-mail usage was becoming mainstream thanks to pioneers such as AOL and Yahoo, so the
founders of RIM crafted a vision for enabling e-mail messaging for people on the go.

The First BlackBerrys

The RIM Inter@ctive Pager, a two-way pager with a small screen and an integrated QWERTY
keyboard, was the first incarnation of this vision. The RIM Pager (shown in Figure I-1)
contained the essential elements that would later come to define the BlackBerry experience,
including a scrollable trackwheel for one-handed operation, a QWERTY keyboard, and reasonable (albeit slow) wireless coverage.

FIGURE I-1: The RIM Inter@ctive Pager model 950 (Courtesy of Research
In Motion Limited)

The original RIM Pager came with wireless data service from Mobitex (BellSouth) and did
not offer any voice capability. RIM's first customers were predictably businessmen — including
portfolio managers, stock traders, and others in the financial sector — whose livelihood depended
on constant communication with customers and co-workers.

RIM followed up on the initial success of the RIM Pager with the very first BlackBerry in 1999.
The BlackBerry improved upon the earlier Pager by offering a larger screen, compatibility
with modern wireless services such as General Packet Radio Service (GPRS) and Code Division

Multiple Access (CDMA) networks, and integration with corporate e-mail through the BlackBerry Enterprise Server (BES). The BlackBerry also was built upon a Java platform, which gave the product a robust foundation for secure communications, as well as a foundation to allow software developers to create add-on software applications and solutions.

Since the introduction of BlackBerry, RIM's devices have grown in both popularity and functionality. Backed by large U.S. wireless carriers such as Sprint, Cingular, Verizon, and T-Mobile, as well as non-U.S. carriers such as O2, Orange, and Vodafone, the BlackBerry devices are now much more available and can easily be purchased through your preferred wireless carrier and added to your existing voice account. Today, according to published estimates, BlackBerry is supported by approximately 200 wireless carriers worldwide and has more than four million handheld customers, and BES is installed at more than 50,000 locations.

The Modern BlackBerry

Today. RIM offers a range of BlackBerry models. The current product line is roughly divided into two form factors: the traditional "waffle" shape with full QWERTY keyboard (seen in the 7200, 7500 and 7700 series) and the newer slim "cell phone" candy-bar shape (found in the 7100 series).

The 7200 series, including the 7290 pictured in Figure I-2, offers the standard BlackBerry device, with voice, wireless e-mail, large color screen, scrollwheel, and QWERTY keyboard. The 7290 also offers Bluetooth support for hands-free headset and car kits, and USB connectivity with desktop computers. The 7270 adds 802.11 wireless IP capabilities, including support for Voice Over IP (VoIP) telephony.

The 7700 series offers a similar configuration as the 7290, albeit with a slightly larger color screen.

The 7500 series also is based on the same standard BlackBerry configuration as the 7200 and 7700, but adds GPS and "walkie-talkie" capabilities and includes a speakerphone, which is noticeably absent on other voice-enabled models. The 7500 is compatible with 800 MHz networks from Nextel.

The 8700 series represents the next generation of data-centric devices that maintain a full QWERTY keyboard layout. Among other improvements, the 8700 models support sharper-looking screens, faster processors, and high-speed wireless connections.

The 7100 Series, introduced in 2004, offers the BlackBerry experience in a slimmer, more cell phone–like form factor for those who prefer a smaller design. Aside from the shape, the most distinct change from the other models found in the 7100 series is the "SureType" keyboard, which combines a standard phone keypad with a QWERTY layout. This scheme relies on multiple-key assignments for each button on the keypad, along with predictive text software, which watches you as you type and does a surprisingly good job of figuring out the characters you intended to type based on a dictionary and your context.

FIGURE I-2: The BlackBerry 7290

Aside from physical differences and slight variations in additional capabilities from model to model, you should note that there are also variations in which model is supported by which wireless carrier networks. For example, the 7100t is offered by T-Mobile and the 7100r is specific to the Rogers Wireless network in Canada, while the 7100g is available on a broader range of carriers. In general, if you obtained your BlackBerry through your wireless carrier, it is "locked" to that network and cannot be used on other wireless networks.

Whom This Book Is For

This book is intended to be rewarding to a wide range of people who are interested in the BlackBerry. Many readers will instantly become more productive with their BlackBerry by learning the shortcuts, tricks, codes, and keystrokes that are unveiled in several chapters. Still others will be delighted to learn of add-on programs that greatly expand the tasks you can use your BlackBerry for. Finally those with a little interest in software programming will enjoy the fun and unique software projects in Part II.

How This Book Is Organized

This book is organized in two parts.

Part I, "Customizing the BlackBerry with Tweaks, Secret Codes, Hidden Keys, and Add-On Applications," is useful to anyone who owns a BlackBerry or is looking to get one, and requires nothing more than a BlackBerry to play with. The chapters in this part provide a wealth of tips, tricks, and shortcuts that can be used in the BlackBerry e-mail, address book, calendar, phone dialer, and other built-in programs. Also covered are a wealth of add-on applications and hacks that enable you to play games, be more productive, search the Web, connect to your PC and network, and much more.

Part II, "Advanced BlackBerry Hacks: Put Your BlackBerry to Fun and Wacky Uses with Creative Software Projects," presents a set of projects of a somewhat more ambitious nature, which highlight how, with a little bit of Java programming, you can get your BlackBerry to play music, act like an Etch-A-Sketch, print wirelessly, and more. A small amount of Java programming background will help you get the most out of these projects, but you can also simply skip the programming part and download the completed programs for your own amusement.

Conventions Used in This Book

In this book, you'll find several notification icons — Note, Caution, Tip, and Cross-Reference — that point out important information. Here's what the four types of icons look like:

 Notes provide you with additional information or resources.

 A caution indicates that you should use extreme care to avoid a potential disaster.

 A tip is advice that can save you time and energy.

 A cross-reference directs you toward more information elsewhere in the book.

Code lines are often longer than what will fit across a page. The symbol ↵ indicates that the following code line is actually a continuation of the current line. For example,

```
var newlat = latpoints[0] + ((latpoints[latpoints.length-1] - ↵
latpoints[0])/2);
```

is really one line of code when you type it into your editor.

Code, functions, URLs, and so forth within the text of this book appear in a monospaced font, while content you type appears either **bold** or monospaced.

What You Need to Use This Book

In order to make the best use of this book, you need a BlackBerry device (any fairly recent model will do just fine) and a wireless data plan from your carrier.

For many of the chapters, that is all you need. For some of the chapters you also need a desktop or laptop computer with an Internet connection in order to download various tools and programs. Finally, you need the USB synchronization cable that came with your BlackBerry, which will help you install and update software on your BlackBerry from your PC.

Part II of this book presents a series of BlackBerry software programming projects that show you how to create your own BlackBerry programs. Although you can always simply load the finished programs from these chapters onto your BlackBerry and enjoy them that way, the chapters will be even more interesting if you follow the steps and learn how these programs are actually created. Doing this requires a basic knowledge of the Java programming language, along with an interest in learning how to write simple BlackBerry programs.

What's on the Companion Website

Additional materials and helpful links for *Hacking BlackBerry* are available on my web page for the book, found at:

> www.bachmannhandheldsolutions.com/hackingbb.htm

The materials can also be found at:

> www.wiley.com/go/extremetech

On both pages you will find errata and updates to *Hacking BlackBerry*, as well as full source code for the projects in Part II.

Although I cannot possibly provide answers and tech support for the entire BlackBerry user population, if you want to drop me a note to say "Hello!" or if you have a development project and want to learn more about my company Bachmann Software, you can use the following e-mail address:

> glenn@bachmannsoftware.com

Summary

In this introduction I've provided a basic overview of the BlackBerry and why it is such a wonderful product to use. Perhaps by now you suspect that I am some sort of paid evangelist for RIM. (I'm not!) But I *am* a BlackBerry lover who's excited to show you the many ways in which you can customize the device and make it your own. This book covers just how to do that.

Hacking
BlackBerry®

Customizing the BlackBerry with Tweaks, Secret Codes, Hidden Keys, and Add-On Applications

part

Secret Codes and Hidden Keys

Welcome to *Hacking BlackBerry*! This book is all about how to do useful, interesting, fun, and different things with your BlackBerry device. I'm going to dive right in with this first chapter, and provide you with information on many undocumented keystrokes and codes that allow you to access and effectively use the helpful, interesting, or just plain obscure features on your BlackBerry.

For information on codes you can use for e-mail, web browser, and security purposes, see Chapters 2, 3, and 7, respectively.

Locating the Important Keys

Although you are already familiar with the BlackBerry keyboard, you should take special note of the key you use most often when executing the shortcuts and key sequences in this chapter. On some devices the ALT key has a half-moon shape on it and is located directly below the A key, in the lower-left corner of your BlackBerry keyboard (see Figure 1-1). On other devices such as the 8700, the ALT key simply has the label "ALT."

You will also use the CAP key a couple of times. This key has an up arrow on it and is located directly to the right of the SPACE key at the bottom of your keyboard.

The backspace key has a left arrow on it and says DEL; it is located on the far right-hand side of your keyboard (directly below the P key).

Finally, the ESC key is located on the right side of your BlackBerry device, just below the trackwheel. The ESC key is generally used to go back, cancel, or dismiss a menu.

Note All the techniques in this chapter work on my BlackBerry 7290 and should function on similar modern devices. If you own a 7100 series device, you may find that some either do not work or require a slightly different keystroke sequence because of the different keyboard configuration.

FIGURE 1-1: The BlackBerry 7290 keyboard layout

Using Typing Shortcuts

As nice as it is to have a QWERTY keyboard on your BlackBerry, typing on it is nowhere near as fast as it can be on your standard desktop or even laptop. Fortunately, the designers of the BlackBerry device were thoughtful enough to augment the keyboard with a number of shortcuts (see Table 1-1) that can be used to speed things up (or at least make it easier on your sore fingers!).

In addition, your BlackBerry has a fantastic feature called AutoText, whose main function is to correct common spelling mistakes. The great news is that you can also use it to define automatic replacement of shortcut letter combinations with any text you wish.

For example, suppose that you want to add a favorite sentence or phrase at the end of every e-mail you compose (such as "Best regards, Glenn"). All you need to do is define an AutoText entry that contains your sentence and select a short letter combination that you can use to invoke the sentence or phrase (such as "brg").

To add an entry to AutoText:

1. Click the trackwheel while typing and choose Edit AutoText. You are presented with a list of predefined AutoText mappings.

2. Press the trackwheel again and choose New from the menu to create your entry.

Table 1-1   Typing Shortcuts

To insert . . .	Do this . . .
A period	Rather than pressing ALT+M, press the SPACE key two times in succession. Not only will your BlackBerry insert a period but it will also capitalize the next letter you type.
A capital letter	Normally you would press the CAP key along with the letter you want to capitalize. With BlackBerry, you can simply press and hold the letter you want to capitalize.
A special character	Press and hold any key while scrolling the trackwheel up or down. You will see a rotating list of characters mapped to that key appear on the screen. Select the character you want by scrolling the trackwheel.
An @ symbol	In any field designed to accept an e-mail address (such as the e-mail field in an Address Book entry), simply type a space for BlackBerry to automatically insert an @ character. This trick works for the period used in e-mail addresses as well.

Accessing System Information

A number of hidden screens and undocumented information codes are available on your BlackBerry device. The key is to know how to access them. This section describes a few system-level screens that can be useful or, at the very least, interesting to take a look at.

The Help Me! Screen

The Help Me! screen is useful because it gathers key information about your device. It displays your operating system version, battery level, wireless signal strength, and available storage.

To access the Help Me! screen:

1. Go to the Applications screen and press ALT+CAP+H.

2. To close the screen, choose the Close menu or press the back button.

The Event Log

The Event Log offers a view into system events that occur on your BlackBerry. It can also be a useful debugging tool to track down what might be going wrong with an application or service on your BlackBerry.

To access the Event Log:

1. Go to the home Applications screen and hold down the ALT key while entering the key sequence LGLG. After a second or two, the event log appears (see Figure 1-2).

Within the Event Log, you can click on the trackwheel to view more details about a given event, clear the log to reclaim some storage memory, or go into the Options menu to fine-tune the types of events that are logged.

2. To close the Event Log and return to your home screen, choose the Close menu.

FIGURE 1-2: The BlackBerry Event Log

The Signal Strength Display Mode

The standard signal strength display on a BlackBerry uses the familiar "five bars" graphic — the more bars you have, the better your signal strength (as shown in Figure 1-1). If you prefer more precision, however, you can have the signal strength display in actual numbers (see Figure 1-3).

To change your signal strength display:

1. Go to the home Applications screen and hold down the ALT key while entering the key sequence **NMLL**.

2. To return to the standard graphical bar display, enter the same key sequence, ALT+NMLL.

Figure 1-3: Signal strength displayed numerically

The numeric signal display represents your signal strength in decibels (dB).

Smart System Codes

You can obtain various types of information about your system by using smart system codes (see Table 1-2). Simply enter the code into any input field, and then press the Enter (or space) key.

Table 1-2	Smart System Codes
Smart Code	Information Returned
myver	Displays the device/version
LD	Displays the local date
LT	Displays the local time
mysig	Displays the information you entered in the BlackBerry Options ⇨ Owner screen
mypin	Displays your handheld's PIN

For example, typing myver in the body of an e-mail and pressing Enter displays the device name and the operating system version, as shown in Figure 1-4.

FIGURE **1-4: The BlackBerry information display after entering the smart code myver in an e-mail**

Working with the Built-In BlackBerry Applications

In addition to the more general-purpose shortcuts listed in the previous sections, many shortcut keys are specific to the built-in BlackBerry applications such as Calendar and Address Book, as well as the standard BlackBerry Applications screen (also known as the home screen). In this section, I present a number of these BlackBerry applications, along with shortcut keys and techniques that apply specifically to those programs.

The BlackBerry Applications Screen

The BlackBerry Applications screen is often referred to as the Home screen or the Ribbon. It supports several shortcut letters to enable you to quickly jump to different programs. Table 1-3 lists known shortcuts you can use to access different applications while in the Applications screen. On newer devices, please note that in order to use these shortcuts, you will first need to disable the Dial from Home Screen option under Options ⇨ General Options ⇨ Phone. When this feature is on, the Home screen assumes that the keystrokes you enter are intended to be part of a phone number you wish to dial.

Table 1-3   Shortcut Keys in the Applications Screen

Shortcut Key	Associated Application or Feature
A	Address Book
R	Alarm Clock
B	Browser
U	Calculator
L	Calendar
C	Compose E-mail
K	Keyboard Lock
M	Messages
D	Notes
O	Options
P	Phone
F	Profiles
V	Saved Messages
S	Search
T	Tasks
W	WAP Bookmarks

Changing the Icon List

Modern BlackBerry devices come with more and more built-in applications, and constantly having to navigate to the same application icons over and over again can become tiresome, especially if these icons happen to be located on the second or third row of icons.

The key to changing the list of application icons that appears on your BlackBerry is to use the key sequence ALT+trackwheel. If you press these two keys together, a hidden menu pops up that allows you to customize the order in which your application icons are displayed, as well as designate which icons are displayed or hidden.

Suppose that you are a big BrickBreaker fan and you are tired of having to always scroll to the BrickBreaker icon. Wouldn't it be great to have BrickBreaker on the first row of icons? Accomplishing this is easy:

1. Navigate to the BrickBreaker icon so that it is the selected icon and press ALT+trackwheel.

2. In the hidden menu that appears, choose the Move Application menu option.

3. Use the trackwheel to move the BrickBreaker icon up to the top position in the applications screen.

The Applications menu can also be used to hide application icons you don't use. This can help you simplify your applications display so that you see only those applications you use regularly.

Suppose that you are not a games person at all and you actually want to remove BrickBreaker from your applications screen. To do this:

1. Navigate to the BrickBreaker icon so that it is selected and press ALT+trackwheel.

2. Select the Hide Application menu option.

Voilà! BrickBreaker is gone. Well, it is really not totally gone — it is still on your BlackBerry, but its icon is just hidden from the Applications screen. If you ever want to bring a hidden application icon back, just press ALT+trackwheel again and choose the Show All menu option. Doing this restores all of the hidden icons.

Switching Between Running Applications

Many people are not aware that a BlackBerry can actually have multiple applications running at the same time. For example, suppose that you are browsing a web site and decide that you need to make a phone call. You can easily call up the list of currently running applications by pressing and holding the ALT key and then pressing ESC, which displays a horizontal ribbon of icons. Use the trackwheel to switch to the application icon you wish to return to.

The BlackBerry Calendar Application

The BlackBerry has a fairly full-featured Calendar application that can synchronize appointments and other events with Microsoft Outlook and other popular calendaring solutions.

The downside of the built-in Calendar application is the awkwardness of navigating through days, weeks, and months using the trackwheel. Fortunately, you can use numerous secret shortcut keys to make navigating your calendar much more pleasant. Table 1-4 describes the various shortcut keys that can be used for quick navigation in the Calendar application.

Table 1-4	Shortcut Keys in the Calendar Application
Shortcut Key	**Meaning**
A	Switch to Agenda view.
M	Switch to Month view.
D	Switch to Day view.
W	Switch to Week view.
G	Go to a specific date. A horizontal band pops up on the screen, enabling you to use the trackwheel to select the month, day, or year. You can then use the keyboard to modify the date component. Select the trackwheel again to jump to the specified date in the calendar. See Figure 1-5 for a screenshot of the Go To Date popup display.

Table 1-4   *Continued*

Shortcut Key	Meaning
T	Go to the current date. Jump to the current date in your currently selected view.
SPACE	Navigate to the next day, week, or month, depending on the current view.
N	Navigate to the next day, week, or month, depending on the current view.
C	Create a new appointment.
ALT+trackwheel	In Day, Week, and Agenda views, navigate forward or backward among the days of the week. In Month view, navigate forward or backward among the weeks in the month.

Note These shortcut keys will not work in the Day view if you are using the Enable Quick Entry option. When you start typing, Enable Quick Entry thinks that you are entering a new appointment rather than accepting what you're typing as shortcut keys. If you prefer to leave Enable Quick Entry on, you will be able to use these shortcut keys in only the Week, Month, and Agenda views.

To turn off Enable Quick Entry, use the trackwheel in the Day view to display the menu and choose Options to bring up the Day View Options screen, then scroll to the Enable Quick Entry item and make sure it is set to No.

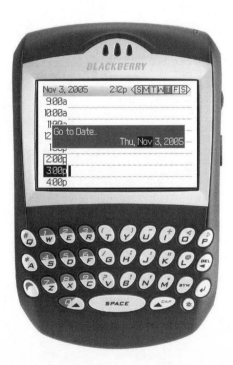

FIGURE 1-5: The Go To Date popup screen that appears after pressing G in the Calendar application

The BlackBerry Address Book Application

BlackBerry users usually call up the Address Book application to quickly find a phone number or e-mail or to enter new contact information. Being able perform these actions quickly is important.

Finding Contacts

If you are like me and have a fairly large list of contacts in your Address Book, quickly finding the right entry when composing an e-mail or making a phone call can be frustrating, especially if you remember only a tiny bit of the contact's information.

For maximum efficiency, start by keeping your Address Book sorted in the same way you are likely to look for contacts. If you are in sales and generally organize your contacts by company, sort your Address Book by company. Similarly, if you are more comfortable searching by last name, set your sort option to use last names.

To change the sort order:

1. Use the trackwheel to bring up the Address Book menu, and choose Options.

2. In the Options screen, change the Sort By field to first, last, or company.

One of the easiest ways to find a contact quickly is to use the proper search technique. In the BlackBerry Address Book list, you can quickly jump to the right contact by taking these simple steps:

1. Type the first few letters of the first name.

2. Insert a space.

3. Type the first few letters of the last name.

This method yields the name you were looking for with a minimum of typing and scrolling because you avoid having to type the full name or scroll up and down within many entries that start with the same letter. Note that this technique works regardless of the sort option you are using.

Editing Contacts

When you add a contact to the Address Book in a hurry, you sometimes enter only the minimum amount of information necessary, such as name and phone number. When editing an Address Book entry, the phone fields (Work, Home, Mobile, and so on) all allow you to enter their values using the number keys. You do not have to use the ALT key when entering numbers for these fields.

The BlackBerry Calculator Application

The BlackBerry Calculator application greatly benefits from the use of special keys. Without them, you are left with only the trackwheel as a means for pressing the various calculator buttons. Table 1-5 lists the known keyboard buttons that can be used with the Calculator application.

Table 1-5   Shortcut Keys in the Calculator Application (Standard Keyboard)

Shortcut Key	Meaning
+ (or L)	Add
- (or U)	Subtract
* (or A)	Multiply
/ (or G)	Divide
) (or Y)	Clear Screen
((or T)	Clear Entry
Return	Calculate and Display Result
V	Square Root
#	Positive (Negative)

The 7100 models with the more phone-centric keyboards do not have labeled keys for add, subtract, multiply, and divide. Instead, you must use the keyboard equivalents shown in Table 1-6.

Table 1-6   Shortcut Keys in the Calculator Application (7100 Keyboard)

Shortcut Key	Meaning
I	Add
U	Subtract
A	Multiply
G	Divide
Y	Clear Screen
T	Clear Entry
Return Key	Calculate and Display Result
V	Square Root
#	Positive (Negative)

Summary

I collected the hacks, tips, and tricks in this chapter from a number of different sources on the Internet. As of this writing, there is no big list of secret BlackBerry codes posted anywhere (a good reason for the existence of this book!). Instead, you can find a few tips here or there in a great many places.

The BlackBerry site has some great information in its customer support materials. Another good source of information is your wireless carrier's website. Several carriers list Frequently Asked Questions and post various tidbits of information in the site's customer support area.

If you are interested in learning more about the codes and hidden screens that BlackBerry users have discovered, several online BlackBerry user forums have a Tips section where users freely post their discoveries or little-known tips and techniques they may have heard about or seen somewhere and simply felt like sharing with others. The following web sites have some good information:

- www.blackberrycool.com
- www.pdastreet.com/forums (navigate to the RIM and BlackBerry discussion forum)
- www.ibbug.org

Who knows? You may even discover some of your own hidden key codes just by experimenting with your own BlackBerry!

Adding Software to Your BlackBerry

Most handheld devices come with a basic set of Personal Information Management (PIM) applications that includes calendar, address book, to-do, and memo options. With wireless devices and smartphones, you also generally get a phone dialer, an e-mail client, and a web browser. Beyond that, perhaps you get a token game or two. To add any other functionality that you would like to have on your device, however, you need to locate and install a third-party application.

Types of Third-Party Applications

Growth in the number of add-on software applications is a relatively new phenomenon for the BlackBerry scene. Compared to the tens of thousands of titles available for Palm and Windows Mobile devices, BlackBerry owners have access to "only" a few thousand programs as of this writing. Still, this is a substantial number of programs that can be added to your BlackBerry to give your handheld new and different capabilities.

Within the universe of BlackBerry programs, titles are available in many different categories. In this section, I describe the most popular ones. To learn where you can find and download these programs, please refer to the section "Finding Third-Party Applications" later in this chapter.

Business and Professional

This category includes software applications that can help the mobile business person be more productive with his or her BlackBerry. Consider these common examples:

- **WorldMate:** Consists of a set of traveler's utilities, including time zone conversion, weather, currency conversion, and travel itineraries.

- **MortgageSolver:** Provides a handy calculator designed for the mobile real estate professional, covering payments, interest rates, and loans.

- **My Time Tracker:** Offers time tracking for meetings, calls, and other daily activities.
- **Expense Report Wizard:** Automates expense tracking and expense report generation.

Business and professional programs such as these are covered in more depth in Chapter 9.

Communications and Wireless

Beyond the built-in e-mail program that comes with BlackBerry, there is a world of add-on wireless programs that can greatly expand your BlackBerry's wireless capabilities. From instant messaging to information retrieval, you will be surprised at how much your BlackBerry is capable of with the right add-on programs!

- **IM+:** This instant messaging application is compatible with MSN, Yahoo, ICQ, and AOL.
- **Minuet Browser:** This HTML browser for your BlackBerry is more advanced than the built-in browser.
- **Gmail Mobile:** This is an e-mail client for Google's popular Gmail service.

More communications and wireless programs like these are covered in Chapters 3 and 4.

Document Management

BlackBerry is one of the few remaining popular smart devices that does not come with some sort of built-in document capability, which seems strange given the built-in BlackBerry keyboard. The following applications can help remedy this situation:

- **eOffice:** Provides viewing and editing of Word and Excel documents.
- **DocHawk:** Includes viewers for PowerPoint, Word, and RTF.
- **BlackBerry Database Viewer:** Enables you to view Access, Excel, and other popular database formats.

Programs such as these are presented in more detail in Chapter 9.

Education and Reference

From dictionaries to educational programs, the following titles can expand your mind:

- **Math Trick Trainer:** A challenging math game.
- **BDicty:** A dictionary program available with a variety of language translations.
- **MSDict Oxford Dictionary of the Bible:** As with the dictionary program, numerous Bible-related texts and references are available.

Entertainment and Games

What would a computer be without a little fun and games? Ringtones, strategy games, and other fun titles abound for BlackBerry owners who are tired of playing BrickBreaker:

- **BlackBerry Ring Tone Megaplex:** Contains over a thousand ringtones for your BlackBerry. If you are one of those people that must have a phone that plays "La Cucaracha" when it rings, this program is for you.

- **Mobile Bartender:** Offers a cocktail recipe guide on-the-go.

- **Aces Texas Hold 'em:** Allows you to play poker anywhere, anytime. Gotta know when to hold 'em and when to fold 'em!

- **Links Scorecard:** Provides the ultimate mobile golf scorecard.

- **Sol Mania:** Offers 24 variations on the classic Solitaire game.

More coverage of program titles in the entertainment category is provided in Chapter 10.

Health and Fitness

A portable handheld device is a natural companion to help you track your exercise and diet regimen. Check out these healthful applications for your BlackBerry:

- **Total Fitness:** Manages nutrition, exercise, and health.

- **Running Log:** Tracks your running workouts.

- **Calorie Counter:** Helps you watch those calories!

Read more about programs such as Running Log for BlackBerry in Chapter 10.

Utilities

In addition to the program categories listed earlier, some programs are useful in a more general way and can help you gain more utility from your BlackBerry. The following are a few examples:

- **MyClock:** Provides an analog clock display.

- **SearchMagic:** Enables you to conduct a full text search on your BlackBerry.

- **Password Manager:** Keeps your passwords and PINs in one safe place.

You can find additional information about programs in the utilities category in Chapter 8.

Finding Third-Party Applications

Through a partnership with the popular online software store Handango.com, RIM has created the Handango Store for BlackBerry. Here, you can browse, learn about, download, and purchase third-party BlackBerry software applications for your device — just as on other popular online stores, such as Amazon, you can browse available software titles by category, popularity, price, or other criteria. Most software programs on the store offer a free trial download.

The Handango Store for BlackBerry is "powered by Handango," which is just another way of saying that the titles available, the shopping cart, and the general store experience is based on Handango's popular online store (found at www.handango.com).

Tip You will find that most of the quality BlackBerry applications listed on Handango are also found on the BlackBerry version of the store. However, you may prefer to shop at Handango.com to get not only a complete listing of titles available for BlackBerry but also a virtual treasure trove of programs for non-BlackBerry handhelds and smartphones.

Why Use the Handango Store?

What is the advantage of using the Handango Store for BlackBerry or www.handango.com over just searching the web? These online software sites offer you the following:

- **One-stop shopping:** A large number and variety of titles are available at one online location.

- **Software quality and security:** When you obtain a software application from the BlackBerry website, you run a lesser risk of downloading a virus or other damaging program to your BlackBerry than you would if you downloaded a program from a less reputable location.

Finding Software Vendor Web Sites

Although the Handango Store provides access to a basic level of information about a program, as well as the ability to download or purchase it, the most comprehensive information about a program is most likely to be found on the software vendor's home website. Going to the vendor directly also usually (but not always) offers the best way of getting technical support and answering questions about the program.

Locating software vendors can be a challenge, but search engines go a long way toward helping find them. Another great way to learn about what is available is to start hanging around the several online discussion forums and news sites that focus on BlackBerry, such as BlackBerryCool and BlackBerryBlog. Here, you will not only read about other people's experiences with various programs, but you can also jump in and participate in the discussion.

- **Customer ratings and reviews:** These can help you determine what programs are right for you.

- **Shopping security:** You know you will get a safe, secure, and reliable shopping experience that will protect your privacy, your personal information, and your payment information.

Although, in general, modern BlackBerry devices are all based on the same operating system, there can be subtle differences from device model to device model, such as screen size. In addition, different device models often come with a slightly different version of the BlackBerry operating system, which may affect how compatible a particular software program is for one model versus another. To ensure that you find programs that are intended for use on your particular BlackBerry model, the Handango site asks developers to list which devices their programs are compatible with, and site visitors to identify which device they own. In this way, Handango can act as a sort of matchmaker, introducing you to the software programs with which you are likely to have the most success.

To navigate the Handango Store for BlackBerry:

1. Go to www.blackberry.com and click the Third Party Applications link in the Own a BlackBerry? section.

2. Now click the Handango link in the Games and Productivity tools section. This takes you to the Handango Store's main page, as pictured in Figure 2-1.

FIGURE 2-1: The main page of the Handango Store for BlackBerry

3. Use your mouse to select your BlackBerry device (for example, "BlackBerry 7250/ BlackBerry 7290"). This takes you to the home page for software that is compatible with your chosen device (see Figure 2-2).

4. From your device's home page, you can search for software by keyword (such as "wireless messaging") or you can browse by category, using the Software Categories navigation bar on the right side of the screen. You can also browse lists of the current best-selling titles, the most recently posted software, or featured programs that the store is promoting at a particular time. A large number of programs is available, so the main idea here is to help you narrow down the list of available programs to those that match your current interests. Regardless of which search method you use, the resulting screen will show a more focused listing of software programs that match your criteria.

5. Click a program title to see the Product Information page for the selected program (see the Product Information page for the popular solitaire program Sol Mania in Figure 2-3).

On the Product Information page, you can read a fuller description of the software program, as well as customer reviews (if any), screenshots, any special compatibility requirements, and other helpful information. You also usually have the option of downloading a limited-time trial version, or you can purchase the software. The purchase process should be familiar to those who have purchased products on the Internet before — as usual there is a shopping cart to hold the items you choose, major credit cards are accepted, and other niceties.

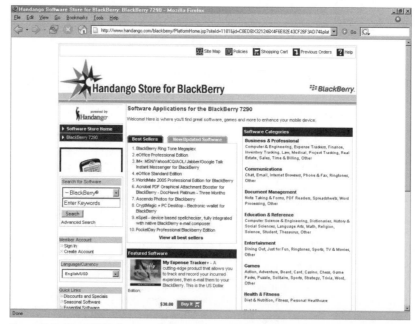

FIGURE 2-2: The 7290's home software page at the Handango Store for BlackBerry

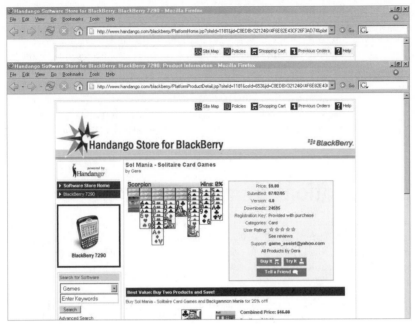

FIGURE 2-3: The Product Information page for Sol Mania

Purchasing Third-Party Applications

The world of third-party BlackBerry applications is populated primarily by small- to medium-sized software companies; you can even find some software posted by software enthusiasts and hobbyists who are not necessarily in it to create a business. Accordingly, you will find some variation in how software is priced and how licensing works. Purchase prices for applications range anywhere from free to over $100, with most titles falling into a range of about $20 to $50. As a general rule, games and other entertainment/consumer-oriented programs tend to be less expensive than business-oriented programs. Just remember that price is not necessarily the most important factor when deciding to download or purchase third-party software. There will be programs that you like and dislike, whether they are free or expensive or somewhere in between.

Note Aside from choosing one product over another to purchase, different purchasing and installation options are available to you, sometimes even within the same product. Software can be purchased as a traditional desktop software installer, which gets run on your desktop computer and installed to your BlackBerry via the USB cable connection. A more recent alternative is to use over-the-air, which allows you to obtain software by downloading directly to your BlackBerry. I cover desktop and OTA installation in more detail later in this chapter.

Software purchasing options are also becoming more varied. The traditional way to purchase software is to pay a one-time cost for a single user license. You then have the right to use that software program, and do not need to pay anything further unless you choose to perhaps upgrade to a newer version. Recently, there has been movement toward a subscription-based model for purchasing software. Instead of paying a one-time fee, you enter into an arrangement in which you are billed monthly or at other regular intervals for your continued use of the software product. Typically, you will find subscription-based options when there is an ongoing need for communication between the software vendor and the customer. A good example of this is a program that has a data component that changes frequently, rather like airline flight schedules, which must be regularly updated and made available to the customer.

Installing Applications from the Desktop

Once you find an application that interests you, you will need to somehow get it installed on your BlackBerry. The traditional way to install add-on software applications to any handheld device, including BlackBerry, is to connect your device to your computer and install via your desktop. To enable this, RIM provides you with the BlackBerry Desktop Manager program.

The BlackBerry Desktop Manager software is a Windows application that manages how your BlackBerry connects to and exchanges data with your desktop computer. Most of the time, the Desktop Manager is used to perform synchronization of data between your BlackBerry and your desktop, including contacts, calendar, and to-do items. The Desktop Manager also performs backup and restore of your BlackBerry. Its most important function in the context of this chapter, however, is that it allows you to add additional applications to your BlackBerry from your desktop.

By default, the BlackBerry Desktop Manager, pictured in Figure 2-4, is configured to auto-start when you start your computer. If you've changed this, or if for some reason the Desktop Manager is not running on your computer, you can run it by going to the Start menu and choosing Programs ➪ BlackBerry ➪ Desktop Manager.

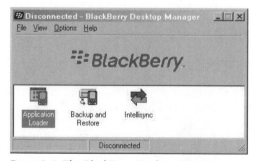

FIGURE 2-4: The BlackBerry Desktop Manager

The Desktop Manager main screen displays a number of icons for each function it supports. The Application Loader icon lets you install BlackBerry applications:

1. Double-click the Application Loader icon to start the Application Loader Wizard, shown in Figure 2-5.

2. The Application Loader Wizard displays the Handheld Application Selection screen (see Figure 2-6), which is a list of all of the applications it sees installed on your BlackBerry.

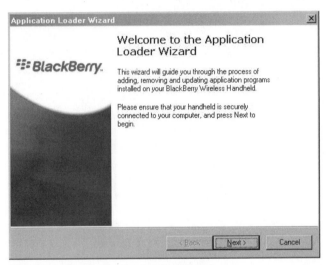

FIGURE 2-5: The Application Loader Wizard

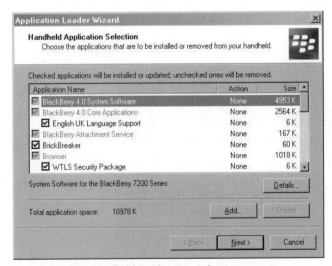

FIGURE 2-6: The Handheld Application Selection screen

Note

If your BlackBerry is not connected to your computer, you will need to connect it before proceeding because the Application Loader will be accessing your BlackBerry's internal storage to determine which programs are installed.

3. Click the Add button to add an application to your BlackBerry. This displays the dialog box shown in Figure 2-7, which allows you to locate the appropriate Application Loader file. Application Loader files have an extension of .alx and accompany the .cod program file in order to provide the Loader Wizard with information about the program you wish to install.

Tip

To remove an application, simply uncheck the box next to the application in the Handheld Application Selection screen.

4. Select the .alx file for the application you wish to add, and then continue with the installation. Your BlackBerry may need to reset; after it re-initializes, you should see the program in the list of icons on your BlackBerry's main screen.

Note

Some programs come as a completely self-contained executable (.exe) file, which automatically interfaces with the Application Loader to add the new program to your BlackBerry.

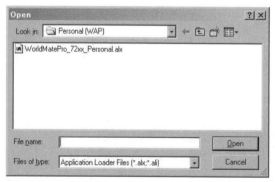

FIGURE 2-7: Selecting an Application Loader file for installation

Installing Applications Over-the-Air

Another, newer way to add software to your wireless handheld is to download programs directly to your BlackBerry using your wireless connection. This method of installation is called "over-the-air" (OTA for short). With OTA installation, you do not need to be connected to your desktop computer; all you need is your BlackBerry, your wireless connection, and your BlackBerry's web browser.

Note If your BlackBerry does not have a web browser, you will not be able to download OTA.

OTA downloads of BlackBerry applications are generally available in the same places where you would find the desktop-installable versions: at Handango.com or at the vendor's web site.

 Note Not all BlackBerry applications are available for OTA download. If an application you are interested in does not support OTA, it could be because the program has a necessary desktop component; the program has multiple components, making it difficult to support with a single download; or the developer simply has not bothered to make an OTA version available.

To learn how to perform an OTA download, you can start by downloading a BlackBerry version of the popular Sudoku game (created by a company called Magmic). The technique described here is applicable to any OTA download:

1. Load your BlackBerry web browser. Once in the browser, click the trackwheel and choose the Go To menu.

2. In the resulting dialog box, enter **bb.magmic.com** and click OK to go to Magmic's OTA download page, shown in Figure 2-8.

3. Scroll to the link for Sudoku, and select it to begin the download.

4. Follow the prompts; the download should take a minute or two to complete.

5. After the download is complete, return to your BlackBerry main screen; you should see the new Sudoku icon. Select and run it, and you are ready to play! Figure 2-9 shows Sudoku in action.

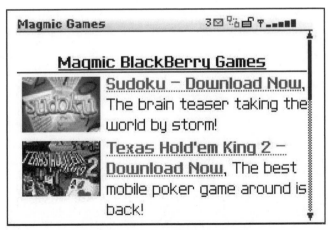

FIGURE 2-8: The Magmic OTA download web page

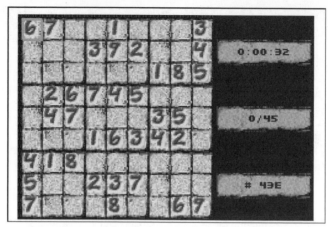

FIGURE 2-9: Magmic's Sudoku

Purchasing OTA Applications

Although the industry is moving toward enabling customers to make purchases directly from a wireless handheld, most OTA downloads are still trial versions. These require you to make an actual purchase of the software from your desktop web browser.

However, a new program called InHand (from Handango) is helping to change this. InHand is a kind of software catalog that loads on your BlackBerry. It contains listings for many BlackBerry titles and allows you to browse, download, and even purchase BlackBerry applications, all directly from the InHand software program running on your BlackBerry.

InHand is a free download, available on both the Handango Store for BlackBerry at www.blackberry.com, as well as the Handango Store's BlackBerry section at www.handango.com.

Summary

Finding and adding a great software program can change your relationship with your BlackBerry, taking it far beyond e-mail messaging. It is without a doubt the easiest way to expand the number of things you can do with your BlackBerry.

The third-party application market for BlackBerry devices is poised for rapid growth as the number of devices shipped demonstrates to software developers that there is potential for reaching new customers. As the number of BlackBerry users grows, so does the pool of enthusiasts, hackers, and other interested people — programmers or otherwise — who will find some needed capability missing from the device, take matters into their own hands, and create their own software solution. The increased number of applications available increases the appeal of the BlackBerry device, which in turn sells more BlackBerry devices and, of course, leads to more programs being created.

With most software programs being so inexpensive, and with the ready availability of free trial downloads, there's no good reason not to dive right in and try out a few!

Advanced E-mail, Voice, and Messaging

This chapter gets right to the heart of why everyone is in love with their BlackBerry devices — e-mail! E-mail is easily the number one reason why people use their BlackBerry, and the BlackBerry is without a doubt the best handheld device or smartphone out there for mobile e-mail and mobile messaging.

In this chapter, you explore all sorts of ways to make the most of your BlackBerry when used for e-mail messaging, instant messaging, and voice phone calls. The chapter covers the usual array of shortcut keystrokes and hidden codes. You also learn how to manage your e-mail signature, work with filters to get control of your e-mail, work with third-party applications for instant messaging and attachments, and even learn how to add custom ringtones to your smartphone!

Shortcuts and Hidden Keys in BlackBerry Messaging

Many keyboard shortcuts are available within the BlackBerry Messages application. You can use these shortcuts to navigate and filter Message Lists and to write, reply, forward, and delete messages.

Special Keys Used in This Chapter

Many of the tips and tricks presented in this chapter require you to enter special key sequences on the BlackBerry keyboard. I will assume that you are already familiar with the basics of typing using the BlackBerry keyboard. However, before you proceed, it's a good idea to make sure you are familiar with the following special keys (the BlackBerry 7290 keyboard layout is pictured in Figure 3-1):

- **ALT:** When I refer to the ALT key, I'm referring to the special "half-moon" key located in the lower-left corner of your BlackBerry keyboard (directly below the A key). Pressing this key in combination with another key changes the functionality of the other key.

- **SHIFT or CAP:** These terms refer to the key with the up arrow on it, located to the right of the SPACE key at the bottom of your keyboard.

- **BACKSPACE or DEL:** This is the key with a left arrow on it, marked "DEL."

FIGURE 3-1: The BlackBerry 7290 keyboard layout

Note Keystrokes can cause different behavior when pressed in different BlackBerry screens. This chapter describes the meaning of special shortcut key sequences in various BlackBerry applications, but keystrokes can behave differently in other applications. For example, observe what happens when you enter the numbers from a phone number in the Phone application as opposed to when you enter those same numbers in a different program, such the Calendar Week screen.

Navigating the Messages List

One of the most attractive qualities of the BlackBerry solution is that it automatically delivers your e-mail to your device, without your having to specifically request it. However, this benefit can often have the unfortunate downside of filling your BlackBerry Inbox with hundreds of message headers if you do not religiously delete unwanted e-mails. In my experience, once you get beyond a page or two of messages, using the trackwheel to scroll up and down through the Messages List becomes tedious and unproductive.

Table 3-1 lists BlackBerry shortcut keystrokes that are extremely handy for performing common navigation commands to help you move through the Messages List, especially when you have several pages of messages in your Inbox.

Table 3-1   Messages List Navigation Shortcut Keys

Shortcut Key	Action
T	Moves the selection to the first message header in the Messages List
B	Moves the selection to the last message header in the Messages List
SPACE	Jumps a page down within the Messages List
CAP+SPACE	Jumps a page up within the Messages List
N	Jumps to the next date header within the Messages List
P	Jumps to the previous date header within the Messages List
U	Jumps to the next unread item
BACKSPACE	Closes the Messages application and returns you to the BlackBerry home screen

Additionally, the shortcut commands in Table 3-2 perform common actions on the selected message in the Messages List.

Table 3-2   Messages List Command Shortcut Keys

Shortcut Key	Action
R	Creates a reply message for the current message, addressed to the original sender
F	Prompts you to select an Address Book entry to forward the message to
L	Creates a reply message for the current message, addressed to all addresses in the original message's recipient list
S	Presents a search screen that allows you to enter criteria for searching your messages
V	Switches to the list of saved messages
C	Opens the Address Book so you can select someone and compose a new e-mail

Filtering the Messages List

Sometimes the fastest way to find the message you are looking for is to filter your Messages List by the type of message. Table 3-3 shows shortcut keystrokes that allow you to filter the Messages List to show only certain types of message entries.

Table 3-3 Messages List Filtering Shortcut Keys

Shortcut Key	Action
ALT+J	Filters the Messages List to show only Incoming messages
ALT+O	Filters the Messages List to show only Outgoing messages
ALT+P	Filters the Messages List to show only Phone Log messages
ALT+S	Filters the Messages List to show only SMS messages
ALT+V	Filters the Messages List to show only VoiceMail messages

Navigating Within the Message Viewer

As most BlackBerry users know, a message can be opened for reading from the Messages List either by clicking the trackwheel and selecting the default Open menu item or by using the shortcut ENTER key.

Once a message is opened, there are a number of shortcut keystrokes that can help you navigate within more lengthy messages, as well as navigate forward and backward through messages from within the message viewer.

Table 3-4 presents a number of shortcut keystrokes that work within the message viewer screen.

Table 3-4 Message Viewer Navigation Shortcut Keys

Shortcut Key	Action
SPACE (or Enter)	Scrolls forward by one screen
ALT+SPACE (or ALT+Enter)	Scrolls backward by one screen
B	Moves to the bottom of the message
T	Moves to the top of the message
U	Moves to the next unread message from the Messages List
N	Moves to the next message
P	Moves to the previous message
BACKSPACE	Closes the message viewer screen and returns to the Messages List

Additionally, the shortcut commands in Table 3-5 perform common actions on the selected message in the Messages List.

Table 3-5   Message Viewer Command Shortcut Keys

Shortcut Key	Action
R	Creates a reply message for the current message, addressed to the original sender
F	Prompts you to select an Address Book entry to forward the message to
L	Creates a reply message for the current message, addressed to all addresses in the original message's recipient list
S	Pops up a search box that lets you search for a word or phrase in the body of the message
V	Switches to the list of saved messages
C	Opens the Address Book so you can select someone and compose a new e-mail

Tip

Have you ever been annoyed by having to scroll forever to get back to where you left off reading a long message? Next time, when you return to your message, just press the G key and the cursor will automatically jump to the place where the cursor was the last time you closed the message!

Composing Messages

When you need to quickly compose a message on your BlackBerry, you don't have time to waste on the formalities of finding the recipient's e-mail address or excessive typing. As mentioned earlier, you can use the C keystroke from within the Message List to automatically create a new message. This brings up the Address Book, so your next challenge is to either find your target recipient in your oversized Address Book or type in your recipient's e-mail address from memory. Not!

Instead, here is an excellent place to employ one of my favorite shortcuts, which is to type partial names in the Address Book listing to quickly find an entry. In most cases, you need to type only the first initial, then the SPACE key, and then the first few letters of the last name, and you will almost certainly have found your contact.

For example, if you were trying to compose an e-mail to me and you thought I was in your Address Book, you would type **g bach** and your Address Book would quickly be filtered down to just a couple (or even one) entries.

Now that you've found your recipient's e-mail address, the following list presents some keyboard shortcuts that can save you time when composing a new e-mail message:

- To type a capital letter, rather than using the CAP key, just press and hold a letter to automatically capitalize it.

- To automatically complete a sentence, just press the SPACE key twice to insert a period (and the next letter you type will be capitalized automatically).

- If you want to add additional recipients in the To or Cc fields and they are not in your Address Book, you may be surprised to know that the SPACE key offers special hidden talents in typing a new e-mail address. When you press the SPACE key in a field intended for e-mail addresses, it automatically knows that it should be an "@" character if it's the first time you have typed it. If it sees there is already an "@" character in the field, it then automatically adds the "." character.

- If you need to type special international or accented characters, press and hold a letter key, and then use the trackwheel to scroll through the available characters and special symbols.

Replying to and Forwarding Your Messages

The following keyboard shortcuts, listed in Table 3-6, offer quick ways to reply to a message or forward a message to another recipient. Note that these shortcuts work both when you have a message selected in the Messages List and when you are viewing the contents of a message.

Keeping Your Messages List Clean

Although your BlackBerry is superb at delivering all of your messages to you, it can be a challenge to stay on top of it all and prevent your device from turning into a sea of old messages. This section shows you several techniques to help clear out old messages and keep your Messages List manageable.

Deleting a Single Message

Yes, there is a specific menu item for deleting the currently selected message, but the fastest way to delete a message is to use the DEL key, also referred to as the Delete or BACKSPACE key. You will of course be asked to confirm your deletion first.

Deleting Multiple Messages

If you really want to clean out your Messages List fast, pressing Delete on each message is too tedious and simply isn't going to cut it. There are two ways to perform a delete of multiple messages at once: deleting by date or by multiple selection.

Deleting Messages by Date

You may have noticed that if you hold on to older messages, when you look at your Messages List, your messages are organized by date, with a date heading separating messages according to which day they were sent to you.

Table 3-6   Message Reply and Forward Shortcut Keys

Shortcut Key	Action
R	Creates a reply to the currently selected message and automatically fills in the To field with the address of the original sender.
L	As with the R shortcut, pressing L creates a reply to the currently selected message but goes further in that it automatically fills in both the To field and the Cc field with all of the original recipients of the original message. This is commonly referred to as a "Reply to All."
F	Creates a new message based on the original, which will be forwarded to a recipient of your choosing. Because the To field is initially empty, you are required to use the Select Address screen, where you may add one or more recipients for the new message.

If you scroll to one of these date headers, click the menu, and choose the Delete Prior menu item, your BlackBerry proceeds to delete all messages from that date or prior to that date. I use this shortcut all the time. Because I often bounce back and forth between my desktop e-mail and my BlackBerry, all of my old messages are ultimately retrieved and stored on my desktop, so there is little reason to retain old messages in my device.

Deleting Messages Using Multiple Selection

The other way to delete multiple messages requires a little more finger exercise but works well if you have a range of messages in a row that you need to delete.

1. Use the trackwheel to scroll to the first message you want to delete.

2. Press the CAP key.

3. Scroll the trackwheel to extend your message selection up or down until you have selected the entire range of messages you wish to delete.

4. Press the DEL key or use the menu item for Delete, and all of the selected messages will be deleted.

Controlling Automatic Deletion of Messages

Aside from manually doing housecleaning in your Messages List, you can also control how long your BlackBerry device holds onto older messages. Because most people use both their BlackBerry and desktop e-mail, most older messages are going to be found on your desktop as well so there is little reason to hold on to older messages on your BlackBerry indefinitely. It takes up additional storage and also makes it harder to find the messages you do wish to open.

To change this setting, go to your Messages List and do the following:

1. Click the trackwheel to bring up the Options menu.

2. Under Options, choose General.

3. Select Keep Messages at the bottom of this screen.

4. Choose Change Option and then choose 15 days, 30 days, 60 days, 90 days, or Forever as the time to keep older messages.

5. Save your new setting, and your BlackBerry will from now on automatically delete any messages that are older than the duration you chose.

Customizing Your BlackBerry Signature

If you have ever received e-mail from someone with a BlackBerry, you are no doubt aware that by default each message gets automatically tagged with the familiar signature "This e-mail was sent wirelessly from my BlackBerry." True, this obviously provides some free marketing and publicity for the BlackBerry folks, and it does tell all your friends and colleagues that you are hip and use the latest technology. But it does also have a more useful aspect in that it clues your recipients in to the fact that you composed your message on-the-go with a thumb keyboard. (At least this way they can cut you some slack and not call the grammar police on you when they see messages from you that read "10am mtg gr8 c u then brng nts.")

Still, most BlackBerry users don't realize that they are not doomed to have every message they send from their BlackBerry formatted this way. Wouldn't it be nice to be able to put a more professional or customized signature on your outgoing messages, as you do in your desktop e-mail program?

Changing Your Blackberry Signature from the Desktop

If you use the BlackBerry Desktop Manager as an e-mail redirector, you can change the default signature by editing your redirector settings:

1. Make sure that your BlackBerry is connected to your desktop computer with the supplied USB cable.

2. Make sure that the Desktop Manager is running, and click the Redirector Settings icon. A number of tabs appear on the next screen.

3. Click the General tab, and you will see the Auto Signature field with the default text in it.

4. Edit the text and save your changes, and your outgoing BlackBerry e-mails should now bear your new signature.

Using Multiple Signatures

Here's a great tip if you like to send messages out to different kinds of people and would like to use different custom signatures for different types of recipients. For example, when you are composing a message to someone at work, you probably want to include your name, title, website address, company name, phone extension, or other work-related information. Likewise, when you are composing a message to your family or friends, you may want to provide a more light-hearted signature or, at the very least, include different contact information.

While the BlackBerry software does not provide for managing and using multiple signatures, you can easily achieve the same effect by making use of the BlackBerry's great Auto Text feature:

1. Make sure you clear the existing default signature text from the Desktop Manager. (See the previous section for how to do this.)

2. On the home screen of your device, go to Options ➪ Auto Text.

3. Create a new Auto Text entry for each custom signature you want to have.

For example, I have an Auto Text entry for my company, Bachmann Software & Services, which I named "bss." It has my name, my company name, and my website URL in it. Now, whenever I want to include this signature on any outgoing business messages, at the bottom of my message I just type the characters "bss" and BlackBerry automatically substitutes the signature I defined. I could, of course, create as many different signatures as I wanted, each with its own Auto Text keyboard shortcut.

Remembering to type the Auto Text shortcut at the end of your e-mails can take a little getting used to, but once you have done it for a while, it becomes pretty automatic.

Cross-Reference Auto Text is covered in more detail in Chapter 1.

Including BlackBerry in Your Signature

While I am still on the topic of custom signatures, I want to point out that just because you don't have to use the default "This e-mail was sent wirelessly from my BlackBerry" signature, it is still probably a good idea to include something in your signature that indicates your e-mail was composed on a BlackBerry. For better or worse, people do form impressions of each other by the way they write e-mail, so doing this can help your recipient understand that you are probably away from your desk and also that you are apologizing in advance for any typing or grammatical errors. Of course, if the recipient of your messages is an important new customer, it may simply be worthwhile to wait until you return to your desk to make sure your messages are crafted in the most professional manner.

Other Messaging Shortcuts

The following sections describe other keystrokes that support special features within the Messages application.

Exchanging Your Contact Information

Back in the days when having a PDA meant that you had a Palm, everyone learned how to "beam" their contact information to one another. This feature does not exist on BlackBerry, but there is still an easier way for you to give someone an e-mail address or phone number than writing it down for them.

Create an e-mail addressed to the person you want to give the contact information to, and then choose the Attach Address menu item. Find the address you want from the Address Book, and the appropriate contact details are added to your e-mail as an attachment. This is a great way to include your other contact information as well, so make sure you have a "Business Card" entry for yourself in your BlackBerry Address Book, and that it is correctly filled out!

Keyboard Shortcuts for Composing Messages

Chapter 1 covers a great many keyboard shortcuts that display interesting information on your BlackBerry. Table 3-7 lists a couple of shortcuts that specifically are helpful when composing or addressing a message. These shortcuts represent fast ways to embed your PIN or phone number in messages so that people can contact you.

Table 3-7	Compose Message Keyboard Shortcuts
Shortcut	*Text Displayed*
Mydcid	Displays your RIM "Direct Connect" ID (Nextel devices only)
Mypin	Displays your PIN, which is your BlackBerry device's unique identifier
Mynumber	Displays your mobile phone number

Receiving Confirmation of Message Delivery

If you would like to get a confirmation message that the message you sent from your BlackBerry was successfully delivered to the recipient, there is a handy shortcut that will do this for you.

When composing your message, just include the phrase "< confirm >" in your message's subject line. The BlackBerry will automatically assume that you want confirmation, and after the message is delivered, you will receive a message back that confirms your message was delivered successfully.

Controlling Your Inbox with Filters

If you are a BlackBerry Internet Service (BIS) user, you may have found that your BlackBerry device is constantly overrun with spam, junk e-mail, and messages that you would rather deal with from your desktop. Wading through your BlackBerry Inbox becomes a tedious process of finding the important messages among the piles of unwanted items. Enterprise BlackBerry users benefit greatly from the messaging controls in place at the corporate e-mail server. Wouldn't it be nice if BIS users could also have some control over the delivery of messages to their BlackBerry?

Many BlackBerry BIS users do not realize it, but you can access and reconfigure your BlackBerry account profile by logging in to your carrier's BlackBerry start page. (Contact your carrier for the exact URL.) Once logged in, you can browse your messages, set up folders, and perform other housekeeping tasks. Additionally, you can set up custom filters to control what messages are delivered to your BlackBerry and how they are delivered.

To access the Filters option, do the following:

1. Click the Filters menu option at the top of the screen after you log in to your BIS profile.

2. Click the Add button, and you will see a screen similar to the one presented in Figure 3-2.

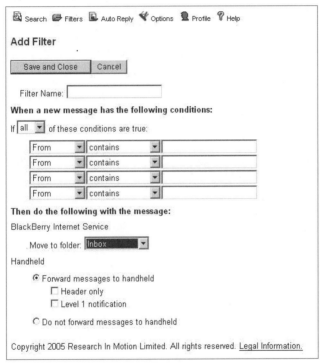

FIGURE 3-2: The BlackBerry Internet Service Add Filter page

3. Starting at the top of this form, each filter you define gets a name, because multiple filters can be associated with your profile.

4. After naming your filter, you may now add one or more "conditions," which will be used to identify messages that you want to forward to (or block from) your BlackBerry. You can set a condition based on the contents of the From, To, Subject, or Body components of each message. Here are some examples of ways you can use conditions:

■ If you want to create a filter condition that can trap all messages that have the word "Urgent" in the subject line, you can choose Subject, Contains, and Urgent as your condition criteria.

- If you decide to set a condition based on the From field, you can set a condition for a specific e-mail address such as john@abc.com.

- You can use a wildcard to trap e-mails from anyone at abc.com, by entering "*.abc.com" as the From address.

5. Once you've established one or more conditions that can trap your messages, you now get to decide what to do with messages that fall under this filter.

- Do you want to move them to your Inbox? Delete them? Block them? The choice is yours, and you can start to see how powerful filters can be in controlling the flow of messages to your handheld.

- You can also forward messages to your handheld. You can use filter criteria to tag specific messages to be sent to your device with "Level 1" notification. This tag can trigger different behaviors on your device, which can be configured in your BlackBerry's device profile settings. For example, if you are working on a critical project with a client, you can associate a Level 1 notification to be sent with any messages from your client and then set your device to immediately notify you with an alert when an e-mail is received from the client.

Instant Messaging Applications

Instant messaging, or IM for short, is a widely popular method of exchanging short text messages directly with other computer or mobile device users. Instant messaging is distinct from e-mail messaging in that it is intended to be very fast and interactive, much more like a live chat than sending and receiving e-mail.

In order to do instant messaging on your BlackBerry, you can elect to use SMS (Short Message Service), which usually requires an add-on subscription from your wireless service provider. Although it costs extra and is not a 100 percent guaranteed service, it is widely supported and thus it is probably more likely that a wider range of recipients will be able to receive the messages you send them.

As an alternative to SMS, a number of messaging applications are now available that integrate with popular instant messaging services from MSN, ICQ, AIM, and Yahoo. These applications do not use SMS to communicate. Instead they use your BlackBerry's data service to communicate with the target messaging service. A clear benefit of going this route, especially if you have an unlimited data plan, is that it can cost a lot less than the available SMS subscription plans from wireless carriers.

WebMessenger Mobile Instant Messenger

WebMessenger Mobile IM provides BlackBerry users with instant messaging/chat capabilities on AOL, MSN, Yahoo, Google Talk, ICQ, and Jabber. WebMessenger Mobile IM requires a subscription from WebMessenger, Inc., priced at $48 per year at the time of this writing. (A free 30-day trial version is available.)

WebMessenger offers advanced support for buddy lists and buddy properties, including buddy groups, filtering, and the ability to import groups from your IM provider. Message settings, filtering, and color-coding add to the usability of the application. The program also includes an interactive chess game that allows you to play against another handheld device user. You can see an example of WebMessenger Mobile Instant Messenger in action in Figure 3-3.

FIGURE 3-3: WebMessenger Mobile
Instant Messenger

WebMessenger is very easy to install. The entire process is handled by a desktop-based "wizard," which is a nice touch. More information on WebMessenger Mobile Instant Messenger, including a free trial download, is available at WebMessenger's website at www.webmessenger.com.

Verichat

Verichat is an award-winning instant messaging application that runs on most handheld devices, including BlackBerry. Verichat supports Yahoo!, ICQ, MSN, and AOL chat networks and lets you carry on multiple conversations at one time with people on your Buddy List.

Aside from person-to-person messaging, Verichat also offers access to numerous added-value services, such as zip code lookup, currency conversion, and more. Verichat presents this list of services to you as part of the menu of actions you can take in addition to messaging.

Verichat's signup and connection process is fairly straightforward, and once you are logged in to your preferred messaging service, chat sessions can be carried on, as shown in Figure 3-4.

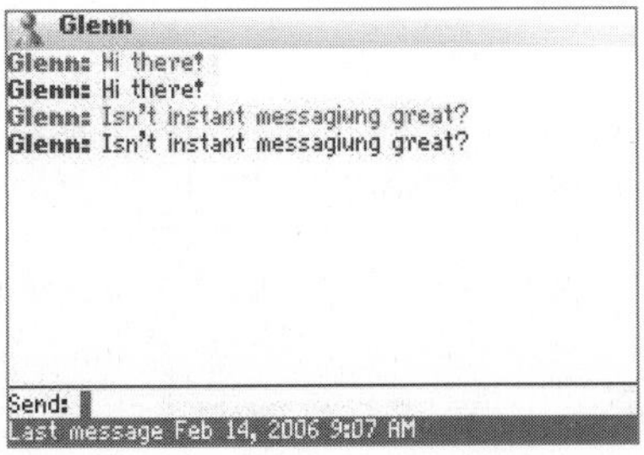

FIGURE 3-4: A chat session using Verichat

IntelliSync's standard version of Verichat is available for $39.95 per year at the time of this writing, or there is a premium version available for $44.95 per year that adds more instant messaging account options. A time-limited free trial version is also available for download. For more information on Verichat, visit www.verichat.com.

IM+ Mobile Instant Messenger

IM+, from a company called Shape Services, supports all of the major instant messaging services including AOL, ICQ, MSN, Yahoo!, Jabber, and Google Talk. Like Verichat, IM+ is available in versions for many other types of devices besides BlackBerry.

IM+ offers a pretty robust array of chat features, including buddy lists, group organization, conferencing, and alerts. Figures 3-5 and 3-6 show IM+ in action.

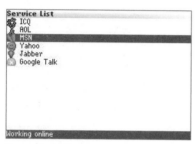

FIGURE 3-5: Choosing among messaging services in IM+

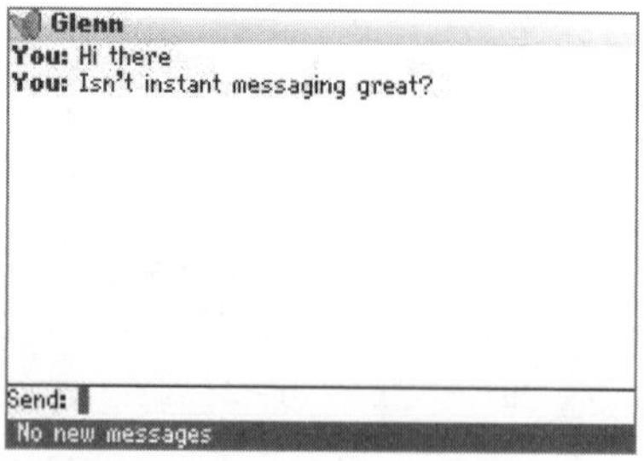

FIGURE 3-6: A chat session using IM+

I did have a little trouble with IM+ at the start when it attempted to try to autoconfigure my network access (see the "About MDS and BES Network Access" section later in this chapter), but I eventually got it configured and connected without too much trouble. If you cannot get past the network connectivity problem, Shape Services also offers a WAP-based version of IM+.

In terms of pricing, IM+ is a little unique compared to the other messaging applications listed here, which require a yearly subscription. At the time of this writing, Shape Services offers

IM+ for a one-time price of $44.95, which is nice if you prefer not to purchase subscription-based software.

For more information on IM+ and other applications from Shape Services, visit www.shapeservices.com.

BlackBerry Messenger

BlackBerry Messenger (see Figure 3-7) is an instant messaging program that is provided free of charge by Research In Motion (the makers of the BlackBerry device itself). Messenger does not integrate with popular instant messaging services such as AOL, ICQ, or MSN. What it does offer is the ability to perform messaging between BlackBerry devices independent of these Internet-based messaging services. Because it relies on the BlackBerry PIN, in order for you to chat with another person with Messenger, that person must be using a BlackBerry and must have installed BlackBerry Messenger on their device.

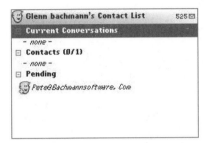

FIGURE 3-7: The BlackBerry Messenger
main screen

Rather than rely on an Internet-based Buddy List, BlackBerry Messenger builds up a messaging contact list out of your existing BlackBerry Address Book. To add to your contact list, just select the contact from your Address Book and a request is sent. Participation is thus by invitation, and you will need to await a confirmation from your target recipient before you can start a conversation with them using Messenger.

If you can live with chatting only with other BlackBerry owners running Messenger, the program can meet your basic messaging needs. Of course, it is a free download so the price can't be beat!

For more information on BlackBerry Messenger as well as access to a free download, please visit www.blackberry.com/messenger. (Note that this web page requires Internet Explorer to work correctly.)

About MDS and BES Network Access

There is one gotcha concerning network-enabled third-party software applications such as the previously described messaging programs, and that is the issue of network access. The built-in mail and browser applications are automatically granted access as "trusted" applications, regardless of your carrier. However, network access is controlled by your wireless data carrier, which may or may not automatically enable direct device-to-host network access from third-party applications on your BlackBerry. Unfortunately, there is no overall consistency across carriers, and there is even some variation among different device models offered by the same carrier in terms of whether network access is enabled.

The basic problem occurs when a non-trusted application tries to make a network connection on your device. If full network access is not configured by your carrier on your device, the network connection request will fail, and the application will not work properly. The problem is most prevalent on older versions of the BlackBerry OS (before 3.8) and in many cases is resolved by upgrading to the most current OS offered by your carrier.

An excellent article that lays out the network configuration steps for each carrier is available at the popular BlackBerryForums.com web portal. The exact web address of the article is www.blackberryforums.com/showthread.php?t=2185. If this link doesn't work, you can search on their website for "How to Configure Full Internet Access."

Using Your BlackBerry with Web-Based Mail

If you are using your BlackBerry with your company's enterprise mail server or if you are using your BlackBerry with your Internet service provider's POP e-mail service, your BlackBerry is good to go as far as sending and receiving e-mail. However, many people who make use of web-based mail services, such as Google's Gmail, Yahoo! Mail, or Hotmail, do not enjoy automatic access to their e-mail accounts on those services. This section describes how to make your BlackBerry work with a number of these web-based mail services.

Google's Gmail

Google's Gmail service is one of the most popular free e-mail services available. Setting up your BlackBerry to work with Gmail requires you to first change your Gmail settings on the web and then configure your BlackBerry Internet Service (BIS) account to access your Gmail account. Perform the following steps:

1. Log in to your Gmail account.
2. Click Settings at the top of the Gmail page.
3. Click Forwarding and POP in the Mail Settings box.
4. Select either "Enable POP for all Mail" or "Enable POP for all mail from now on."
5. Click Save Changes.
6. Now go and log in to your BlackBerry Internet service account.
7. Click the Profile link at the top of the page.
8. Click Other Email Accounts in the e-mail accounts section of your BIS profile.

9. Click Add Account.

10. Now enter the information for your Gmail account, including e-mail address, username, and password.

11. To complete the change, click Submit.

At this point, if your Gmail account has been properly set for POP access, you should be able to send and receive Gmail on your BlackBerry.

Yahoo! Mail

In order to integrate your Yahoo! Mail account with your BlackBerry, you must first subscribe to the Yahoo! Mail Plus service. (Unfortunately, regular Yahoo! Mail accounts are not supported.)

1. Log in to your BlackBerry Internet Service account.

2. Click the Profile link at the top of the page.

3. Click Other Email Accounts in the e-mail accounts section of your BIS profile.

4. Click Add Account.

5. Now enter the information for your Yahoo! Mail Plus account, including e-mail address, username, and password.

6. Click the option "I have enabled POP access to my Yahoo! mailbox and want to add it." Then click Next.

7. To complete the change, click Submit.

Hotmail

To integrate your Hotmail account with your BlackBerry, you need to upgrade to MSN Hotmail Plus, which is a paid subscription.

1. Log in to your BlackBerry Internet Service account.

2. Click the Profile link at the top of the page.

3. Click Other Email Accounts in the e-mail accounts section of your BIS profile.

4. Click Add Account.

5. Now enter the information for your MSN Hotmail Plus account, including e-mail address, username, and password.

6. To complete the change, click Submit.

Note that if you try this procedure with a regular (non-Plus) Hotmail account, you will receive an error message such as "Cannot integrate the email account."

Outlook Web Access

To integrate your Outlook Web Access account with your BlackBerry, perform the following steps:

1. Log in to your BlackBerry Internet Service account.
2. Click the Profile link at the top of the page.
3. Click Other Email Accounts in the e-mail accounts section of your BIS profile.
4. Click Add Account.
5. Enter the information for your Outlook Web Access account, including e-mail address, username, and password.
6. Under Microsoft Outlook / Exchange, choose the option "I can access my mailbox using a Web browser (Outlook Web Access)."
7. Click Submit.
8. In the Outlook Web Access URL field, type the Outlook Web Access account URL.
9. In the Mailbox Name field, type the Mailbox name for your Outlook Web Access account.
10. Select the option "Leave messages on mail server."
11. Click Submit.

iNotes

To integrate your iNotes account with your BlackBerry, perform the following steps:

1. Log in to your BlackBerry Internet Service account.
2. Click the Profile link at the top of the page.
3. Click Other Email Accounts in the e-mail accounts section of your BIS profile.
4. Click Add Account.
5. Enter the information for your iNotes account, including e-mail address, username, and password.
6. Under Lotus Notes/Domino, choose the option "I can access my mailbox using a Web browser (iNotes)."
7. Click Submit.
8. In the iNotes URL field, type the iNotes account URL. Be sure to include the location of the .nsf file and the connection type (http or https).
9. Select the option "Leave messages on mail server."
10. Click Submit.

Working with E-mail Attachments

Although the earliest BlackBerry units were capable of viewing only the body text of e-mails, modern BlackBerry devices come with a basic ability to view e-mail attachments of different file types, including Word documents, Excel spreadsheets, and PDF files. Attachment handling is actually turned on as the Attachment Service on the BlackBerry Enterprise Server (or by your carrier's BlackBerry Internet Service).

About the BlackBerry Attachment Viewer

The Attachment Service works by intercepting your incoming BlackBerry e-mail, scanning it for attachments it knows how to handle, and performing a conversion of any attachments to a standard viewable format. On your device, when you open an e-mail that has an attachment, an Open Attachment menu item becomes available that will then retrieve the attachment in viewable format and display it on your handheld screen.

This attachment handling scheme has some advantages. For one, the conversion process breaks down the attachment into logical sections, kind of like the chapters in a book. This means that you don't need to burden your handheld with the task of retrieving a file that can potentially be many megabytes in size all at once. Another advantage is that you don't need separate programs on your device to handle, convert, and view attachments of various file types. They are all handled by the BlackBerry attachment viewer.

Despite these advantages, there are some drawbacks to using the Attachment Service and associated attachment viewer. The breakup of documents into logical sections helps reduce waiting time for downloads, but it also makes the reading and navigation of your attachments a different experience than that of your desktop computer, and if you are not sure where in the document the information is that you are looking for, it can be very tedious to retrieve and view the sections one by one.

Another disadvantage is that some file formats lose quite a bit in the conversion process. Much of the formatting in Word documents, and especially PDF files, is lost or poorly translated.

Note For information on third-party programs that offer more fully functioning attachment and document editing functionality, see the section "Third-Party Attachment Programs" later in this chapter.

The physical nature of the BlackBerry device also presents a challenge with some file formats. Navigating through even a moderately sized Excel spreadsheet with just the trackwheel on a small screen is a far cry from what happens on your desktop.

Attachment Viewer Keyboard Shortcuts

Tables 3-8, 3-9, and 3-10 present a number of keyboard shortcuts that can speed up and augment your viewing of e-mail attachments. Separate tables are provided for the Document Viewer, Spreadsheet Viewer, and Image Viewer.

Table 3-8   Attachment Viewer Navigation Shortcut Keys (Document Viewer)

Shortcut Key	Action
V	Switches between table of contents and full content view
T	Goes to the top of the page
B	Goes to the bottom of the page
F	Opens the Find dialog box (and repeated pressing finds each next occurrence)
J	Goes directly to an embedded link under the cursor
G	Opens the Go To Page dialog box
N	Goes to the next page
P	Goes to the previous page

Table 3-9   Attachment Viewer Navigation Shortcut Keys (Spreadsheet Viewer)

Shortcut Key	Action
Trackwheel	Scrolls vertically
ALT+trackwheel	Scrolls horizontally
V	Switches between table of contents and full content view
T	Goes to the top left of the current worksheet
B	Goes to the bottom right of the current worksheet
F	Opens the Find dialog box (and repeated pressing finds each next occurrence)
G	Opens the Go to Cell dialog box
N	Goes to the next sheet in the workbook
P	Goes to the previous sheet in the workbook

Table 3-10   Attachment Viewer Navigation Shortcut Keys (Image Viewer)

Shortcut Key	Action
ALT+trackwheel	Pans horizontally across an image
3	Zooms in on an image
9	Zooms out on an image
. (period)	Rotates an image

Third-Party Attachment Programs

A number of third-party applications have arrived on the scene to fill the gaps in attachment handling functionality. This section reviews three of the most popular of these "attachment plug-ins."

Viewing PDF Attachments with DocHawk

Terratial Technologies offers a number of document and attachment utilities for BlackBerry devices, but it is perhaps best known for its DocHawk attachment service. DocHawk allows BlackBerry users to open and view PDF attachments in their original format — a vast improvement over the text-oriented representation offered by the standard BlackBerry attachment service.

DocHawk has two main components: a conversion host service that prepares PDF attachments for viewing on the handheld and a device application that inserts itself into the BlackBerry e-mail application. Once installed on your BlackBerry, DocHawk becomes available as a new menu item when you open e-mails with PDF attachments (shown in Figure 3-8).

FIGURE 3-8: The Open With DocHawk menu option

If you highlight an attachment and choose Open with DocHawk, DocHawk asks you to confirm that you wish to submit your attachment to the DocHawk host conversion server (see Figure 3-9). If you choose Submit, DocHawk contacts the host service and prepares an appropriate conversion of your PDF for viewing on the device.

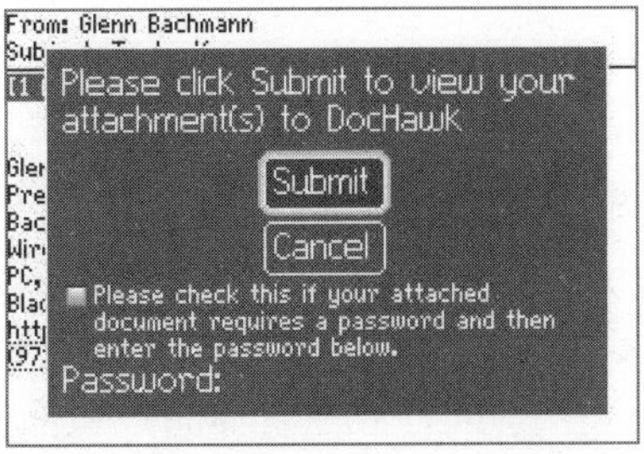

FIGURE 3-9: The Submit dialog box in DocHawk

This process can take some time to complete (their documentation claims up to a minute, your mileage may vary), especially for larger documents, but when it is complete what you get is a PDF viewing experience that is reminiscent of what you would expect when viewing a PDF attachment from within your desktop e-mail application. Your PDF document is rendered in all its glory, graphics, formatting, and all. Additional viewing features are offered to help with readability on the small screen, including the ability to zoom out to various levels.

Besides opening attachments from within e-mails, the other way to use DocHawk is as a standalone application. DocHawk can be run from its application icon on the BlackBerry home screen, and it will present you with a list of PDF attachments that can be viewed. This can be a preferable method of accessing your PDFs if you want to avoid navigating through your e-mails to find your attachments.

DocHawk is priced as a subscription service and, at the time of this writing, can be purchased for $59.95 per year or $19.95 per quarter. You can get a trial download, as well as more information on DocHawk and other Terratial products, at the Terratial website at `www.terratial.com`.

Viewing Attachments with Repligo

Repligo Professional for BlackBerry, by Cerience Corporation, offers an attachment conversion service and attachment viewers for many popular file formats, including Word, Excel, PDF, PowerPoint, Zip, fax, and image. As with DocHawk, Repligo preserves your document's original formatting, including fonts, graphics, colors, images, tables, and other features.

Like DocHawk, Repligo offers both an on-device file viewer as well as a host-based conversion service. Attachments may be viewed from within the context of the original e-mail, or separately from the Repligo Document List. The trial version of Repligo lets you download a short list of sample documents from the Repligo host, as shown in Figure 3-10.

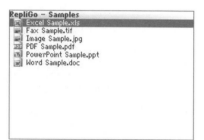

FIGURE 3-10: The Repligo Sample Document list

From within the document list, you can select a document for viewing. Doing this submits a request to the Repligo host to convert the document for viewing on the handheld. Conversions occur one page at a time and are fairly quick. Once a page is retrieved, it can be quickly zoomed in or out, and a number of navigational aids allow you to move around the document.

Figure 3-11 shows a sample Excel spreadsheet with a graph included, highlighting Repligo's ability to preserve the original document's graphics and formatting.

FIGURE 3-11: A sample Excel spreadsheet, viewed in Repligo

Repligo is priced as a subscription service and can be purchased for $99.95 per year or $29.95 per quarter at the time of this writing. A limited functionality trial download, as well as more information on Repligo, can be obtained at the Cerience website at www.cerience.com.

Viewing Documents with eOffice

eOffice from Dynoplex takes a somewhat different approach than DocHawk and Repligo in that the emphasis is on providing a full Office suite, including document editing, creation, and viewing on the BlackBerry device. eOffice goes far beyond attachment viewing and attempts to fill a fairly prominent gap in the BlackBerry bundle of included software applications. While Dynoplex does not replicate the exact same level of formatting as found in Microsoft Office, it does offer a much fuller suite of document functionality to those users who require Office-type features on their handheld.

eOffice claims to support Word, Excel, PDF, PowerPoint, text (Notepad.txt), as well as many image formats. Among these formats, Word and Excel are also supported for creation of new documents as well as editing of existing documents.

For handling attachments, eOffice adds to a message that contains an attachment a custom menu, "Save to eOffice." Selecting this menu option on an attachment brings up a screen similar to the one in Figure 3-12, from which you can open the attachment directly in eOffice or save it to a "folder" on your handheld.

FIGURE 3-12: Saving an attachment to eOffice

After choosing the "Save Attachment" option, eOffice submits a request to have the attachment run through the Dynoplex document converter host. Depending on the size of your document this can take a few seconds to a few minutes. Your next step is to run the eOffice utility, which is accessible from your home screen. This utility presents an interesting Explorer-like view of files and programs on your BlackBerry. Document attachments are stored in the Local\Mail Attachments folder, as shown in Figure 3-13.

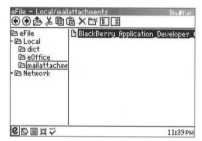

FIGURE 3-13: Locating a saved attachment in the eOffice file explorer

Working with attachments in eOffice can be a bit more cumbersome and take a few more steps than in DocHawk or Repligo, but in exchange you are rewarded with a richer feature set and a taste of full Office functionality on your BlackBerry.

At the time of this writing, eOffice is available for purchase in Basic ($119), Standard ($149), and Professional ($199) editions, at a one-time (non-subscription) cost.

For more information on eOffice as well as access to free trial downloads, visit Dynoplex at www.dynoplex.com.

Spell Checking Your E-mail

BlackBerry users understand that doing e-mail on a BlackBerry is all about mobility, e-mail everywhere, and quick communications. Formatting, grammar, and spelling definitely take a back seat to getting a quick message out. Yet the non–BlackBerry-carrying world doesn't always see it that way, and it can be downright embarrassing to have an important client or customer read your e-mails when they are full of spelling mistakes and incomprehensible abbreviations.

The folks at Dynoplex have created a spell checker for BlackBerry called eSpell. eSpell integrates seamlessly into the Compose Message menu screen, so all you have to do before you send your message off is to select the Spell Check menu item and you can run your typing through a nice spell checker. Figure 3-14 shows eSpell in action on a poorly typed e-mail message.

eSpell is available from Dynoplex at www.dynoplex.com and is part of their eOffice suite of applications (described earlier in the "Working with E-mail Attachments" section).

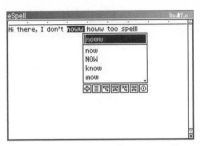

FIGURE 3-14: eSpell catches my spelling
mistakes

Faxing from Your BlackBerry

Perhaps you might by now consider faxing to be a retro, oh-so-1990 thing to do, but look in any business and odds are you will find a trusty old fax machine, sending and receiving several faxes each and every day. Faxing remains a fixture in today's world because of its unique ability to produce a physical, paper copy of a message or document in a recipient's hands with virtually no effort other than dialing a phone number and inserting the source document into the fax paper feed.

Wouldn't it be great to be able to send a fax right from your BlackBerry? Its not as easy as you might think. These days, wireless carriers have either blocked analog faxing traffic on their networks or at the very least have made it inconvenient to figure out how to set it up. One answer is to sign up for a faxing service that can convert an e-mail to a fax on your behalf.

If you do a search on the Internet, you will find a great many email-to-fax services. One such service is eFax (www.efax.com). With eFax, you need to sign up for an account, but once you have done that, all you need to do is compose an e-mail and then send it to a special e-mail address. The eFax service then creates your fax electronically for you, and redirects it to the fax machine you specify. eFax offers many different service plans, including a free limited-functionality plan, all of which may be viewed on the www.efax.com website.

Shortcuts and Hidden Keys in the Phone Application

The BlackBerry Phone application supports a number of shortcuts for making calls more quickly and efficiently.

Using Speed Dial

Although you may not realize it, your BlackBerry does have a Speed Dial screen. This screen is accessible from the View Speed Dial menu in the Phone application.

Speed Dial supports the use of keyboard letters, which can be assigned to specific contacts. Because you can make use of the entire alphabet, the BlackBerry speed dial is arguably more powerful than that on standard phones.

To assign a speed dial letter:

1. Go to the Phone application and press and hold the letter you wish to use.

2. You will see a prompt appear asking if you wish to assign the letter to a speed dial. Click Yes and you are then presented with the address list.

3. Scroll to the Address Book entry you wish to associate with the speed dial letter. Select the address entry to successfully assign a speed dial letter to that entry.

To make a call using speed dial, simply press and hold the speed dial letter. The Phone application automatically dials the associated number. You can use this feature from either within the Phone application or from the home Applications screen.

One Speed Dial assignment is automatically made for you: your voice mail number. To quickly dial your voice mail, just press and hold the 1 key.

Note To quickly redial the last number you called, press the SPACE key from within the Phone application.

Dialing from the Home Applications Screen

Besides being able to dial a number directly in the Phone application using the numeric keypad, you can also conveniently dial while in the BlackBerry Applications screen.

To enable this feature:

1. In the Phone application, go to the Options menu and choose the General Options category.

2. Choose Dial From Home Screen and make sure the option is set to Yes.

With this option enabled, just start dialing a number from the Applications screen and the Phone application automatically starts for you.

Dialing Using Letters

Some phone numbers are familiar not by their number, but by the word or phrase conjured up by the telephone keypad letters that map to the number (for example, BLK-BRRY is 255-2779).

Although the BlackBerry assumes that you are dialing using numbers when you are in the Phone application, you can still dial letters as part of a phone number. To do this, hold down the ALT key and press the letter you wish to use.

Working with Live Calls

The tricks described in this section are employed during a live BlackBerry phone call.

- **Using the mute function:** Press the Phone button.
- **Adjusting the volume:** Roll the trackwheel up (to make the audio louder) or down (to make it softer).
- **Making a three-way call:** Accomplishing a three-way call can be a mystery even on a standard landline phone. It is, however, remarkably easy on your BlackBerry.

    1. Press the trackwheel and choose the Hold menu item. This places your current call on hold.

    2. Dial the number for the third party. Your screen lists both parties as connected.

    3. Press the trackwheel again and choose the Join menu to engage your call.

        Once a three-way call is engaged, you can make use of the Split menu option, accessible from the Trackwheel menu, to switch among the active connections. The Split menu option enables you to speak privately with one of the callers while on a multiple-party call.

Seeing Missed Calls

By default, the BlackBerry notifies you of a missed call by displaying a tiny icon at the top of your screen. It's easy to miss this subtle notification.

Fortunately, you can change your BlackBerry's settings to pop up a window when you have missed a call. To do this:

1. Go to the Phone application and use the trackwheel to select the Options menu.

2. Go into General Options and set the Phone List View option to Call Log.

You can also specify that a Missed Call entry be added to your Messages List in the Call Logging option.

Installing and Playing Custom Ring Tones

Listen to enough of the millions of cell phones ringing every day, and a good percentage of them will be playing a familiar tune such as Beethoven's *Fifth Symphony*, the theme from *Jaws*, or some new-wave hit from the 80s. Depending on your perspective, ringtones are an entertaining diversion, a useful way to recognize callers on your phone, or an annoying plague on society. Whether or not ringtones appeal to you, there is no denying that millions of people love putting custom ringtones on their cell phones.

Clearly, BlackBerry owners want to be invited to the ringtone party as well. One of the questions asked most often on the many BlackBerry online discussion boards is "How do I add ringtones to my BlackBerry?" This section describes how to add ringtones to your BlackBerry, using available third-party software.

Understanding Hardware Capabilities

First, let's set some expectations on what you will hear. Because of differences in the audio hardware and software, the BlackBerry model that you own will determine the quality of the tones that can be played. In general, if you own a 7100, 7130, or 8700 model, you can take advantage of "polyphonic" ringtones. Older models can still play tones, but they will be reduced to "monophonic." The terms "polyphonic" and "monophonic" simply refer to how many tones can be played at once by your BlackBerry model. Polyphonic ringtones sound better and more true to the original tune, but if you have an older model that supports only monophonic, don't despair; monophonic ringtones sound perfectly fine as well.

Using BlackBerry Ringtone Megaplex

One of the most popular BlackBerry programs available today is a product called BlackBerry Ringtone Megaplex, by Terratial Technologies (the same company that produces DocHawk, described earlier in this chapter).

Like many of the products described here, Ringtone Megaplex is both a host-based service as well as a software program that you load onto your BlackBerry. In the case of Ringtone Megaplex, the host service part consists of a website that allows subscribers to access, browse, and download from over 1,000 different custom ringtones. Each ringtone is a downloadable file that is wirelessly transferred to your BlackBerry through the BlackBerry web browser. Once downloaded to the device, you can then associate your ringtone with one or more of your BlackBerry profiles. On older devices, profiles are managed in the Options application, which is found on the BlackBerry home screen. Newer devices running BlackBerry OS 4.1 or better have access to the Profiles icon directly from the home screen.

My goal when I set out to write this section was to be able to change the ringtone from the humdrum standard tones available with my 7290 to a recognizable tune that everyone around me will love (or hate) to hear. Following are the steps that I took to get there.

Signing Up for the Ringtone Megaplex Service

BlackBerry Ringtone Megaplex is one of those rare programs that is not available as a free trial download. However, at $19.99 for an entire year's subscription, the cost is not too bad, especially if you are addicted to ringtones! So, before you can try out Ringtone Megaplex, go to Terratial's website at www.terratial.com (or an online software store such as www.handango.com) and plunk down your $19.95.

Immediately after you purchase your subscription, you are sent a confirmation e-mail with instructions on how to download the handheld software as well as how to access the library of available ringtones.

Browsing and Downloading Ringtones

After downloading and installing the BlackBerry Ringtone Megaplex software on your device, you are able to browse and download ringtones. Ringtone Megaplex installs with a visible application icon on your BlackBerry home screen, but this icon really is just there to display instructions on how to obtain ringtones and associate a ringtone with your BlackBerry profile. To actually begin the process, you instead need to follow these steps:

1. Use your BlackBerry web browser to connect to the web page containing the ringtone library. Note that this page is for subscribers only and is password protected so you need to log in with the information that was sent to you when you purchased the product.

2. Once you've logged in, you are prompted to select the link that matches up with your BlackBerry device model (such as 7290 or 7100t).

3. After selecting your model, you will see a screen on your browser like the one pictured in Figure 3-15, presenting you with a list of ringtone categories such as Classical, Movie, or Rock.

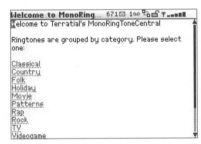

FIGURE 3-15: Browsing the Ringtone Megaplex library

After you have selected a ringtone category, you are presented with a list of available ringtones for download. In my experiment, I went into the Classical category and chose Ravel's "Bolero."

4. Once selected, an audio player window appears and, as a preview, begins playing the ringtone you've chosen on your BlackBerry speaker, as shown in Figure 3-16.

FIGURE 3-16: Previewing a selected ringtone

5. You can stop and restart the ringtone preview using the onscreen Play and Stop buttons.

6. If you are happy with your selection, use the trackwheel to choose the third button (which looks like a playlist icon), and from the popup menu choose Save. This will save the ringtone to a special folder on your BlackBerry device and add it to your own library of downloaded ringtones.

Setting a Ringtone in Your BlackBerry Profile

You must perform one more step in order to set your custom ringtone on your BlackBerry, and that is to change your BlackBerry profile to use the ringtone instead of the currently configured tune. To do this, follow these steps:

1. Return to your BlackBerry home screen and choose the Profiles icon.

2. Your BlackBerry normally has a list of available profiles, each of which defines how your device will behave in various circumstances such as appointment alarms, incoming calls, and so on. One of these profiles is the Default profile. Select this profile, and scroll to the Phone item.

3. Open the Phone item, and you will see a screen that allows you to customize how your BlackBerry responds to an incoming phone call. This screen allows you to set different settings for when your BlackBerry is in or out of the holster.

4. Scroll to the Out of Holster or In Holster settings, and choose the Tune setting. Use the trackwheel menu to change the option. You should see a drop-down list like the one pictured in Figure 3-17, displaying a list of available tunes. If you've downloaded one or more ringtones, these will appear by name in the drop-down list, just like my "Bolero" ringtone in Figure 3-17.

```
Phone in Default            bolero_320271603
Out of Holster:             BlackBerry 1
Tune:                       BlackBerry 2
Volume:                     BlackBerry 3
Number of Beeps:            BlackBerry 4
Repeat Notification:        BlackBerry 5
In Holster:                 BlackBerry 6
Tune:                       Ring 1
Volume:                     Ring 2
Number of Beeps:            Ring 3
Repeat Notification:        Ring 4
Do Not Disturb:             Ring 5
                            Ring 6
                            UK Ring 1
                            UK Ring 2
                            UK Ring 3
```

FIGURE 3-17: Selecting a ringtone for your BlackBerry profiles

5. Once you've chosen your new ringtone, save and close the Profile program.

You should now be all set with your new ringtone. To test it out, just dial your BlackBerry from some other phone, and when your BlackBerry rings, your new ringtone will play! In my case, the "Bolero" tune has been ringing all day, and I am dying to change it. I wonder what I should change it to? Hmmm . . .

Specifying a Unique Ringtone for Individual Contacts

The steps I outlined establish a new ringtone for all incoming calls. But what if you want to be able to tell who is calling you, just by the ringtone that is played? I won't go into all of the reasons why you might want to know if it is your boss, your wife, or your best buddy calling you, but suffice to say there might be many reasons.

If you are using a BlackBerry that is running a version of the BlackBerry OS earlier than version 4.1, you are out of luck. You cannot assign different tunes to different contacts. But if you are using a newer model that runs OS 4.1 (such as the 7130 or the 8700) or if your carrier has provided an upgrade to OS 4.1 for your device model, you can indeed assign unique tunes to different contacts.

To do this, follow these steps:

1. Go into your Address Book from the BlackBerry home screen.

2. Select a contact, click the Trackwheel menu, and choose Edit.

3. If you scroll to the very end of the contact fields, you can push the trackwheel in and select the Custom Tune menu item.

4. From the drop-down list, choose the tune from your list of built-in or custom ringtones in your device library.

5. Click Save.

From this point on when this contact calls, the tune associated with him or her plays.

Summary

Many BlackBerry users simply are not aware that there is more to BlackBerry messaging than scrolling up and down the Messages List and opening e-mails. In this chapter you learned how to transform the way you perform BlackBerry messaging into a much more efficient and personalized experience through the use of special shortcut keys, custom signatures to your outgoing messages, attachment handling, and fun and distinctive ringtones.

Armed with these tips and techniques, it's a cinch that you'll be more productive in how you handle e-mail. Just don't be surprised to find people looking over your shoulder as you work on your BlackBerry, saying "Hey! Can you show me how to do that on my BlackBerry?"

Unleashing the Wireless Web

G iven the built-in wireless capability that comes with BlackBerry, it makes sense that BlackBerry users want to make the most of their device by taking advantage of as much of the wireless world as they can. As you've seen, e-mail and messaging in general are the first and most obvious features that BlackBerry users gravitate toward. But what about the Web? For desktop and laptop users, the Web is the Internet. So how much of the Web can a BlackBerry user expect to be able to access on his or her device?

In this chapter, you explore the built-in BlackBerry Browser and uncover hidden shortcut keys that can help speed up your use of the mobile Web. You also see some of the more mobile-friendly websites that exist and cater to users who access them from BlackBerry devices. You also step outside of the browser itself and take a look at tools for subscribing to and accessing information and news feeds from RSS, and even how to blog with your BlackBerry!

Built-in Web Browsing Tools

Before you dive into the various ways to extend and enhance your access to the wireless Web on your BlackBerry, it is worthwhile to do a quick review of what is available in terms of the built-in web browser software that comes on a standard BlackBerry device.

Comparing the WAP Browser and the Internet Browser

Modern BlackBerry handhelds generally offer two primary web browser configurations. The first web browsing configuration is called a WAP browser. WAP, which is an acronym for Wireless Access Protocol, is a network protocol that can serve up and display specially formatted pages from a WAP gateway. These pages must be written using a special syntax called Wireless Markup Language, or WML for short. WML was designed many years ago as a kind of sister page description language to HTML, one that is optimized for use on slower networks and less capable browser displays. Although you can find some pages around the Internet that are formatted using WML, the WAP browser is not going to be able to work with standard HTML web pages on the public Internet. Instead, the WAP browser is perhaps most suited for internal corporate applications that deliver custom data between a host server and a BlackBerry device.

The second web browser configuration is a BlackBerry implementation of a standard HTML browser. This browser is known either as the "BlackBerry Browser" (if it is provisioned as part of an MDS corporate server) or the "Internet Browser" (if it is provisioned as part of an individual wireless data plan). Starting with BlackBerry OS 4.0, wireless carriers began offering the standard HTML browser with new BlackBerry devices, so just about any new BlackBerry device comes equipped with an HTML-capable browser. Also, depending on the wireless carrier, if you have an older BlackBerry and can upgrade it to BlackBerry OS 4.x, you should automatically get the web browser as part of the upgrade. If you are running BlackBerry OS 4.x and don't see an icon for the Internet Browser on your screen, check with your IT administrator or your wireless carrier to see if you can get the browser software.

Note In some cases you will find that your BlackBerry user documentation refers to the browser by some other name. This is simply a case where a wireless carrier has chosen to "re-brand" the built-in browser for whatever purpose.

The Surf's Definitely Not Up

Looking at both browser configurations, it is easy to see that for most BlackBerry owners the Internet Browser is by far the more useful browsing option because it offers the chance to visit standard websites and pages around the Internet. However, before you start thinking that you will be happily surfing the Internet on your BlackBerry, that is unfortunately not the case. Despite steady improvements in wireless connection speeds, screen displays, and handheld processing power, surfing the Web on a handheld device (any device, not just a BlackBerry) is still a pretty frustrating experience.

This is not to lay the blame on the BlackBerry web browser software. As a matter of fact, the current version is quite feature-rich. The main problem is that the vast majority of websites out there assume the user is sitting in front of a powerful desktop or laptop computer with a big screen and a broadband network connection, and are weighed down with slow-loading images, complex screen layouts, navigation bars that assume a mouse, and complex scripts and style sheets. If you are using an enterprise BlackBerry, MDS helps with these tasks on the server side by reducing images and filtering out inappropriate HTML formatting. Nevertheless, these pages can take quite a long time to download and render on your BlackBerry, and even when they do, the end result is not very pleasing — often ranging from barely readable to downright unusable. It seems likely that until (or unless) web designers start taking into account the possibility that their visitors just might be trying to view their sites on a teeny-tiny screen, the general web surfing experience on any handheld browser is not going to get much better.

Still, despite these challenges, the built-in Internet Browser can be quite useful in the following circumstances:

- Performing quick information searches, using a simple search page such as www.google.com

- Directly accessing a mobile-friendly web page or download URL from a saved bookmark

- Accessing news, weather, and other information via a mobile-friendly web portal

- Downloading applications "over-the-air" directly to your BlackBerry

- Accessing internal HTML pages from a corporate server that are specifically designed for use by a BlackBerry device

Given a direct URL to a mobile-friendly web page, it is amazing how much better the experience can be on a BlackBerry!

Web Browser Keyboard Shortcuts

Within the built-in Internet Browser are a number of helpful features and shortcuts that can help smooth over some of the awkwardness of trying to get around. Table 4-1 lists shortcut keys you can use within the Browser.

Table 4-1   Internet Browser Shortcut Keys

Shortcut Key	Action
spacebar	When typing a web page address, enters a period (.). When viewing a web page, performs a page down.
Shift+spacebar	When viewing a web page, performs a page up.
H	Jumps to your browser's home page from whatever page is currently being viewed.
ESC	Goes back to the previously viewed page.
R	Refreshes the currently viewed page.
F	Lets you search for a keyword on the current page.
G	Jumps to the Go To page screen.
O	Jumps to the browser Options screen.
K	Jumps to the Bookmarks screen.
T	Jumps to the top of the currently viewed page.

Table 4-1 *Continued*

Shortcut Key	Action
B	Jumps to the bottom of the currently viewed page.
A	Prompts you to add the currently viewed page as a bookmark.
I	Jumps to the browser History screen.
N	Goes to the next page in the browser History list.
L	Brings up the address for the currently selected link and allows you to copy the address to the clipboard or to e-mail the address.
P	Brings up the address for the currently viewed page and allows you to copy the address to the clipboard or to e-mail the address.
S	Saves a link to the currently viewed page as a Saved Message.
D	Switches the web browser to the background and lets you switch to a different application without having to close your browser session.
U	Toggles between full-screen mode and normal viewing mode. Full screen mode omits the title bar and status bar to give you slightly more screen real estate to view a web page in.
C	Brings up an interesting Connection Information screen that shows details about your current browser session and connection. You can copy this information to the clipboard if you wish.

Many of these shortcut keys can save you a considerable amount of repetitive and monotonous thumb-scrolling and menu-clicking. As with some of the other BlackBerry shortcut keys and techniques covered in Chapter 1, once you master these keystrokes, you'll wonder how you ever got along without them!

BlackBerry-Friendly Websites and Portals

The key to success with BlackBerry's Internet Browser (or any mobile device browser, for that matter) is to make sure you fill your bookmarks with links to mobile-friendly websites. If at all possible, you want to avoid visiting a website that is designed with a full-screen desktop computer in mind. If, in fact, such a web page loads at all, often you will find that it takes forever, it is very hard to read, and navigation is next to impossible.

So what makes a website *mobile-friendly*? Some websites are already mobile-friendly without necessarily being designed with mobile devices such as the BlackBerry in mind. Probably the most obvious example of such a website is Google (www.google.com). Google's main page loads lightning-fast on a desktop computer and with good reason — aside from the Google logo, the main page is free of graphics and is amazingly sparse given how powerful and popular a place it holds in today's world. Google does offer mobile versions of its web services, but even the standard Google main page loads quite nicely on a mobile device. Contrast the main Google page with the home pages for Yahoo or MSN. Certainly both of these pages contain tons more information, but then again they also take an eternity to load on a mobile web browser.

Many websites have pursued a strategy of providing both a full-featured desktop layout as well as a more stripped-down version that is more appropriate for mobile devices. Some of these sites automatically recognize the fact that you are browsing from a mobile device and will load the appropriate mobile-friendly pages. More often, you need to know a special URL that points to the mobile-friendly pages.

Unfortunately for users of BlackBerry and other mobile devices, there is at present no really good way to know which websites offer mobile versions of their pages. Even for those sites that do, finding the correct URL often means first visiting the website on your desktop and looking for information on mobile device support. While this is better than nothing, it isn't very helpful to someone traveling far from home with just a BlackBerry as his or her only way to access the web.

A few scattered directories of mobile-friendly web pages have popped up here and there. While Table 4-2 is by no means comprehensive, it does offer a starting point for some good sites to bookmark in your BlackBerry Browser.

Figures 4-1 through 4-3 illustrate how these websites have taken their full-featured web content and reformatted it for use on a BlackBerry device.

Table 4-2   Mobile-Friendly Websites

Website	Content
www.usatoday.com	*USA Today* (news)
www.usnews.com/usnews/textmenu.htm	*US News and World Report* (news)
www.nypost.com/avantgo	*New York Post* (news)
Pda.businessweek.com	*Business Week* (business news)
www.prnewswire.com/tnw/tnw.shtml	*PR NewsWire* (press releases)
Wireless.cnn.com	CNN (news)
www.mapquest.com/pda	MapQuest (maps and directions)
Ppc.sportsline.com	SportsLine (sports news)
Mobile.espn.go.com	ESPN (sports news)
www.amazon.com/mcommerce	Amazon.com (online shopping)
www.google.com	Google (search engine)
www.motleyfool.com	Motley Fool (investment/financial)
Wireless.tvguide.com	*TV Guide* (TV listings)

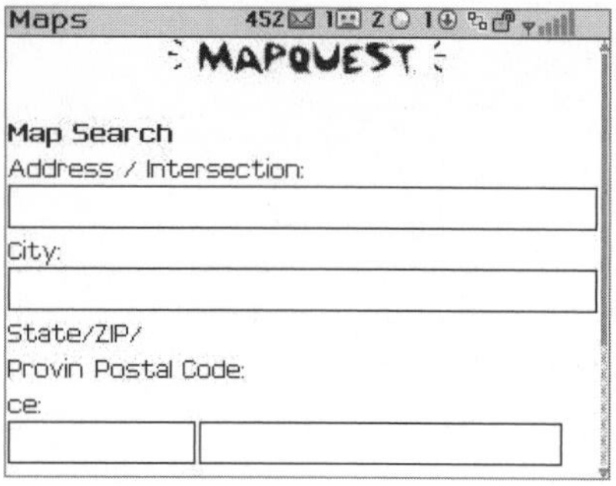

FIGURE 4-1: MapQuest as shown in the
BlackBerry Browser

FIGURE 4-2: SportsLine's mobile-friendly site

FIGURE 4-3: *TV Guide*'s wireless website

A good strategy I recommend is to spend a few minutes on your desktop computer finding a couple of good mobile-ready websites that cover the information categories you care most about and pre-load your BlackBerry Internet Browser with bookmarks for those sites. Later when you have only your BlackBerry to depend on, you'll be glad you did!

Third-Party Web Browsers

For just about any given product in the world, there are almost always at least a couple of alternatives to choose from. Competition and customer demand tend to ensure that this happens. Even on Windows desktops, just when the web "browser wars" were long thought to be over and Internet Explorer declared the winner, security concerns exposed a hole in IE and those users who were worried about security started looking for alternative browsers that would give them a safer browser environment. The Firefox browser was among the alternative browsers that gained significant exposure and growth because of this. IE still represents the majority of web browser users, but because Firefox answered a need that IE did not fulfill, it was preferred by many Windows users.

Although by now modern BlackBerry devices come equipped with the BlackBerry Browser, there continues to be demand for alternative browsers. A couple of years ago there was a clear need for a third-party HTML-capable browser, simply because no built-in solution was available from RIM. Today, with new BlackBerrys coming with the built-in BlackBerry Browser, the need is less clear, but depending on what device you have and what you are trying to do, you may want to investigate this option.

Why Use a Third-Party Browser?

You might want to consider using a third-party web browser on your BlackBerry device for several reasons. First, if you have an older device, your wireless carrier may not provision your BlackBerry device with the BlackBerry Browser. Sometimes this can be remedied by upgrading your device to a newer version of the BlackBerry OS, but your company's IT department may prohibit this, or you may not wish to go through the hassle yourself. Another reason may be that you are using an Enterprise device and your company has an IT policy that prohibits the provisioning of the browser. Last, there may be a specific website or a specific browser feature that is not supported well in the BlackBerry Browser but that enjoys a better level of support with one of the available third-party browsers.

Opera Mini

Opera Mini is a proxy-based web browser designed with phones in mind. It runs on the MIDP/J2ME platform and will run on a BlackBerry device. Opera Mini is referred to as a proxy browser because it does not directly retrieve and format web pages on the device. Instead it offloads this task to a server whose job it is to evaluate any requested web pages and reformat them so that they will work well on a phone's small screen. Depending on the web page you are trying to access, this approach can result in faster web page downloads and better looking pages because the device no longer has to do all of the hard work.

Besides the proxy-based feature, Opera Mini (pictured in Figure 4-4) also has some user-interface niceties such as an optimized home page with ready-to-use search, bookmark, and history sections. Opera also features a unique "speed dial" option for quickly accessing commonly used bookmarks; just press ALT+* and the number of the bookmark from your list, and Opera will retrieve the referenced web page.

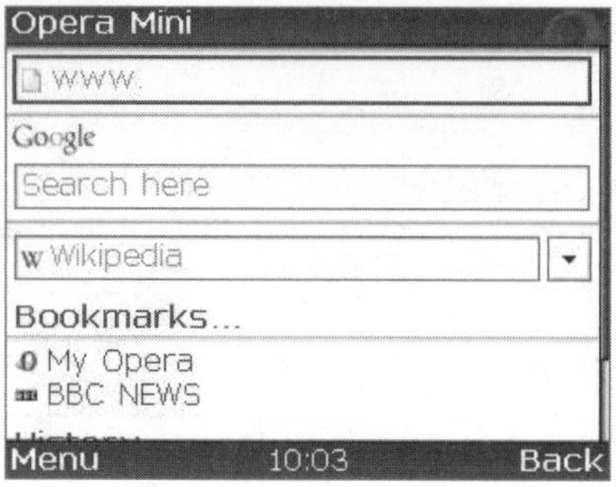

FIGURE 4-4: Opera's home screen

Opera Mini is a free download and is available at the Opera website, www.opera.com.

Minuet

Minuet, developed by TriPrince at TriPrince.com, is another popular alternative web browser for BlackBerry devices. In contrast to Opera, Minuet claims to use no proxy middleman servers and does all of the brute-force web formatting and rendering on the device itself via a direct connection. Other advantages that TriPrince claims with Minuet are background web page loading, image display optimizations, better security, and caching.

As with Opera, depending on which device you have and which web pages you want to access, you may find that Minuet provides a better experience for you than the built-in BlackBerry Browser. Note that Minuet is a native BlackBerry program and does require BlackBerry OS 4.*x* or better.

To get more information on Minuet including a trial download, visit Handango at www.handango.com or www.TriPrince.com.

Assisted Web Search and Information Aids

The well-known search engines such as Google and Yahoo offer powerful access to a humongous index of websites and information. These search engines are designed to be self-service: Just go to the search engine's home page, enter your search words, and then sift through the resulting links until you find what you need.

Recently, a new category of web service has arrived on the scene that I tend to call "assisted search." Why would you need help with something as ridiculously simple as a Google search? To understand the need for assisted search, you have to imagine that you are in a situation in which using standard search tools might be difficult, awkward, or even impossible. First, take away any notion of access to a desktop or laptop computer, so at best your only tool is your BlackBerry, the built-in Internet Browser, and an acceptable wireless data connection. Now, imagine a scenario in which you are in a rush, under pressure, in an unfamiliar location, on the go, or even in a tight spot. (Remember that although a search engine may be optimized for the small screen, the actual search result links will not be.) In such a situation, using the standard BlackBerry Browser and tediously wading through pages of search hits may not work for you.

This is where assisted search comes in handy. Although not exclusively designed with BlackBerry users in mind, assisted search services do cater to people who need information quickly but may not have access to a fast web connection and desktop computer (or indeed access to any computer at all). Assisted search comes in many forms, some examples of which are described in the next few sections.

AskMeNow

One example of such an assisted search service is called AskMeNow, located at (you guessed it) www.askmenow.com. The premise of AskMeNow is that you sign up for the service, and whenever you need information you pose your question to the AskMeNow service by placing a phone call or by submitting a question from the AskMeNow software. Your answer is then sent as a text message to your phone via your wireless data connection.

AskMeNow claims that they can answer "virtually any question for which the answer can be found on the Internet." Questions that can be answered automatically, such as 411 info, driving directions, directory listings, or movie times, are free. AskMeNow also offers a service called AskMeAnything, which allows you to ask any question at all for a per-question fee of $0.49. These questions may require an actual person to research the answer for you (for example, "Why is the sky blue?").

Although you can use AskMeNow by simply calling in your question and receiving the answer as a text message, you can download software that lets you interact with the service from your BlackBerry. The optional software loads as a BlackBerry icon.

When you first run AskMeNow on your BlackBerry, you just need to enter your mobile phone number so that the AskMeNow service can correctly send the answer to your question as a text message. You are then presented with the main AskMeNow screen (see Figure 4-5), a series of icons representing 12 different categories of information, including weather, sports, stock quotes, driving directions, flight status, hotel listings, and more. Within each category is an entry form formatted specifically for that category, so for example if you want to know the score of today's Mets baseball game, you choose Major League Baseball as the sport and Mets as the team. Similarly if you want driving directions, enter the starting and ending address.

FIGURE 4-5: The AskMeNow software program

As advertised, in my testing of AskMeNow, I consistently received a text message in my BlackBerry inbox within a minute of submitting my question, complete with the answer to my question. This was quite amazing. Without opening up a web browser or connecting to the Internet, I was able to get answers to questions in seconds that would have taken me at the very least several minutes (and quite possibly much longer) to find. Especially in the case of something like driving directions (which I often struggle with), this service is incredibly useful.

A small, unobtrusive advertisement was included at the end of the received message, but considering that AskMeNow's service is free, I found this to be quite acceptable. For more information on AskMeNow, visit their website at www.askmenow.com.

Berry 411

Berry 411 is a software program that acts as a front end to the BlackBerry Internet Browser. As its name suggests, Berry 411 aims to give you the Internet equivalent of the 411 telephone information service and make it easily accessible from a BlackBerry device.

Berry 411 delivers on this goal with a deceptively plain-looking software program that loads on your BlackBerry. You run Berry 411 as you do any other BlackBerry application, and Berry 411 presents you with a simple form (shown in Figure 4-6) with two pieces of information to fill out: your location and one or more keywords representing what you are searching for.

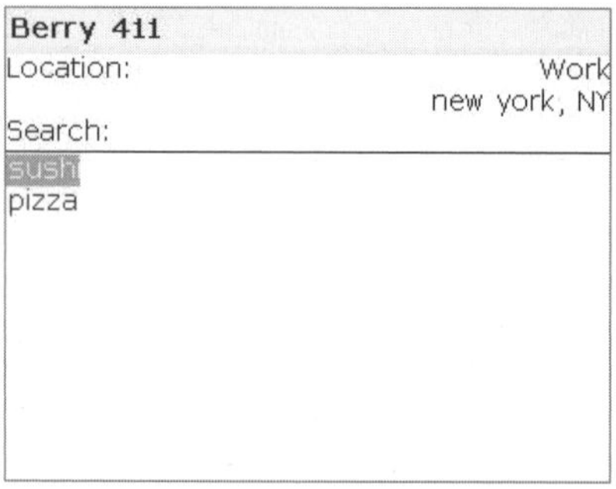

Berry 411
Location: Work
                                    new york, NY
Search:
sushi
pizza

FIGURE 4-6: The Berry 411 search form

Your location is pre-filled with your work, home, or other location. These locations can be entered when you first run the program and can be changed at any point when you do a search. Once you enter your search terms, clicking the trackwheel menu brings up a list of search choices that you can target with your search. Selectable options include the Yellow Pages, White Pages, Google, Weather, Shopping, Movies, and Sports. Selecting a search option then submits your search terms to the selected service and launches the BlackBerry Browser with the matching search results.

For example, I performed a search for "sushi" in my work location of New York City, and within a few seconds I was presented with a listing of available restaurants (shown in Figure 4-7) where I could get my hands on a spicy tuna roll with extra wasabi.

FIGURE 4-7: Berry 411 search results

Notice that the listings are all formatted consistently with name of the restaurant, phone number, and street address. Finding this same information without Berry 411 would have involved either a Google search and wading through a hodgepodge of results or else finding a mobile-friendly restaurant listing web page. Even nicer, with Berry 411's software front end, I didn't even have to connect to the Internet until I was ready to submit my search!

Believe it or not, Berry 411 is freeware and is downloadable from www.berry411.com.

YubNub

YubNub is neither a software application nor an information service. Instead, www.yubnub.org is a website that offers what it refers to as a "command line for the Web." The idea behind YubNub is that you can execute a much more specific, directed search for information by typing a complete command line that describes what you want YubNub to do. YubNub offers a wealth of predefined commands that cover weather, sports, news, music, stock quotes, and more.

For example, to get the weather for New York City, you go to the YubNub page and enter **weather 10001** in the input box (10001 is one of New York's zip codes). YubNub quickly brings you to a page from The Weather Channel that offers the current weather conditions for New York! Similarly, typing **allmusic Bob Dylan** brings up a page from the popular music site www.allmusic.com, with information on the musician Bob Dylan.

You can also direct your search commands to use mobile-friendly search results that are stripped of images or other bandwidth- and screen-hogging elements. For example, the command to search Answers.com is **a**, and you can direct YubNub to use the mobile-friendly version by adding **mo** to the command, as in **amo** thunder, which will return the Answers.com page containing the definition of "thunder," optimized for mobile devices. Pretty cool!

Figure 4-8 shows YubNub on the standard BlackBerry Internet Browser. While not a BlackBerry-specific service, YubNub is a boon to BlackBerry users in that it speeds up the search process and lets you retrieve information using few keystrokes. Instead of having to go to a specific website (which may not be mobile-friendly at all) and enter your search criteria, you can do it all from the YubNub site, which loads on a BlackBerry in a matter of seconds. YubNub also leans on something that is a natural fit for BlackBerry — a preference to use the keyboard to type in a specific command, rather than tediously mouse clicking through multiple web pages.

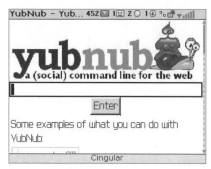

FIGURE 4-8: YubNub

Working with RSS Feeds

RSS, which stands for Really Simple Syndication, has grown over the past several years to become the de facto standard method for distributing information such as news, discussions, and blog postings over the Internet. Websites that want to provide information in the form of an RSS feed simply need to "publish" it in a standard XML format. These sites provide visitors with a special RSS link and, typically, an orange XML icon on their pages, which tells the visitor that some of the site's information is available via RSS. The formatted feed is then downloaded, read, parsed, and made viewable by a special software program called an RSS Client.

For example, say you are a news junkie and you are particularly interested in politics. There are many, perhaps even hundreds, of RSS feeds around the Internet that offer news feeds in this specific area, but for this example you will choose CNN as the source. On the CNN.com home page is the RSS link and familiar orange XML icon that tells you that CNN.com offers RSS feeds. Clicking this icon leads you to a page that lists all of the news topics for which there are feeds. Scanning down the list, you can see that the Politics news feed has a URL of `http://rss.cnn.com/rss/cnn_allpolitics.rss`. All you need to do to start receiving regular updates of CNN's political news stories is to add this URL to your RSS client program's list of subscribed feeds.

An RSS Client can be thought of as a manager for all of the RSS-compatible websites you subscribe to. When you find or learn about an RSS-compatible website that you wish to subscribe to, you add a special URL to your RSS client's list of subscriptions, and thereafter the website can be checked, either manually or automatically, for new or updated information. There are now a considerable number of these RSS client programs (also commonly referred to as *readers*) available, and you can find versions for Windows, Macintosh, and Unix, as well as for most handheld and smartphone platforms, including (of course) BlackBerry.

Note On my Windows desktop, I use a great RSS reader called FeedDemon (www.feeddemon.com), and I subscribe to over 50 different RSS feeds covering topics such as world news, technology, music, and more. FeedDemon provides me with excellent organization of my many subscriptions. In many cases it can automatically subscribe me to a feed I am looking at in my browser. It also has an embedded browser window that makes reading full articles possible without ever leaving the FeedDemon main window. As a BlackBerry user, I'm in search of an RSS client that can give me some of these same reading features I enjoy in FeedDemon. As you will discover, none of the BlackBerry readers available today comes close to the functionality of FeedDemon, but I expect developers of these products will recognize this need and continue to improve them.

RSS Clients for BlackBerry

In this section I present a couple of the better available RSS clients for BlackBerry devices. There are others you can check out, and more readers/clients are being published all the time, so be sure to frequently check online at BlackBerry software sites such as Handango.com (which, by the way, offers an RSS feed of new BlackBerry software titles published!) for new programs.

BerryVine RSS Reader

BerryVine RSS Reader, shown in Figure 4-9, is an RSS client for BlackBerry devices, developed by a company by the name of Razab-Sekh Information Company B.V. (RSIC).

```
Find:
 BBC News
 Blackberry Cool
 CNN
 MSNBC Business
 MSNBC Entertainment
 MSNBC Sports
 MSNBC Technology & Science
 MSNBC Top News
 MSNBC Weather
 Reuters Sports News
 Reuters Top News
 The NY Times Business
 The NY Times Movie News
 The NY Times Sports
```

FIGURE 4-9: BerryVine's main screen

As you can see from Figure 4-9, the main screen for BerryVine is a list of the RSS feeds you are subscribed to. Many RSS clients start you with a blank list and leave it up to you to find and subscribe to your first RSS feeds, but I liked the fact that BerryVine populates your subscription list with 18 preconfigured feeds, including feeds from popular sources such as Yahoo, CNN, the *New York Times*, and Reuters.

Loading a Feed

To retrieve the latest news items from a feed you are subscribed to, just select the feed you wish to read, click the trackwheel menu, and choose Load Feed, as shown in Figure 4-10.

FIGURE 4-10: BerryVine's main feed menu

Choosing Load Feed causes BerryVine to connect to the Internet, contact the URL associated with the feed you have selected, and download all of the latest items or stories that are published. As an example, in Figures 4-11 and 4-12, I've chosen the RSS feed for the popular BlackBerryCool website for BlackBerry enthusiasts and asked BerryVine to retrieve the latest stories.

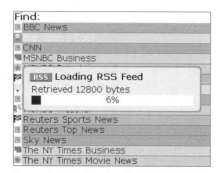

FIGURE 4-11: Retrieving the latest stories

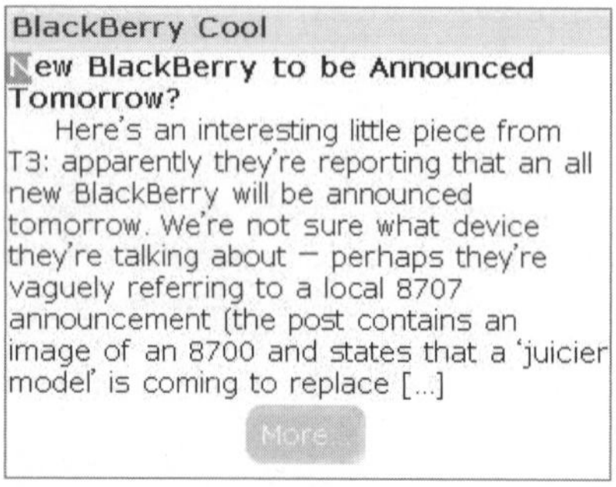

FIGURE 4-12: BerryVine's list of BlackBerryCool stories

To read any of the stories listed, just select an item and click the trackwheel View Item menu. As shown in Figure 4-12, BerryVine then displays a short preview snippet of the selected story. If you decide you want to read the full story, you can click the More button, which then launches the full story in the BlackBerry Browser. In practice, this is a bit awkward in that it requires you to keep bouncing back and forth between BerryVine and the BlackBerry Browser as you read multiple stories.

Adding a New Feed

Although BerryVine comes with many preconfigured RSS feeds, the experience becomes much more personal when you start adding additional feeds that are closely aligned with your own areas of personal (or business) interests. To add a new feed to BerryVine, go to the main screen, click the trackwheel menu, and choose Add RSS Feed. This brings up the screen pictured in Figure 4-13.

FIGURE 4-13: Adding a Handango news feed to BerryVine

In the previous example, I wanted to find a way to learn about new BlackBerry software applications as they are released. Because I knew that Handango.com keeps such a list, I went to the Handango website from my desktop web browser, clicked on the XML icon, and discovered that the URL for a feed of newly released BlackBerry apps is:

```
http://service.handango.com/ampp/ContentRequestGenerator?id=
123&password=rss20content&platformId=5&maxCount=50&optionId=5
```

To add this feed to BerryVine, simply fill out the form as shown in Figure 4-13, including the URL. (Yes, I know this is tedious on the BlackBerry keyboard.) If you are careful and enter the URL correctly, you can then load stories for this feed, as shown in Figure 4-14.

Getting Updates

Some desktop RSS readers automatically check for updates on each subscribed feed, but in BerryVine's case you need to manually check each feed on your list when you want to see if new items are posted.

FIGURE 4-14: The Handango RSS feed shows me the latest BlackBerry applications released!

Where to Find Out More

To learn more about BerryVine, check the program listing at Handango or visit the BerryVine website at `www.berryvine.com`. BerryVine currently retails for a one-time price of $6.50 and also is available for a free trial download period.

PicoNews

PicoNews is an interesting combination of a software program and an online service that come together to create a very nice RSS news reader solution for BlackBerry devices. Like BerryVine, PicoNews is a downloadable BlackBerry software application that installs onto your device. But whereas BerryVine then works more or less like a traditional RSS client, PicoNews takes advantage of the PicoNews online website, at `www.piconews.com`. The website's main benefits are:

- An online catalog of known RSS feeds from a wide variety of categories.

- Registered PicoNews users can manage their subscriptions and feed options from their desktop web browser, rather than having to do so from their device.

- Automatic "push" of new stories and items for your subscribed feeds down to your device.

Figure 4-15 shows the main PicoNews screen as seen on a BlackBerry device.

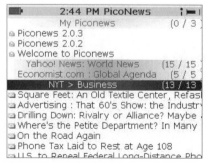

FIGURE 4-15: The PicoNews main screen

PicoNews's user interface is based on a series of folders, with each folder containing the news items for a given subscription. Folders can be opened or closed by clicking on the folder title bar with the trackwheel. Figure 4-15 shows the *New York Times* Business feed opened.

PicoNews can be used in a manner similar to BerryVine: opening your subscribed feeds, obtaining the latest items using the Get All News Items trackwheel menu, and opening and reading the news items that are of interest to you. As with BerryVine, you are given a snippet of the article, and in order to read the full article contents, you will need to launch the article in the BlackBerry Browser.

To me, the main difference between BerryVine and PicoNews is the added value provided by the PicoNews website. When you install PicoNews to your BlackBerry, you are automatically given an account that you can use to sign on to the PicoNews website at www.piconews.com. Once you are signed in, you have access to your list of currently subscribed RSS feeds, and you can even add new subscriptions from the growing PicoNews RSS catalog or by entering the direct URL. Back on the device, to add a new subscribed feed to your folder list, just choose the menu option Synchronize Subscriptions, and your folder list is updated to match the list of subscriptions on your piconews.com account.

What's more, PicoNews.com will automatically "push" new and updated news items to your device, so that rather than having to manually check each of your subscribed feeds, your news-feeds are updated and waiting for you each time you open PicoNews. This is a really nice feature, especially as your subscription list grows.

As of this writing, PicoNews is offered free of charge as a download from either Handango.com or www.piconews.com and includes the online PicoNews.com account option.

Blogging with Your BlackBerry

Everybody likes to express their thoughts, views and opinions at one time or another. But up until very recently making your voice loud enough to be heard by the general public has been limited to the domain of a privileged few: newspaper editors, politicians, and umm . . . oh yes, book authors! Of course the Internet has changed so many aspects of modern life, but one of the best innovations it has brought is how it grants equal visibility to anyone who cares to put up a website or join a discussion group. On the World Wide Web, JoesDelicatessen.com is on equal footing with Amazon.com in terms of having its place in the sun.

The Popularity of the Blog

There has been a tremendous growth recently in the use of tools that enable social interaction and personal musings online. Probably the most well known of these tools is the web log, or blog. Some blogs are designed to be shared with a very few close friends and family. Other blogs are created for the purpose of expressing your views to the entire world. Blogs are also used for marketing or publicity purposes. For example, a politician running for office might create a blog where she can state her positions on a variety of issues.

But a blog is more than the published musings of an individual. Blogs can be interactive as well. The owner of a blog may post an opinion, and if permitted, others may post their own thoughts on the same topic in response. Some blogs are restricted to allow only the owner to make postings, others allow moderated discussion, and still others are wide open. Thus a blog can be thought of not so much as a solitary diary, but more like a cross between a diary and an e-mail thread.

A number of online tools allow authors to design, create, and maintain blogs. I use one called Blogger, at www.blogger.com, because I found it very easy to use and it provided me with the help I needed back when I knew nothing about blogs. Blogger.com is also free, which certainly helps, especially when you are just getting started. Of course, Blogger.com is by no means the only blogging tool; you can find a wide variety of available tools with a simple web search.

Blogging and BlackBerry

So what does all this have to do with BlackBerry? Well, if you think about it, there are two main things you want to do with a blog: read it and post to it. Say you know of a blog that's out there which is of interest to you. Wouldn't it be great if you could keep up-to-date with new postings to the blog by reading them on your BlackBerry, wherever (or whenever) it is convenient? Likewise, if you are either the author of a blog, or an authorized contributor to someone else's blog, it would be very convenient if you could use your BlackBerry to write your thoughts and post them to your blog immediately, rather than waiting until you got back to your desktop computer.

These aren't just ideas. Using a sample blog that I created on blogger.com, I can show you how to set your blog up so that you can read your blog on your BlackBerry. I'll even show how to post new articles to your blog, right from your BlackBerry — instantly!

Reading a Blog from Your BlackBerry

Most blogging tools offer blog authors a way to publish the contents of a blog as a specially formatted XML file. Depending on the blog authoring tool you are using, this format can be one of several different variations of commonly accepted syndication formats. For example, Blogger.com, which I will be using in this discussion, offers me the ability to automatically publish my blog as an Atom feed. Atom is, in fact, very similar to RSS, which was covered earlier in this chapter, in that it is a commonly understood format for describing a series of articles published from a given website. The next time you visit someone else's blog home page, look for the familiar orange button labeled RSS, XML, or Atom, which indicates to you that the blog author has enabled his or her blog to be published via one of these formats.

If you were following the earlier section on RSS, you might now be wondering whether one of the RSS client programs out there for BlackBerry can subscribe to an Atom feed. In fact, the PicoNews RSS reader you read about earlier supports the Atom format, so any blog that publishes its content in Atom XML format can be subscribed to by PicoNews.

My little test blog is published at www.bachmannsoftware.com/atom.xml so Figure 4-16 shows the Add Feed screen for PicoNews, which adds my test blog to the list of subscribed feeds.

```
Feed parameters
Name: bachmann blog
Url: http://bachmannsoftware.com/atom.xml
Category:                          Misc.
Language:                       English
☐ Private
                 Request sent
```

FIGURE 4-16: Adding my test blog to PicoNews

After adding the feed, my blog now shows up in the PicoNews main list for my subscriptions, as shown in Figure 4-17.

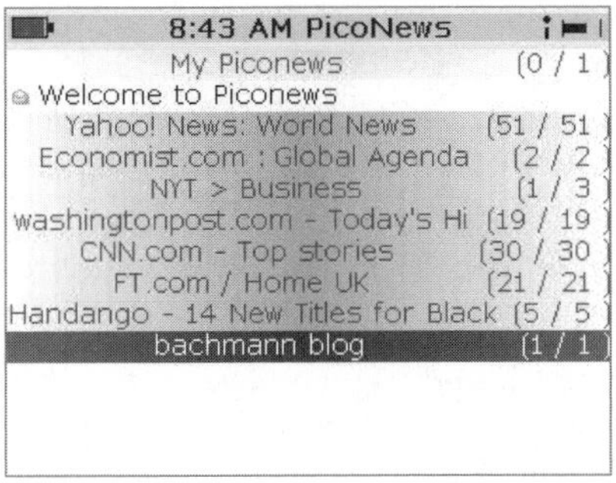

```
◼▸         8:43 AM PicoNews      ┇ ▬ |
        My Piconews              (0 / 1 )
◔ Welcome to Piconews
      Yahoo! News: World News   (51 / 51 )
  Economist.com : Global Agenda  (2 / 2 )
        NYT > Business           (1 / 3 )
washingtonpost.com - Today's Hi (19 / 19 )
    CNN.com - Top stories       (30 / 30 )
        FT.com / Home UK        (21 / 21 )
Handango - 14 New Titles for Black (5 / 5 )
        bachmann blog           (1 / 1 )
```

FIGURE 4-17: I am now subscribed to receive articles from my blog.

Posting to a Blog from Your BlackBerry

Anybody can subscribe to any blog, as long as the author of the blog has published his content in one of the previously described syndication formats. Posting a new article or comment to a blog, however, is subject to the permissions granted by the blog author. As I noted earlier, depending on the author's goals for the blog, the blog may allow postings only by the author himself, or it may be limited to registered members, or it may be wide open for comments by anyone.

Assuming that you are either the author of your blog or someone who has permission to post to a blog, it would be great to be able to post blog comments from your mobile BlackBerry device. As thoughts, ideas, or new experiences occur in your life, you can immediately blog them, making the blogging experience that much more interactive.

Blogging from your BlackBerry is done via e-mail, which is perfect given how wonderful the BlackBerry is at messaging. The only requirement is that the target blog have been configured by the author to allow comments to be submitted via e-mail. Note that this is not the default setting for new blogs at www.blogger.com, so the author has to specifically turn on this feature.

If you are the author of a blog at www.blogger.com and want to give yourself (and potentially others) the ability to comment to your blog via e-mail, log into your Blogger account, and on the Settings tab for your blog, choose the Email section to see a field called the Mail-to-Blogger Address, as shown in Figure 4-18.

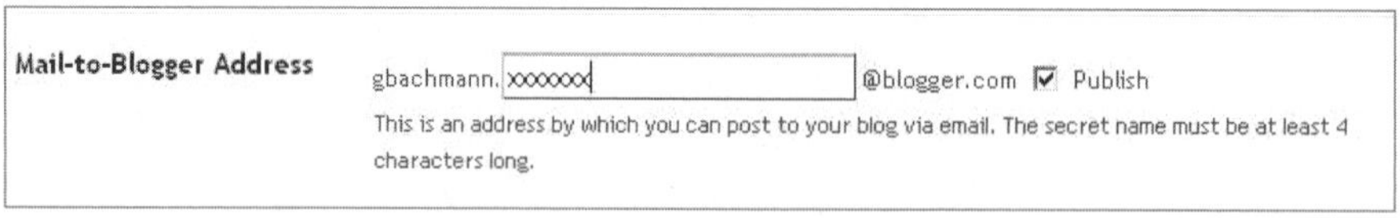

Mail-to-Blogger Address	gbachmann. xxxxxxx @blogger.com ☑ Publish
	This is an address by which you can post to your blog via email. The secret name must be at least 4 characters long.

FIGURE 4-18: Configuring my test blog to allow e-mail postings

The Mail-to-Blogger address is a special e-mail address that you can use to post to your own blog, and it is in the form *username.secretname*@blogger.com, where *username* is your Blogger username and *secretname* is a name you choose that will be unique for your Mail-to-Blogger address. Check the box labeled Publish if you want e-mailed comments to be posted to the blog immediately, or leave it unchecked if you want to have the opportunity to moderate or preview these comments before they are posted.

One thing to note about the Mail-to-Blogger address. Regardless of how you as the author specified your blog's rules about who can post comments to your blog, anyone who uses the Mail-to-Blogger address can post to your blog! As long as you understand this and take appropriate steps to safeguard this e-mail address, it should not be a problem. If the e-mail address does accidentally get into the wrong hands and you start getting unwanted posts, you can either change your settings so that e-mail comments are not immediately published, or of course you can simply change the Mail-to-Blogger e-mail address to something different, which will have the effect of disabling any e-mail comments from those who have the older address.

Once the Mail-to-Blogger setting is enabled, you can post comments to your own blog by simply creating an e-mail containing your comments and sending it to the e-mail address you specified as your Mail-to-Blogger address. This capability is not limited to BlackBerry posting. You can now post to your blog via Outlook, web mail, or any other means you have available for sending an e-mail message. But e-mail posting is especially wonderful for BlackBerry users because it gives you blogging options wherever you may be.

For my test blog, I composed an e-mail on my BlackBerry, and set the "to:" address to be my blog's Mail-to-Blogger address. I then sent it. I then went to my laptop's web browser to check my blog, and sure enough, my post was immediately reflected at the top of the blog (see Figure 4-19).

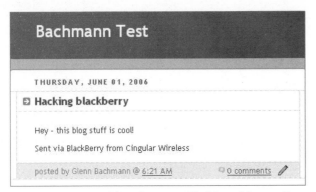

Bachmann Test

THURSDAY, JUNE 01, 2006

Hacking blackberry

Hey - this blog stuff is cool!

Sent via BlackBerry from Cingular Wireless

posted by Glenn Bachmann @ 6:21 AM   0 comments

FIGURE 4-19: My test blog shows my BlackBerry blog post!

Of course, if you've followed the steps described earlier in the section "Reading a Blog from Your BlackBerry" and are using PicoNews, you can also see this blog posting on your BlackBerry.

Summary

In this chapter you learned how to start using your BlackBerry's browser to access content from the World Wide Web, and you became familiar with a series of hidden keyboard short-cuts that can be used to make the built-in BlackBerry browser more convenient to use. You also saw how BlackBerry web access can go way beyond viewing websites in a tiny browser window. Programs such as AskMeNow and Berry 411 leapfrog the browser entirely and deliver the online information you need without your having to navigate through page after page of slow-loading web content.

Bringing the BlackBerry into the world of social networking, you also saw how to use your BlackBerry to participate in the fast-growing world of RSS feeds and web logs (blogs), both as a reader and even as an active participant. These capabilities are not difficult to add to your BlackBerry and greatly enhance your access to online news, headlines, and discussions.

Using Your BlackBerry as a Wireless Dialup Modem

If you are like many laptop users, sooner or later you travel someplace where your laptop cannot get Internet access, wireless or wired. You could be in a car, at an airport, in a client's building, or at any of a number of other places where a network hub or Wi-Fi is simply not an option for you.

If you are ever in that situation, you may just find yourself staring at the BlackBerry, which is happily connected to the Internet and delivering your e-mail. You may be wondering, "Hmmm. I have this great wireless device that can connect to the Internet just about anywhere. I wonder if I could somehow use it to get wireless Internet on my laptop."

It turns out that you are not alone in wondering about this. How to use your BlackBerry as a wireless modem is one of the most often asked questions on BlackBerry discussion and customer support pages. Unfortunately, it is discussed so frequently because the information on how to actually make it work is so hard to find. Also, the information that is out there is based on guesswork or trial and error and is often confusing, outdated, or simply wrong. Research In Motion, in its own online support knowledge base, currently takes an official stance that using BlackBerry as an Internet modem is "not supported." Even worse, the information that does exist needs to be regularly updated based on the arrival of new BlackBerry devices, new BlackBerry desktop software, and differences among the various wireless carriers that officially either support or do not support this feature.

Despite all this, I can personally attest that it is indeed possible to use a BlackBerry device as a wireless modem on your laptop. I have made a successful connection, surfed the Web on my laptop, and retrieved my Outlook e-mail, using my BlackBerry wireless data service. There was definitely some voodoo that had to occur to get there, and it was a mighty struggle, but in the end it worked!

While my success does not guarantee that it is easy (or even possible!) to make this connection with every BlackBerry device, carrier, and laptop, in this chapter I will at the very least describe the basic steps for configuring your computer to use a BlackBerry as a modem and offer you further information, tips, and resources on how to try it on your own.

What Does a BlackBerry Modem Give You?

In a nutshell, using your BlackBerry as an external modem can provide your laptop with Internet access wherever your BlackBerry has wireless coverage. Instead of being limited to Wi-Fi hotspots for Internet access, depending on your chosen wireless network you can get to the Internet virtually anywhere, be it in a car, on a boat, on a park bench, or wherever.

One thing to note is that your connection speed will vary depending on your device and your wireless carrier, but certainly you should expect it to be noticeably slower than Wi-Fi. Still, it should perform better than a lowly 56K dialup modem, and if you have a faster wireless connection such as EV-DO or EDGE on your BlackBerry, it can in fact be quite reasonable.

 A major caveat is that you should make sure that if you use this feature, you have an unlimited data plan. The bytes and megabytes add up quickly when you retrieve your e-mail or surf the Web, and you definitely want to avoid getting socked with a big bill the next time you get your wireless account statement.

Finally, it is probably a good idea to check with your wireless carrier to see if you need to add any special features to your wireless data plan in order to enable dialup modem usage. Depending on whom you get on the phone, they may not even know what you are talking about, but it's worth a try and it may save you headaches (or even additional charges) later on.

 Wireless carriers can and sometimes do change their service plans, and wireless bills are notoriously difficult to comprehend, often using fine print or strange terminology to notify you of changes in your billing. It is a good idea to regularly review your bill and watch out for any change in the amount of your bill, just to be sure you aren't being charged in error.

Supported Devices

Research In Motion claims in its knowledge base that a BlackBerry can be used as an external modem to connect a laptop computer to the Internet. It lists the BlackBerry models 7100, 7250, 7290, and 8700 as those to which this statement applies. However, it must be noted that despite this statement, RIM also does not offer any promise of user support for customers who try to use a BlackBerry for this purpose. Essentially this means that the potential is there to use your BlackBerry as an external modem, but you can't expect to get help from Research In Motion if it doesn't work or if you have questions about it. Rather than take on responsibility for this feature directly, RIM defers to the wireless carrier for any support issues related to the use of a BlackBerry as a modem.

What seems to be true is that these devices have the potential to be used as tethered modems for laptops. Whether in practice you can be successful achieving this will depend on other factors, including what version of the BlackBerry OS and desktop software you are using and especially whether your wireless carrier supports this feature at all.

Note At present, some wireless carriers claim to support using a BlackBerry as a dialup modem, others say they don't allow it, and still others simply say nothing about the feature. My guess is that as a result of the increasing demand for this useful capability, more and more carriers will support it and offer documented steps for how to make it work, but at present it is hit or miss, so make sure you check with your carrier periodically.

I've personally had success with both a 7290 and an 8700, using AT&T and Cingular. Various postings from www.blackberryforums.com and other sites around the Web testify success or failure with these and other devices using different carriers. So rather than making any sort of sweeping statement about which devices and carriers you can use the external modem feature with, let me simply recommend that you follow the steps and try it. The worst that can happen is that it won't work, but you may just be able to get it to work and enjoy a really useful new possibility with your BlackBerry!

Connection Options: USB vs. Bluetooth

In order to make an external modem connection between your laptop and your BlackBerry, you will need to tether your BlackBerry device to your laptop using the original USB cable that came with your BlackBerry.

Newer BlackBerry devices, as well as select older models such as the 7290, support Bluetooth, a wireless radio that can connect your BlackBerry to other Bluetooth-enabled devices such as headsets, GPS units, and Bluetooth-enabled computers. However, the bad news for those seeking to try the external modem feature is that the Bluetooth capability included in the currently available BlackBerry devices cannot make a modem connection.

Steps for Setting Up Windows

The actual steps for setting up Windows to recognize your BlackBerry as a valid GPRS modem are fairly straightforward and involve three main tasks:

1. Connecting the device with BlackBerry Desktop Manager

2. Configuring the BlackBerry modem in the Control Panel

3. Creating a new network connection profile

At present, a description of how to perform these steps is on RIM's support pages, but I found the information to be actually wrong, at least for my device (in this case, an 8700 on Cingular).

In the following sections, I cover the basic steps for each of these tasks, using my Cingular configuration as an example throughout. Just be aware that some details will vary based on your wireless carrier, and if at all available you should seek out the most updated instructions from your specific carrier on its support pages. If the carrier supports the feature, it is the best source for this information.

Connecting the Device with BlackBerry Desktop Manager

In order to enable modem support in your BlackBerry, you need to connect your BlackBerry to your laptop using the supplied USB cable. In addition, you need to be running the BlackBerry Desktop Manager. It is Desktop Manager that installs the drivers that make an attached BlackBerry appear to be a "virtual" modem attached to your laptop.

If the BlackBerry Desktop Manager does not automatically run when you start your laptop, you at least need to run it during the following configuration steps, as well as whenever you wish to use your BlackBerry as a modem.

Configuring the Modem

The next task is to find the modem entry for your BlackBerry in Windows Control Panel and to customize it to communicate properly on your carrier's wireless network.

To do this, follow these steps:

1. Run Control Panel on your laptop.

2. Choose the Modem Options icon.

3. When this panel opens, choose the Modems tab.

4. Here you should see an entry called Standard Modem assigned to a COM port such as COM4 or COM11. (If you actually have a real modem attached to your laptop you will also see other modem entries in this list). Select the Standard Modem entry.

5. Click the Properties button.

6. Click on the Advanced tab.

7. In the Advanced tab is a field called Extra Initialization Commands. Here is where you need to enter the special modem commands that will initialize the BlackBerry modem interface with your carrier's wireless network. My wireless carrier is Cingular, and according to Cingular's support site, the proper initialization string to enter is:

```
at+cgdcont=1,"IP","isp.cingular"
```

Note   After much frustration, I discovered that this initialization string is slightly wrong. It should be `wap.cingular` and not `isp.cingular`. This is a perfect example of why it is so hard to guarantee success with this feature. There are several configuration steps and the slightest error in each step will prevent the feature from working!

Figure 5-1 shows the correct initialization string as entered in my Modem properties page.

8. Once you have carefully entered the initialization string, click OK and close the Control Panel.

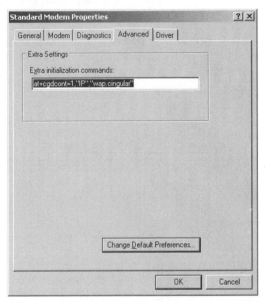

FIGURE 5-1: The BlackBerry Modem Initialization String (for Cingular networks)

At this point you have successfully configured your BlackBerry's modem support (or so you hope!) for use with your laptop. This is the rough equivalent of purchasing an actual external modem and installing it as a modem on your computer. Now the next step is to create a network connection that uses your new modem.

Creating a Network Connection

To create a Windows Network connection that uses your BlackBerry modem to connect to the Internet, follow these steps:

1. Go to Control Panel.

2. Double-click the Networks icon.

3. Choose the New Connection Wizard.

4. Indicate that you wish to create an Internet connection.

5. Choose to set up the connection manually.

6. Choose the Connect Using a Dialup Modem option.

7. Select your Standard Modem from the list of modems that appears.

8. Name your new connection, calling it **BlackBerry Modem** (or some other name that will help you remember what it is), and click Next.

9. Enter the phone number to use when dialing out to the Internet with your BlackBerry modem. Here is another carrier-specific setting. According to Cingular, the number to use is *99#. This can and will be different for other carriers, so again, check your service provider's support page to determine the correct phone number to use.

10. The final pieces of information you need to enter will be a username and password to use when registering your connection on the network. For Cingular, I am instructed to use ISP@CINGULARGPRS.COM as my username, and CINGULAR1 as the password (again, check with your service provider as necessary).

11. After entering this information, save and finish your new connection configuration.

That's it, you are ready to connect (or try to, anyway)!

Testing the Connection

First, make sure your BlackBerry is connected to your laptop via your USB cable and that BlackBerry Desktop is running. If you created a desktop icon for your network connection, you can now double-click it, or you can choose Start ➪ Connect To ➪ BlackBerry Modem. You should be prompted to confirm your username and password, and then Windows will attempt to dial out to the Internet using your connection settings, as shown in Figure 5-2.

Figure 5-2: Dialing up using Cingular settings

Now cross your fingers, hold a rabbit's foot, and hold your breath while you watch the progress of your dialup connection.

If you are successful, you are greeted with a happy new network connection in your Windows system tray, and you are on the Internet. Double-click this connection icon, and you should see a connection status window, similar to the one shown in Figure 5-3. If this happens to you, congratulations!

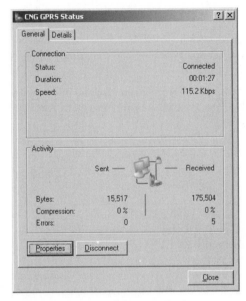

FIGURE 5-3: A successful connection!

If the connection fails, you may experience a variety of error messages and codes, unfortunately none of which will be very helpful in determining what went wrong.

One thing to check that might just fix it is to make sure that IP header compression is turned off in your network connection. You can check this by following these steps:

1. Choose Properties ➪ Networking.

2. Then select the Internet Protocol item.

3. Choose Properties again to access the TCP/IP Settings page.

4. Click Advanced.

5. Under PPP Link, make sure that Use IP Header Compression is unchecked.

If this does not improve things, my best advice is to retrace your steps in the three configuration tasks you just covered and also to double- and triple-check the modem initialization string, dialup number, username, and password supplied by your wireless carrier.

Where to Obtain Further Information

As mentioned before, the first place you should check for the most accurate information on using your BlackBerry as a modem is your wireless carrier's customer support page. This is a feature that is being asked for by an increasing number of customers, so it seems increasingly likely that it is in the carriers' best interest to provide the information to those customers if they are going to support it at all.

Another place to obtain information about this feature is the group of discussion forums found at www.blackberryforums.com, in particular the valuable and informative postings by Mark Rejhon. The information there is updated frequently by both Mark and the generous postings of the BlackBerry user community. They provide additional tips and tricks that just might make the difference between success and failure for your specific device.

Finally, RIM's BlackBerry site is another resource, and there is some helpful information there, although again in my experience most of the issues you will need to overcome in getting this feature to work are specific to your wireless carrier.

Summary

In this chapter you've seen how to dramatically add to the value of your BlackBerry by leveraging its built-in wireless data capability for use as an add-on dialup modem for your laptop. Although support for this feature can vary a great deal depending on wireless carrier and device model, getting it to work successfully means you will be able to get online with your laptop anytime, anywhere, without needing a phone jack or Wi-Fi hotspot. Given the potential benefit, I feel it is definitely worth the effort to try to get this feature enabled on your BlackBerry. With a little luck and perhaps even some support from your carrier, let's hope you'll be online in more places than ever!

The Ultimate Remote Control: Controlling Your Desktop Computer from Your BlackBerry

As BlackBerrys become more powerful, add more storage space, and support faster wireless connections, we will naturally rely on them for more and more of our daily computing. Already we use our BlackBerrys to do e-mail, work our calendars, access the Web, and even work with attachments.

Yet no matter how many useful tasks you use your BlackBerry for, Murphy's Law says that there will always be some file, some piece of information, or some task for which you will need to connect back to your computer and network server. Perhaps I forgot to bring an important document on my business trip. Maybe I am at home and I get an e-mail from a client requesting a file that is back on my office network. Or maybe I'm on the road and need to access my desktop computer and perform some daily or weekly maintenance task.

Whatever the reason, the ability to connect back to a desktop computer or network server is a very common need. Indeed, for mobile laptop users a great many software solutions are available that can provide various kinds of remote access. In this chapter, I present an amazing and surprising variety of remote access programs that work on your BlackBerry. These programs let you use your BlackBerry as a remote terminal, grab files off of a server, and even view and control the screen of a desktop computer!

Remote Control/Remote Desktop Tools

Remote control, which is sometimes also referred to as *remote desktop*, is a term applied to any software that allows one computer to control another computer over some type of wired or wireless connection. There are, of course, many ways in which a computer can command and control the behavior of another computer. For the purposes of this section, "remote control" means that when connected, your computer screen displays the host computer's screen, and when you type on your keyboard or move your mouse, those actions are relayed over to the host computer. It is as if your computer becomes the host computer, just as if you were sitting right in front of it, typing away.

Remote control has been around for almost as long as computers have been connected to one another. The uses of remote control software are many and varied. For technical support, it allows a support rep to see the problem the customer is seeing and potentially even fix it from a separate location. For customer meetings, it allows remote participants to interact with your presentation. It allows applications running on a single computer to be shared among many users. And for travelers on the road, it allows access to a home or office computer whenever needed.

Before you look at remote control for BlackBerry, you first should understand how remote control is currently implemented for desktop computing.

Desktop Remote Control Solutions

Many popular commercial remote control software programs are available. Perhaps the oldest and most well known is Symantec's PCAnywhere. PCAnywhere is an example of a traditional client-host remote control solution. PCAnywhere's host component is installed on the computer that you would like to access, and PCAnywhere's client component is installed on a remote computer that will access and control the host's screen and keyboard. The PCAnywhere client and host components communicate directly with one another in a peer-to-peer fashion.

As the Internet and web browsing became ubiquitous, a new breed of remote control software arose that made use of HTTP and standard web browser technology to achieve a remote control connection. GotoMyPC is a good example of this type of solution. Browser-based remote control has an advantage over peer-to-peer remote control in that it is less complicated to install and configure. Browser-based remote control also interacts well with firewalls, which by default block proprietary protocols such as the type used by PCAnywhere users but accept HTTP-based connections.

Microsoft Terminal Services

Terminal Services is a component that is built into Microsoft's Windows 2003 and XP operating systems. Terminal Services, based on Remote Desktop Protocol (RDP), allows a remote computer user to access applications and data that reside on a networked computer. In order to access these applications and data sources, the host computer must be running Terminal Services, and the computer that wants access must be running a Terminal Services Client. This client can be Microsoft's Terminal Services Client, or it can be a third-party application that has implemented RDP and thus can access a Terminal Services–enabled remote computer.

For individual users looking to provide remote access to a single computer, Terminal Services is somewhat inconvenient in that the remote client actually logs in as a Windows user, and while that user is logged in, the target computer cannot be used, nor can it be accessed by another remote access client. Depending on your needs, this issue may or may not be relevant.

VNC

VNC stands for Virtual Network Computing. VNC allows a computer to connect to and control another computer over the Internet. VNC is different from more traditional proprietary remote control software products in the following ways:

- **Cross-platform compatibility:** The client computer does not have to be the same type of computer as the host. For example, a Windows computer can control a Linux computer.

- **Cost:** It is generally available for free (assuming it is for personal use).

VNC software is available from www.realvnc.com, www.ultravnc.com, and other sources.

Common Connection Issues

Aside from installing and using a good remote control solution, a successful remote control connection is generally dependent on two things: identifying the target computer's IP address and getting past the firewall.

Identifying the Host IP Address

Each computer on a TCP/IP network is assigned a unique IP address. In order to remote control a computer, you generally need to know that computer's IP address. For some kinds of networks, this can be trickier than it sounds. For one, although many computers have a fixed "static" IP address, many others are configured for dynamic IP address assignment. This means that each time the computer is connected to the network, it requests and is assigned an IP address by a designated server. This IP address is very often different each time, which creates a problem for some remote control software products that depend on knowing a reliable IP address. Another IP address issue occurs when you are trying to access a computer that is behind a router on an internal network. In many instances, the internally assigned IP address of a computer on these networks is different from the "public" IP address. In such cases, a router feature called "port forwarding" must be enabled in order to have IP communications "forwarded" to the proper computer via the router.

Getting Past the Firewall

The other problem in successfully using remote control is in getting past the firewall. Today, virtually every network is protected by some kind of firewall that is either built into a router or attached as a standalone appliance. The firewall blocks all IP communications except those that are considered "safe." This is generally done at the firewall by blocking specific *port numbers*, which can be thought of as doorways through which programs can communicate. Aside from a few core port numbers, such as the ones assigned to well-known protocols such as HTTP and POP3, most other ports are blocked by default. Needless to say, a port that has the potential to allow someone else to access and control your computer would be frowned upon by the firewall!

Of course additional ports can be opened on your firewall if you have permission and you know how to reconfigure your router, at your own risk.

In addition, the most recent versions of Windows include a software firewall that runs on each computer. As with the firewall that protects the entire network, the Windows Firewall also blocks all but the most core protocols and ports and requires reconfiguring in order to allow additional ports to be used.

The firewall issue presents a bit of a challenge for users who want to use a proprietary remote control package such as PCAnywhere or even a free solution such as VNC. In these cases, you need to make sure any firewalls that stand between your computer and the host computer will allow the necessary ports to be opened.

BlackBerry Remote Control Solutions

Now that you've reviewed the basics of how remote control works, it's time to take a look at what is available to allow a BlackBerry to connect to and control a remote desktop computer.

Idokorro Mobile Desktop

Idokorro is a software company that offers a number of BlackBerry remote access applications. Mobile Desktop is an application that installs on your BlackBerry and supports remote control of a desktop computer over a network. When installed on your BlackBerry, Mobile Desktop can connect to remote computers that are running either VNC or Microsoft's Terminal Services.

Terminal Services comes bundled with Microsoft XP, although the service is typically inactive by default and thus will likely need to be activated and configured for use. If you decide to go the VNC route, Idokorro lists supported VNC implementations that may be downloaded freely for personal use. I chose to use VNC with my tests and found RealVNC (www.realvnc.com) to be simple to install and configure as a VNC service on my desktop computer. (As mentioned earlier, firewall and IP address issues may need to be resolved as well.)

Note The firewall issues discussed in this chapter are negated if your BlackBerry service is connected to a corporate network running the BlackBerry Enterprise Server (BES). The Mobile Data Service (MDS), which is part of BES, provides a safe and secure pipe for trusted applications to use in communicating with computers behind the firewall.

Mobile Desktop itself installs as a standard BlackBerry application. Once installed, you have the ability to define one or more remote computers that you wish to access and control. For each remote computer, you must specify the method used to connect (Terminal Services or VNC) as well as the IP address for the computer. Figure 6-1 shows the configuration screen for a remote computer connection.

If you've done everything right and you have ensured the VNC or Terminal Services protocols are allowed through your firewall, you should now be able to connect to your target computer!

Figure 6-2 shows Mobile Desktop in action, allowing me to remotely access Excel on my computer, although you can just as easily access iTunes or other software.

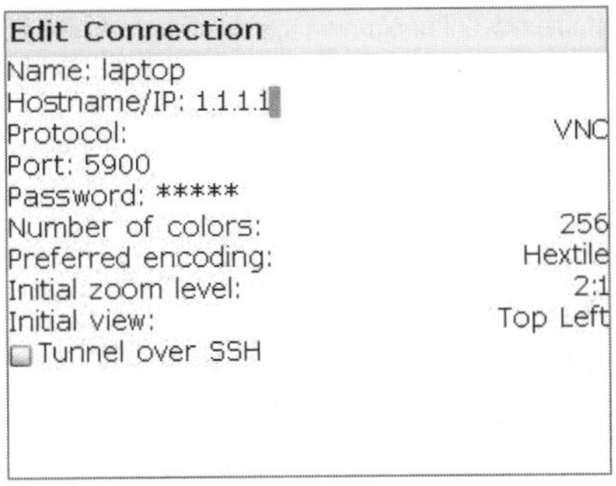

```
Edit Connection
Name: laptop
Hostname/IP: 1.1.1.1
Protocol:                              VNC
Port: 5900
Password: *****
Number of colors:                      256
Preferred encoding:                 Hextile
Initial zoom level:                     2:1
Initial view:                     Top Left
☐ Tunnel over SSH
```

FIGURE 6-1: Configuring Mobile Desktop
to access a remote computer

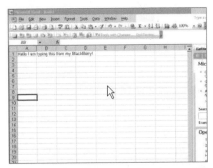

FIGURE 6-2: Working on an Excel spreadsheet
from my BlackBerry with Mobile Desktop

So what was it like to be viewing and controlling my computer screen from my BlackBerry?

Well, from a technical perspective alone, just the ability to see and work with my computer remotely from my BlackBerry is an amazing achievement. I can control iTunes and play music whenever I want! However, in my experience you need to level-set your expectations somewhat for the following reasons:

- The difference in screen dimensions between a typical desktop computer and a BlackBerry is dramatic, and you will be able to see only a portion of the remote screen at any one time. Even given that, text on the remote screen can be so small as to be barely readable.

- I ran Mobile Desktop on a BlackBerry 8700, which is much more powerful than many commonly used BlackBerrys. I also use Cingular's EDGE high-speed wireless network. Even with these advantages, redrawing the screen as I moved up and down was painfully slow, incurring waiting times of half a minute or more. On some occasions, the screen never updated, so I had to disconnect and reconnect to get things back on track.

- Using the "mouse" pointer to click the correct spot on the screen can be tricky, not to mention tedious.

Still, I found that Mobile Desktop worked as advertised. You certainly would not want to work in remote access mode for any extended period of time, but if you need to check up on how an application is working or maybe run a quick command-line procedure, I would think Mobile Desktop could prove to be incredibly useful.

Mobile Desktop is available for $45 per BlackBerry device from Idokorro's website at www.idokorro.com. It is also available for a free 30-day trial download.

TSMobiles and Remote Desktop for Mobiles

A company called ZZZ Software provides an alternative to Idokorro's Mobile Desktop for BlackBerry users. ZZZ Software offers two different remote control solutions. Its TSMobiles product is a Terminal Services client application that uses Windows' Remote Desktop Protocol (RDP) to remotely access a Windows desktop computer. Naturally, the desktop computer must be running Terminal Services in order for the solution to be successful. ZZZ Software also offers a product called Remote Desktop for Mobiles, which performs a similar function but uses proprietary protocols to achieve remote control.

TSMobiles and Terminal Services

TSMobiles has a simple setup that allows you to define a remote computer in a kind of Address Book. You will need the IP address of the remote computer, as well as a valid Windows login and password for the remote computer. As I noted earlier, a disadvantage in using Terminal Services compared to a separate client-server remote access solution is that a Terminal Services connection takes over the login for the computer being controlled. This means that when a connection is made from your BlackBerry, you will be asked if it is okay to log out of the existing Windows user session so that the Terminal Services session can take over. See Figure 6-3 for an illustration of how this is handled from the perspective of the BlackBerry user.

FIGURE 6-3: Windows Terminal Services needs to take over the remote computer's Windows login session

I want to point out that this step is not specific to ZZZ Software's Terminal Services product. Rather, it is a "feature" associated with Windows' Terminal Services implementation. True, if you are accessing your computer remotely, it is probably okay if you force the computer to log out and log in to make a connection. But if the remote computer is a shared resource or if someone else is using the computer while you are out, this can be a nuisance. What's worse is that if you choose Yes to the prompt, a new Windows login session is started, and I don't know about you, but my Windows computer can take a minute or more to completely log in and be ready for use. Plus there are those alerts and popups from the taskbar that you always need to dismiss. That is not a problem when you are sitting at your desktop, but they are mighty annoying when you have to dismiss them one by one remotely on a BlackBerry!

Still, I found TSMobiles to work reasonably well as a remote access/Terminal Services product. As with Idokorro's Mobile Desktop, expect wait times of 30 seconds to a minute for a full-screen redraw, so it's really best suited for quick and easy remote operations.

Remote Desktop for Mobiles

ZZZ Software's other offering is called Remote Desktop for Mobiles, and this product does not use Terminal Services for remote access. Instead, Remote Desktop installs a special server component on your desktop that offers proprietary remote control services to ZZZ Software's BlackBerry client application. Of course this means that both your Windows firewall and your network firewall will need to be modified to allow Remote Desktop's communications to go through. (Remote Desktop uses port 6100 by default, although this can be changed if you wish.)

When you install Remote Desktop for Mobiles on your BlackBerry, the client offers a similar main screen and Address Book as the TSMobiles product, but that's where the similarity ends. In my experience, Remote Desktop for Mobiles is a superior solution for BlackBerry remote desktop access for a couple of reasons:

- It does not use Terminal Services, so the remote desktop can remain logged in and in use while your remote control session goes on.

- I found Remote Desktop for Mobiles to offer much faster screen redraws and overall responsiveness than TSMobiles and even Idokorro's product.

Figure 6-4 shows my BlackBerry 8700 controlling my laptop. (It has the Remote Desktop for Mobiles web page displayed in my laptop's Firefox browser.)

FIGURE 6-4: Remote Desktop for Mobiles controlling my laptop screen

Aside from the faster performance I observed, I also noted that ZZZ Software makes available an online service called RDM Online which helps to resolve the issue of connecting to a computer that does not have a reliable IP address. As mentioned earlier, home computers with dynamic IP addressing and computers behind a network router both can create challenges in counting on a reliable IP address. The RDM Online service is described as a sort of a proxy on the Internet for Remote Desktop in that the BlackBerry client does not need to communicate directly with the target computer. Instead, the connection goes through a proxy server at RDM Online that makes sure that the connection is made properly.

Remote Desktop for Mobiles retails for $35 for a single user license, and comes with a free three-month subscription to RDM Online Service if you need an IP-independent way to connect. If you need to use RDM Online Service for more than that amount of time, it is available for three months at a time for $30 or for a full year for about $100. ZZZ Software's Terminal Services is simply a $35 single user license.

For more information about TSMobiles and Remote Desktop for Mobiles, visit ZZZ Software's website www.zzzsoftware.com.

Remote control on BlackBerry devices is a fairly new concept, so I would expect the available solutions to get better and faster over time, and new products and players may become available. Which remote control solution is the best one really depends on your needs, computer, and network configuration. My recommendation is to give both Idokorro's and ZZZ Software's products a try and see which one works best for your specific situation.

Remote File Access Tools

The prior section presented a number of programs that allow you to access and control the screen, keyboard, and mouse of a remote computer. While this gives you considerable power and lets you perform virtually any task on the computer you are connected to, it's overkill if all you want to do is grab and download a file. In this section, you take a look at software solutions that fall in the category of Remote File Access.

Avvenu

Avvenu is a file sharing solution that allows users of mobile devices and Internet-connected computers to access their files from their desktop computer. Avvenu is installed as a software application on your desktop computer, and after successful completion of the installation process, folders and files on your computer can be accessed from any computer or mobile device using just a standard web browser.

A nice feature of this approach is that because Avvenu uses only standard web protocols, no security issues should exist in terms of allowing the software to operate through your Windows or network firewall. Once installed on your desktop, you can go to your BlackBerry's HTML Web Browser, enter the special Avvenu access URL of http://share.avvenu.com, and log in using your personal username and password. You are then greeted with a web browser screen displaying folders and files from your computer desktop.

Figure 6-5 shows my BlackBerry browsing the folders and files from My Documents on my desktop computer.

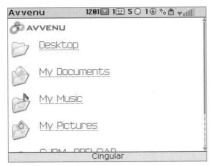

FIGURE 6-5: Using Avvenu in the BlackBerry Browser

The capability to browse and access your desktop files sounds great, but there are some problems with using a solution such as Avvenu on a BlackBerry device:

- Browsing through large folders can be very tedious. Only five or six listings are shown per page, so if there are dozens or perhaps hundreds of files, and you have to click Next to page through a folder, it will take a very long time to locate the file you want.

- Making the Avvenu client browser-based means that users don't have to install special software on the device; all they need is the BlackBerry Browser. But it also means that their user experience in browsing their desktop files will suffer the same limitations and frustrations as browsing through web pages. Pages are slow to display, images take a long time to render, and drilling down to subfolders and back up can be quite painful.

- This is not really Avvenu's problem, but a BlackBerry does not have any built-in way to work with common document file types such as Word, Excel, PowerPoint, or PDF. This means that Avvenu users on a BlackBerry will not be able to download these file types to their BlackBerry. Certain browser-ready file types such as JPG and TXT are recognized and display nicely on the BlackBerry, but many (perhaps even most) of the file types you would want to access on your desktop will simply give you an error if you try to download them to your BlackBerry.

- Even if you were to go and purchase one of the several document solutions available for BlackBerry, those solutions do not work with native file types on the device, so that does not help in the Avvenu scenario, which totally depends on the ability of the web browser to recognize the file type.

Despite these drawbacks, Avvenu does indeed work on a BlackBerry device and can be a worthwhile solution to look at if the supported file types you need to access are among the limited list of types that can work with BlackBerry.

Avvenu is free for a basic level of service. There are also "plus" levels of service that you can pay for, which take advantage of Avvenu's hosting service, giving you guaranteed access to files even if your computer is turned off or unavailable.

For more information on Avvenu, visit www.avvenu.com.

I'm In Touch

I'm In Touch is, like Avvenu, a web browser–based remote access solution. Like Avvenu, I'm In Touch relies on a desktop application that is installed on your computer and makes your files and other information available to you when you connect from another computer — in this case, your BlackBerry.

However, for BlackBerry device users, I'm In Touch goes above and beyond the basic file/folder access capability offered by Avvenu and lets you actually view most document types on your BlackBerry. I'm In Touch manages to do this by including a document converter utility with the desktop application. What happens is that when you select a document using I'm In Touch on your BlackBerry Browser, the I'm In Touch desktop service converts the selected document to a web-viewable format and then serves it to you in the browser itself. While this is still not quite the same as being able to download and work with a document in Microsoft Word, the ability to at least access and view the contents of a document can be very useful.

I'm In Touch does not limit you to accessing files and folders, either. When you log in from your BlackBerry, you are presented with a menu that lists the various types of information that can be accessed remotely, as shown in Figure 6-6.

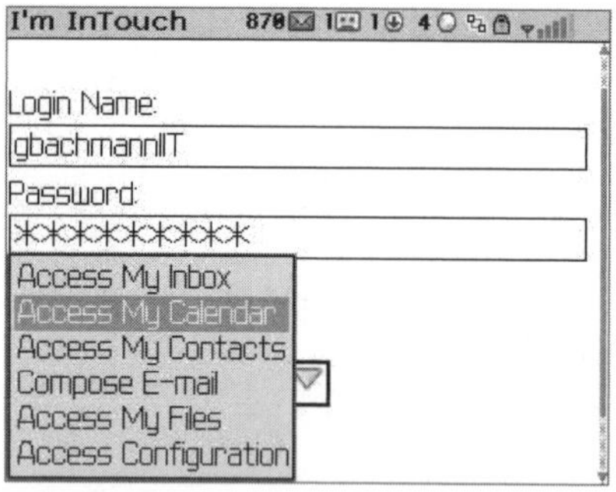

FIGURE 6-6: I'm In Touch remote access options

As you can see from Figure 6-6, besides files and folders, I'm In Touch can also remotely access your desktop calendar, contacts, and Inbox. You can even create an e-mail remotely and attach a file from your desktop to the e-mail!

I'm In Touch is available from 01 Communications at www.imintouch.net, and at the time of this writing, a subscription costs $99.95 per year or $9.95 per month.

EasyReach

EasyReach is a somewhat different product in that it focuses on the problem of searching for and finding information on your desktop. EasyReach indexes all of your documents, e-mail, contacts, appointments, tasks, and other information on your desktop, which then enables it to provide very fast searching of your data based on keywords. On top of general-purpose desktop search, EasyReach also lets you define projects that organize all of your content related to a specific topic in such a way that it is always collected together for you.

EasyReach is primarily oriented as an information search and organization tool for desktop users, but the product's relevance in this discussion is that it also offers remote users access to this information from a web browser or from a special BlackBerry software client that is installed to the device.

When you run the EasyReach BlackBerry client, you are prompted to log in with your user name and password. After doing this, you are greeted with a very simple search form where you enter keywords that match the content you are searching for. As shown in Figure 6-7, you can specify the scope of your search to include documents, appointments, e-mail, tasks, contacts, or all of the above.

FIGURE 6-7: Specifying a search in EasyReach

EasyReach then submits your search criteria directly to your desktop computer and returns any matching results, as shown in Figure 6-8.

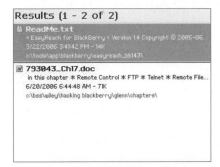

FIGURE 6-8: My EasyReach search results

Because the EasyReach client is not web browser–based, the results returned are very easy and intuitive to navigate. It is not very different from navigating in other BlackBerry applications such as Messages or Calendar.

Although EasyReach does not offer viewing capabilities for BlackBerry users, it does provide a workaround: You can ask EasyReach to e-mail your document to you on your BlackBerry. If you are using the BlackBerry Attachment Service, your document is then converted to a viewable attachment for your BlackBerry. The full menu of actions available once you've selected a document is shown in Figure 6-9.

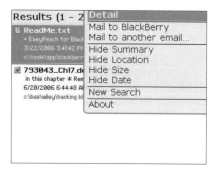

FIGURE 6-9: My EasyReach available actions

A free trial download of EasyReach is available from EasyReach Corporation at www.easyreach.com. At the time of this writing, the basic EasyReach "Find" desktop software sells for $49.99 per computer and includes a 1-year subscription to the remote access service. The full desktop Workspace edition is $99.99 per computer.

Mobile Administration Tools

So far you've been focusing on remote control and remote access tools that can help you connect to your desktop computer from your BlackBerry. Another practical use of remote access is for performing maintenance on servers, web sites, and FTP sites, either as part of your daily job or as an occasional task. This section provides a brief overview of the available tools that target this need.

Idokorro Mobile FTP

File Transfer Protocol, more commonly known as FTP, is one of the oldest Internet protocols around. FTP runs on TCP/IP, and an FTP connection consists of an FTP server, which manages the files stored on a destination computer, and an FTP client, which runs on your computer and allows you to connect to, upload, download, and perform file and folder operations on the destination computer.

People use FTP for many reasons. Employees use it to download applications and other files from company web sites. Web site designers and administrators use FTP to maintain, upload, and download HTML files, images, and other web content on their web sites. Individual users may utilize an FTP site as an easy alternative to e-mail attachments for transferring large files to colleagues and friends. An FTP server can also theoretically be used on your work or home computer in order to allow you to remotely access your files while away from your desk.

FTP is not an actual software product; it is just a protocol, and as such there are perhaps hundreds of server and client implementations of the FTP standard. An FTP server is now a standard part of just about any type of server operating system, and FTP client programs are available for every computer platform, be it Windows, Macintosh, Linux, or even (you guessed it) handhelds and smartphones such as BlackBerry.

As you've seen with other software tools, remote file access has its challenges on the BlackBerry platform because of the lack of native document support on the device. Theoretically you could download and upload files on your BlackBerry, but you would have no way of creating, viewing, or editing them. While this does somewhat limit the usefulness of FTP on BlackBerry, many types of FTP usage require only folder operations to be performed on the server, such as renaming, deleting, or moving files among different folders. Furthermore, those files that do need to be edited are typically in plain text format, such as HTML files, which make up the bulk of web content.

Idokorro's Mobile FTP product, along with Mobile Desktop (reviewed earlier in this chapter), is part of Idokorro's Mobile Access Solutions product line. As with other FTP client programs, Mobile FTP enables you to create, configure, and store FTP connection profiles for each server that you need to access. Typically you will need at least the host name (domain or IP), user ID, and password in order to connect.

Once you've entered the necessary configuration for the destination FTP site, you are connected to the server, and a list of files and folders residing on the server is displayed, as shown in Figure 6-10.

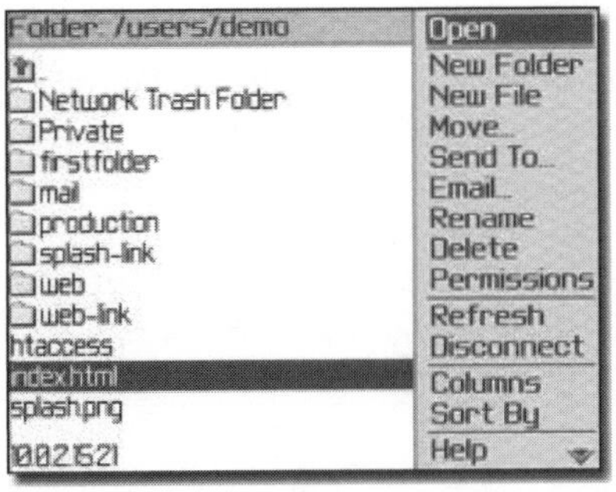

FIGURE 6-10: Idokorro Mobile FTP

Once the file listing appears, you can select a file and use the trackwheel menu to create, view, edit, rename, move, and delete folders and files; view images; change permissions; or even e-mail files as attachments to a specified e-mail address.

Mobile FTP is available from Idokorro's web site www.idokorro.com for $35 per license, and a free trial download is also provided.

Other Networking Tools

Although not as widely used among the general computer user population, network administration and computer support professionals use a number of other handy software utilities, including tools for server maintenance, password management, remote secure shell, and other administrative tasks.

As with Mobile Desktop and Mobile FTP, Idokorro once again steps in and provides a fine set of tools for this purpose with their Mobile Admin suite as well as Mobile SSH and Mobile Telnet. Idokorro Mobile Admin is a toolbox in and of itself that provides BlackBerry users with many features. Following are just some of the highlights:

- Managing Windows computers and networks
- Managing Microsoft Active Directory, Exchange, and SQL Server
- Managing Lotus Notes/Domino
- Managing BlackBerry Enterprise Server

Like many of the tools reviewed in this chapter, Idokorro Mobile Admin consists of a desktop/server application and a BlackBerry application "client" that runs on the device. The desktop/server component controls access to the various Mobile Admin functions, and the client connects your BlackBerry to the desktop Mobile Admin service on your computer. In an enterprise installation, Mobile Admin even provides you with the ability to connect to and administer multiple servers within your network.

After installing the Mobile Admin client application to your BlackBerry, you will need to enter the IP address for the computer on which you installed the desktop software. You will also need to make sure that the port number (4054 by default) for Mobile Admin is allowed through your network and computer firewalls. Security is managed either by your BES server connection or if you are not using BES/MDS by using HTTPS to safeguard the data flow to your desktop.

Once you have connected, you will see a screen of icons that represent all of the various utility functions you can perform with Mobile Admin (see Figure 6-11).

FIGURE 6-11: Idokorro Mobile Admin's main icon screen

Summary

In this chapter I've shown you a variety of tools that enable you to use your BlackBerry as a remote control, remote command console, or remote administration tool for accessing networked desktop computers. If you are away from your desktop for much of the time, these tools can truly be a lifesaver by enabling you to do things such as find and forward an important file to your customer, execute a quick procedure on a server, or perform a remote backup.

With the introduction of more powerful BlackBerry devices, better screens, faster processors, and faster wireless connections, these tools will no doubt become more capable and even more essential for performing remote tasks. In particular, process- and data-dependent tasks such as remote screen control and remote file access are just now appearing, and if current trends continue, should become more usable in the future.

Storage on the Go: Your BlackBerry as a USB Thumb Drive

Modern BlackBerry device models are being sold with 32 megabytes and even 64 megabytes of memory storage on board, giving valuable breathing room for more e-mail messages, more contact records, more software applications, and more of everything. Yet it's a pretty safe bet that most BlackBerry owners make use of only a fraction of that available memory. After all, current BlackBerry models do not come with MP3 or video capability, nor do they have built-in document editing support, so there are fewer things that BlackBerry owners can put on their device, versus someone who owns a Palm Treo or Windows Mobile handheld.

They say that nature abhors a vacuum, and indeed the tendency among computer users is to try to fill any unused memory storage with more files. After all, why have a BlackBerry with 64MB of memory if you aren't going to make full use of it? And for that matter, what exactly *is* on a BlackBerry, and how do you get files on and off of it?

This chapter unlocks some of the mystery of what is stored on a typical BlackBerry device and how data is stored by BlackBerry programs. I then go further and show you how to copy files to and from your BlackBerry, effectively turning your BlackBerry into a kind of portable USB "hard drive."

Understanding BlackBerry Memory Storage

Like most handheld and smartphone devices, BlackBerry devices ship with built-in flash memory, which is used for storage of applications, files, and application data. In addition to flash memory, BlackBerry devices also come with SRAM, or Static Random Access Memory. SRAM is a fast form of memory used as working memory by both the operating system and any running applications. When a device is using too much SRAM, data in working memory gets swapped in and out of flash storage as necessary by the operating system.

Comparing Memory on BlackBerry Devices

BlackBerry devices have evolved over the years, and just like any other computer product they have come with an ever increasing amount of built-in flash memory storage. The increase in storage capacity is driven by lower flash memory costs, miniaturization and, of course, customer demand.

Table 7-1 looks at selected BlackBerry models and charts the increase in flash memory storage capacity over the years, from the early RIM Pagers to the more recent 8700 and 7130 BlackBerry models.

Table 7-1   Memory Configurations for Selected BlackBerry Devices

Device Model	Memory Storage Capacity
RIM Pager 857/957	8MB
6750	10MB
7510	16MB
7100	32MB
7290	32MB
7130	64MB
8700	64MB

Obviously, the trend has been toward increasing capacity with each new device model or series. How much memory will come with future BlackBerry models is anyone's guess, but it's a pretty safe bet they will come with more than previous models.

Currently, no BlackBerry devices have an expansion card slot, but a quick glance at flash memory SD card prices shows that cards with 256MB are incredibly inexpensive, and even 1GB, 2GB, and 4GB card configurations are all available for less than $100. So it is clear that how much memory comes on a given model is less a technical hurdle than it is simply a product pricing and customer demand issue for Research In Motion to work out. The technology to load up a small handheld with gigabytes of storage is here (as proven by Apple's iPod).

About the BlackBerry File System

In contrast to the laptop or desktop computers we work with, which come with gigabytes of memory as well as file explorer programs to help manage and organize your files, a BlackBerry device offers very little visibility into how files are stored. Is there even a file system on a BlackBerry?

Certainly there is no built-in file explorer program to let you browse the BlackBerry file system, and there is no facility for creating or using file folders such as we are familiar with on Windows or Apple computers. In fact, the only visible evidence of any sort of file system is buried under the Settings icon, in the Applications category, where you can selectively delete programs you no longer want and also see how much memory you have available on your device.

A review of the software developer documentation that comes with the BlackBerry Java Development Environment (JDE) sheds little light on the mystery. There are wispy references to a File class that offers a way to navigate a file system, but it also comes with an admonition that the class is not available on any but a very few device models.

Beyond the File class, programmers are given the option to make use of a Java facility called the MIDP Record Store if they need to store data. Alternatively, they may use the BlackBerry Persistence Model to store object data. Neither option describes anything like a standard folder file system like we are used to seeing on desktop computers.

If software programmers are not given the tools to interact with the file system, how is it possible for the average BlackBerry user? The following sections explore methods you can use to list the files residing on your BlackBerry.

Spelunking the BlackBerry File System with JavaLoader

A barely mentioned, little-documented program that Research In Motion includes as part of its software development toolkit is called JavaLoader. If you download and install the BlackBerry JDE on your desktop computer, you will find the JavaLoader program buried under the /Program Files/Research In Motion/BlackBerry JDE/bin folder.

JavaLoader is nothing fancy, a humble-looking command-line utility that runs from a Windows command prompt. Yet take a look at the feature set that JavaLoader offers:

- Connects to your BlackBerry over USB
- Obtains device information
- Provides application and file directory listings
- Takes screenshots of your BlackBerry device
- Loads application programs onto a device
- Erases application programs from a device
- Wipes (cleans) a device

Now, I'd say that's quite a feature list for a program that is hardly mentioned anywhere in the BlackBerry documentation!

As I mentioned, JavaLoader runs from an MS-DOS–type command line. In order to get JavaLoader to perform any of the previously mentioned programs, you need to open a DOS command prompt and type **javaloader**, followed by the command-line options that will tell JavaLoader what you want it to do. The most useful JavaLoader command-line options are shown in Table 7-2.

Table 7-2   JavaLoader Command-Line Options

Command	Meaning
-usb	Connects over USB.
Dir	Produces a directory listing of all files on the device. Adding –d also lists dependent modules, and adding –s shows program's "sibling files."
Deviceinfo	Provides information about the connected device.
Load	Loads a BlackBerry program specified onto the device (program must be a .cod file).
Save	Retrieves a file from the handheld to the desktop.
Info	Provides info on the specified device file.
Wipe	Completely wipes the device. Use –f to wipe only the file system or –a to wipe only applications. *Use this with caution!*
Erase	Erases the specified module from the device.
Screenshot	Takes a screenshot from the device and stores it as a .bmp file on the desktop with the specified name.

It goes without saying that you should use JavaLoader with extreme caution. Erasing the wrong file or wiping your device can have undesirable consequences and can even wreck your device! To be safe, always make sure you have a recent backup of your device before playing with a utility such as JavaLoader.

Listing System Files with JavaLoader

To obtain a directory listing showing the files on your device, connect your BlackBerry to your desktop using the USB cable and then type the following into a DOS command prompt:

```
javaloader -usb dir
```

On my device, this command produces a listing, as shown in Figure 7-1.

Each entry in the listing is a file that is currently stored on your device. Some are system files, some are applications, and others are resource files that support an application.

A full listing of files on my device from JavaLoader shows 196 entries. This list scrolls far too quickly on my computer, so I use a handy DOS option called "redirection," which causes the output from the JavaLoader command to be sent to a file instead of the screen, as follows:

```
javaloader -usb dir > "FileListing.txt"
```

```
Command Prompt                                                          _ □ X
C:\Program Files\Research In Motion\BlackBerry JDE 4.1.0\bin>javaloader -usb dir
RIM Wireless Handheld Java Loader
Copyright 2001-2005 Research In Motion Limited
Connected
Name                              Version        Size      Created
-----------------------------------------------------------------------
net_rim_os                        4.1.0.194      507800    Sat Nov 12 12:33:36 2005
net_rim_smartcard                 4.1.0.194      26536     Sat Nov 12 12:35:30 2005
net_rim_wap                       4.1.0.194      66884 *   Sat Nov 12 12:36:32 2005
net_rim_event_log_viewer_app      4.1.0.194      12400     Sat Nov 12 12:36:21 2005
net_rim_io_contentstore           4.1.0.194      63044     Sat Nov 12 12:36:24 2005
net_rim_cldc_io_rim_impl          4.1.0.194      64684     Sat Nov 12 12:35:19 2005
net_rim_runtime_resource          4.1.0.194      2728      Sat Nov 12 12:34:30 2005
net_rim_runtime_resource__en      4.1.0.194      11308     Sat Nov 12 12:34:31 2005
net_rim_bb_activation             4.1.0.194      38084     Sat Nov 12 12:39:43 2005
net_rim_bb_addressbook_app        4.1.0.194      93636     Sat Nov 12 12:39:48 2005
net_rim_bb_addressbook_gal        4.1.0.194      25160     Sat Nov 12 12:36:58 2005
net_rim_bb_addressbook_models     4.1.0.194      13016     Sat Nov 12 12:36:43 2005
net_rim_bb_addressbook_groupaddress 4.1.0.194    15920     Sat Nov 12 12:39:56 2005
net_rim_bb_alarm_app              4.1.0.194      16136     Sat Nov 12 12:40:11 2005
net_rim_bb_apps_framework         4.1.0.194      98588     Sat Nov 12 12:36:51 2005
net_rim_bb_attachment             4.1.0.194      5324      Sat Nov 12 12:37:21 2005
net_rim_bb_browser_field_api      4.1.0.194      10308     Sat Nov 12 12:37:02 2005
net_rim_bb_browser_push           4.1.0.194      32876     Sat Nov 12 12:38:00 2005
net_rim_bb_calendar_app           4.1.0.194      80796     Sat Nov 12 12:41:14 2005
net_rim_bb_calendar_lib           4.1.0.194      79192     Sat Nov 12 12:37:24 2005
net_rim_bb_calendar_ota           4.1.0.194      56404     Sat Nov 12 12:39:37 2005
net_rim_bb_email                  4.1.0.194      265820    Sat Nov 12 12:37:06 2005
net_rim_bb_profiles_tunes         4.1.0.194      18872     Sat Nov 12 12:45:00 2005
net_rim_bb_remindermanager        4.1.0.194      14984     Sat Nov 12 12:45:12 2005
net_rim_bb_ribbon_app             4.1.0.194      123832    Sat Nov 12 12:45:19 2005
net_rim_bb_messagesearch_lib      4.1.0.194      45680     Sat Nov 12 12:41:30 2005
net_rim_bb_itadmin                4.1.0.194      9308      Sat Nov 12 12:44:25 2005
net_rim_bb_applicationdelivery    4.1.0.194      11792     Sat Nov 12 12:40:15 2005
net_rim_bb_resource               4.1.0.194      6008      Sat Nov 12 12:45:15 2005
net_rim_bb_resource__en           4.1.0.194      46392     Sat Nov 12 12:45:17 2005
net_rim_bb_mc_app                 4.1.0.194      9668      Sat Nov 12 13:07:51 2005
net_rim_bb_password_wizard        4.1.0.194      4300      Sat Nov 12 13:08:17 2005
net_rim_cldc_io_tcp               4.1.0.194      56744     Sat Nov 12 12:35:25 2005
net_rim_tcp_options               4.1.0.194      3516      Sat Nov 12 12:45:46 2005
net_rim_bb_addressbook_simapp     4.1.0.194      46828     Sat Nov 12 12:40:04 2005
net_rim_sel3nettable              4.1.0.194      42840     Sat Nov 12 12:36:29 2005
net_rim_bb_globalsearch_app       4.1.0.194      14180     Sat Nov 12 12:41:56 2005
net_rim_MIDPRootCerts             4.1.0.194      11416     Sat Nov 12 12:34:23 2005
net_rim_bbapi_mailv2              4.1.0.194      43888     Sat Nov 12 12:37:44 2005
net_rim_bbapi_mail                4.1.0.194      1964      Sat Nov 12 12:38:54 2005
net_rim_bbapi_menuitem            4.1.0.194      5500      Sat Nov 12 12:38:59 2005
net_rim_bbapi_pim                 4.1.0.194      64912     Sat Nov 12 12:38:49 2005
net_rim_bbapi_pim_todo            4.1.0.194      8692      Sat Nov 12 12:39:03 2005
net_rim_pdap                      4.1.0.194      69144     Sat Nov 12 12:37:51 2005
net_rim_pdap_resources            4.1.0.194      1672      Sat Nov 12 12:37:49 2005
net_rim_pdap_todo                 4.1.0.194      10132     Sat Nov 12 12:37:57 2005
net_rim_bbapi_pim_res             4.1.0.194      1992      Sat Nov 12 12:39:07 2005
net_rim_bbapi_pim_res__en         4.1.0.194      2572      Sat Nov 12 12:39:08 2005
net_rim_bbapi_options             4.1.0.194      2700      Sat Nov 12 12:39:01 2005
net_rim_bbapi_browser             4.1.0.194      5332      Sat Nov 12 12:38:45 2005
net_rim_bbapi_phone               4.1.0.194      10332     Sat Nov 12 12:38:56 2005
net_rim_bbapi_invoke              4.1.0.194      6292      Sat Nov 12 12:47:03 2005
net_rim_serialformats             4.1.0.194      43044     Sat Nov 12 12:36:46 2005
net_rim_bb_phone_entry            4.1.0.194      2552      Sat Nov 12 12:23:14 2005
net_rim_locationapi               4.1.0.194      22424     Sat Nov 12 12:20:03 2005
net_rim_bb_ribbon_skin_svg        4.1.0.194      9580      Sat Nov 12 12:44:08 2005
net_rim_bb_contentinjector        4.1.0.194      7784      Sat Nov 12 12:52:17 2005
net_rim_bb_explorer_picture       4.1.0.194      10056     Sat Nov 12 12:41:24 2005
net_rim_plazmic_mediaengine       4.1.0.194      60112     Sat Nov 12 12:34:55 2005
net_rim_plazmic_mediaengine_pme02 4.1.0.194      25312     Sat Nov 12 12:46:41 2005
net_rim_plazmic_mediaengine_pme10 4.1.0.194      73596     Sat Nov 12 12:46:44 2005
net_rim_plazmic_mediaengine_bundle 4.1.0.194     5216      Sat Nov 12 12:46:39 2005
net_rim_bb_standardcalculator_app 4.1.0.194      17504     Sat Nov 12 12:45:36 2005
net_rim_font_european_sff         4.1.0.194      123872    Sat Nov 12 12:33:59 2005
net_rim_bb_idlescreen_app         4.1.0.194      13856     Sat Nov 12 12:44:11 2005
net_rim_device_api_games          4.1.0.194      6508      Sat Nov 12 12:39:11 2005
net_rim_theme_blackberry_320x240  4.1.0.194      884828    Sat Nov 12 13:04:18 2005
net_rim_bb_backdrops_320x240      4.1.0.194      502796    Sat Nov 12 12:40:20 2005
net_rim_theme_bb_dimension_list_320x240 4.1.0.194 184736   Sat Nov 12 13:03:26 2005
```

FIGURE 7-1: Using JavaLoader to obtain a listing of files on my BlackBerry

Although not a true file utility, JavaLoader directory listings provide you with insight not easily obtainable by other means into what files are on your BlackBerry. It is interesting to see the system components as well as which files are consuming the most space.

Loading a File onto the Device with JavaLoader

JavaLoader's `load` command-line option offers you the ability to add a BlackBerry module (a .cod file) onto the device over a USB connection. In this respect, it effectively duplicates the Application Loader feature from the BlackBerry Desktop Manager program. Unfortunately, JavaLoader is not capable of loading non-BlackBerry files onto a device, but it can serve as an alternative means of installing a BlackBerry program or other file onto a connected device.

As an example, the following syntax could be used to add a program called "HelloWorld" onto a connected device:

```
javaloader -usb load HelloWorld.cod
```

Getting a File from the Device to Your Desktop

Although it is hard to imagine many reasons why you would want to copy one of the BlackBerry files from your device to your desktop, you can do it by executing the following command:

```
javaloader -usb save HelloWorld.cod
```

Taking a Screenshot with JavaLoader

Perhaps the most widely useful feature of JavaLoader is its ability to take a device screenshot. As a matter of fact, I've used this very feature extensively in writing this book. All the BlackBerry device screenshots were taken using JavaLoader.

To take a screenshot of your BlackBerry, connect your device over USB, and then go to your BlackBerry and navigate to the screen you wish to take a picture of. Now on your desktop, execute the following JavaLoader command:

```
javaloader -usb screenshot myscreen.bmp
```

This takes a snapshot of what is currently displaying on your device and stores it as a standard Windows bitmap (.bmp) file on your desktop. You can then open the bitmap file with Microsoft Paint or another image viewer program and rename it or do whatever you wish with it.

Besides taking snapshots for books, this feature is quite useful for product documentation, web site demonstrations and discussions, PowerPoint presentations, or any other situation where you wish to show others an example of a BlackBerry screen.

What's Missing?

JavaLoader is definitely a nice find for anyone interested in learning more about what is going on with the internal file system of a BlackBerry. But the fact that it able to work only with BlackBerry files is an unfortunate limitation that makes it not quite as useful as it would be if we were able to copy other kinds of files to and from a device, such as MP3 files or documents. For that, you look to another software utility called eFile.

Copying Files Between BlackBerry and Desktop

eFile is a free BlackBerry software program from the folks at DynoPlex, makers of the eOffice BlackBerry office suite. When you install eFile, you wind up with a program that installs and runs on your BlackBerry, as well as a companion program called eFile Desktop that runs on your desktop computer.

On a BlackBerry device, eFile is clearly intended to play a role similar to the one File Explorer plays in Windows. Indeed, the main screen for eFile (pictured in Figure 7-2) strongly resembles the folder tree/file listing layout familiar to most Windows users.

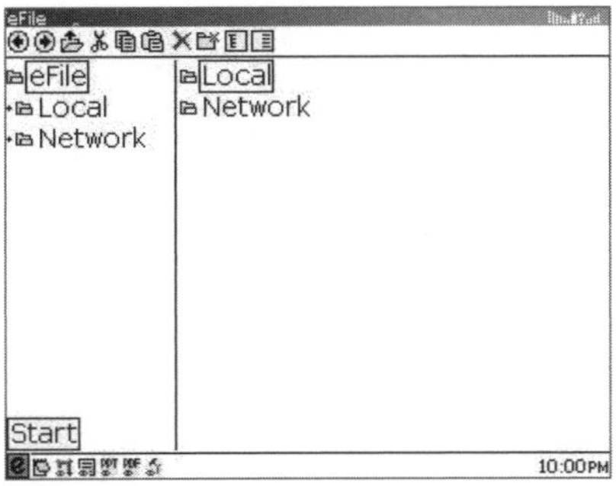

FIGURE 7-2: The main eFile screen layout

As shown in Figure 7-2, on the left side of the eFile screen are folders for Local and Network files. On the right side of the screen, you see the files in the currently selected folder. Navigation between the panels and around the folders and files is supported using either the trackwheel or the menu system that pops up from the Start button at the lower left.

One of the first things you notice is that upon initial installation, there aren't any files in any of the folders. This seems a bit perplexing at first. What's the point of a file explorer if it doesn't show you the files on your BlackBerry? This requires a bit of explanation. eFile does not actually show you any of the BlackBerry files, such as system files or programs, that reside on your device. Although that function would arguably be useful to some people, the real purpose of eFile is not to let you mess around with the built-in system files, but rather to let you copy ordinary documents, spreadsheets, and other file types from your desktop to your device.

So how do you copy files from your desktop to your BlackBerry? This is where the eFile Desktop program component comes in. When you run eFile Desktop from your Windows Start button, it opens as a window with two panels, as shown in Figure 7-3.

On the left side is a view of the folders and files on your computer. The drop-down list at the top lets you move up or down within the drives and folders on your computer. Below the drop-down is a list of files that reside in the currently selected desktop folder. On the right side of the eFile desktop display is a representation of the files on your BlackBerry that are managed by eFile.

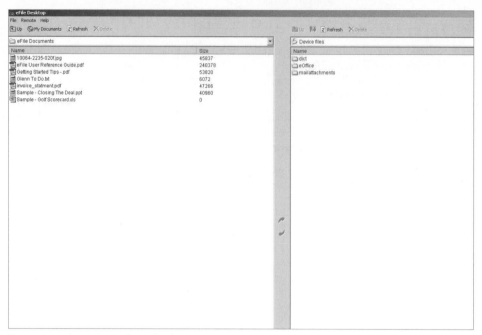

FIGURE 7-3: The eFile Desktop display

To copy a file from your desktop to the device, simply select the file or files you wish to place on your BlackBerry, and click the arrow icon in the center that points to the right. eFile Desktop will then place the files in the list on the right side panel. During this process, eFile Desktop attempts to "convert" any files for which it has a file type plug-in. DynoPlex offers alternative programs for Word and Excel, and because of this, eFile automatically converts files of those types to its own internal eWord and eExcel formats. For other file types, no conversion is performed and the file is left intact, which generally means that the file will not be viewable on your BlackBerry. (If you do not want a Word or Excel document to be converted, you can change the file extension, for example .ddd instead of .doc.)

The actual file transfer is triggered by invoking a synchronization session with your BlackBerry using BlackBerry Desktop Manager. The eFile synchronization process is then run by Desktop Manager and will automatically process any file actions necessary. Figure 7-4 shows the eFile BlackBerry display after successful synchronization and file transfer.

To delete files from your BlackBerry, simply use eFile Desktop's right side panel to select the files to remove and they will be removed from your BlackBerry on the next synchronization. Additionally, you can copy files from your BlackBerry to your desktop.

eFile is available as a free download from www.dynoplex.com.

FIGURE 7-4: eFile shows me the files I copied
to my BlackBerry

Summary

Despite the lack of tangible evidence on a standard BlackBerry device, there are some (barely documented) methods for discovering what files are actually stored on your BlackBerry and even for copying files between your BlackBerry and your desktop. With a little knowledge, BlackBerry owners can even exploit the information presented here to use their devices as a kind of portable external storage drive.

It is pretty clear that eFile is intended to encourage users to try out the full eOffice suite, in order to enjoy the ability to launch into, view, and edit documents. But as simply a means for getting standard desktop files onto and off of a BlackBerry device, eFile does the job well enough on its own. The only real issue with using it as a way to turn a BlackBerry into a portable hard drive is eFile's habit of trying to convert files to eOffice format, but that can be worked around. Given enough available storage on your BlackBerry, eFile can be used in a pinch to transport files such as MP3, video, or even Windows programs and other files between your home and work computer or between any two computers. Of course you also need to have eFile Desktop installed on any computer you wish to copy files to from your BlackBerry, but given that it is a free download, this should not be a problem.

Keeping Your BlackBerry Safe

Most people find that once they start using their BlackBerry, it becomes the repository for much of the information they need in their personal and work lives. Certainly, your BlackBerry routinely and automatically delivers your e-mail messages to you. Your e-mail account settings and passwords are stored on your device. Plus, even simple e-mails sometimes carry important document attachments filled with important and perhaps even secret or proprietary information. It is likely that all of the addresses and phone numbers for your friends, family, customers, clients, and colleagues are stored on your BlackBerry. Also on your BlackBerry Calendar is likely to be a precise schedule for your whereabouts and activities on a daily basis. Finally, if you make use of any other BlackBerry software applications or services, other tidbits of information about you or your company are also possibly stored on your device.

This is all good news, right? I mean, the whole point of carrying a great handheld device such as a BlackBerry is to have instant access to your important information. But what if your BlackBerry is lost, stolen, or even borrowed? You got it — the fact that you will be without your constant BlackBerry companion is perhaps the least of your worries. Perhaps even more upsetting is the idea that all of your precious private data is now in the hands of someone else.

It is a bit disturbing to think of all of your personal information being read by another person who has your BlackBerry. And just think about how your employer might feel if he or she knew that company e-mails, contacts, and activities were all out in the open. Think about the implications of all this for a moment, and I am sure you will realize that security on your BlackBerry is an issue that you want to learn more about.

This chapter delves into methods of protecting against the loss or theft of the data stored on your BlackBerry. I cover how to use the BlackBerry's built-in password protection mechanism to secure your data. I describe available data backup and restore features to make sure that you have good backup copies of your data. I also present several third-party applications that can give you peace of mind by storing, securing, and even encrypting your BlackBerry data.

in this chapter

☑ Securing your device with passwords

☑ Protecting your BlackBerry from Bluetooth devices

☑ Backing up and restoring your device and data

☑ Wiping and resetting your BlackBerry

☑ Extending your battery's life

☑ Securely storing your personal information

Setting Your Owner Information

One of the easiest and most overlooked options for protecting against the loss of your BlackBerry data is to use the Owner screen in the Options application to record your name, phone number, address, and other information that might help someone who finds your BlackBerry return it to you. Certainly this simple method will not prevent you from losing your BlackBerry either through carelessness or outright theft. But just like putting an address label on your luggage when you travel, it gives the person who finds your BlackBerry at least some way to contact you and ship your device back to you.

To set your owner information:

1. Run the Options application from the BlackBerry home screen.

2. In the Options screen, scroll down the list of alphabetical option categories until you see Owner. Select and open the Owner option with the trackwheel, and you are presented with the Owner screen, as shown in Figure 8-1.

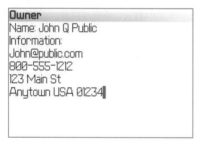

FIGURE 8-1: The Owner information screen

3. The Owner screen has only two fields: Name and Information. Enter your name in the Name field; in the Information field, enter as many clues as possible that could help someone who has found your BlackBerry contact you. Although you can't enter much text (the input field supports only 128 characters), at minimum it is a good idea to provide an e-mail address, a phone number, and a physical mailing address to which your device can be shipped.

Password-Protecting Your BlackBerry

BlackBerry devices have a built-in password protection facility that can be used to prevent unauthorized access to the applications and data stored on the handheld. By default, this password feature is disabled, but if you have any security concerns, you should indeed set a password. When a password is set, a screen saver displays on your handheld after a defined period of inactivity, as shown in Figure 8-2. In order to gain access to the handheld after the screen saver is displayed, you must enter the correct password.

FIGURE 8-2: The password challenge screen

To set a password on your BlackBerry:

1. Go to the Options application, and scroll down the alphabetical list of options until you find the Security category. Use the trackwheel to display the Security screen (shown in Figure 8-3).

Security	
Password:	Enabled
Security Timeout:	1 Min.
Lock Handheld Upon Holstering:	No
Content Protection:	Disabled
Content Compression:	Enabled
Allow Outgoing Call While Locked	No
Services:	
✱✱✱ no services ✱✱✱	

FIGURE 8-3: The security options screen

2. Position the trackwheel on the Password field and click to enable the Password feature; when you go to Save, you are prompted to enter your password.

Note Passwords are required to be between 4 and 14 characters in length, and the device is smart enough to reject passwords that are considered to be "weak," such as an obvious sequence like "abcd" or "0000." Any time you set your password, you are also required to re-enter and confirm your password a second time.

The Security Timeout field, also found on the Security Options screen, goes hand in hand with the password option, as it determines the amount of time your handheld is inactive before a password must be supplied to use the BlackBerry. By default, this is set to 2 minutes, but you can change it to be as short as 1 minute or as long as 1 hour. Set this to whatever time you are comfortable with. Don't set it so short that you are annoyed by having to constantly re-enter your own password, but don't set it to be so long that you run the risk of unauthorized access if you accidentally leave it behind on your airplane seat.

You can also set an option in the Security Options screen to automatically lock the device if you place your BlackBerry in its holster, requiring a password to use the device once it is removed again from the holster.

Now, remember the owner information you set in the previous section? As a bonus, on the screen where you unlock your BlackBerry with a password after a period of inactivity, your owner information is displayed in the background on the screen saver. This is a nice feature that helps anyone who finds your handheld know who the owner is without having to be knowledgeable enough about a BlackBerry to navigate to the Owner screen in the Options application.

As protection against someone trying to guess your password, if an incorrect password is entered ten times in a row, your BlackBerry will automatically perform a "hard reset," wiping the device clear of any user data. Of course, you usually don't want to lose any data, especially in the event of an unanticipated hard reset. That is why it is always best to regularly back up your information, which is discussed in the section "Backing Up and Restoring Your BlackBerry."

Note You can use this feature on purpose if you want to wipe your handheld data for some reason (such as if you are returning it to your employer or to the store where you purchased it).

Protecting Against Bluetooth Discovery

If your BlackBerry supports Bluetooth (as the 7290 does), it is theoretically possible (although perhaps unlikely) for other Bluetooth devices to connect to your BlackBerry. Once connected, that device can retrieve some of your stored information, including your contacts, e-mail messages, or calendar items.

If you are particularly paranoid — or even if you simply do not have any use for Bluetooth — you can easily turn off the Discoverable feature of your BlackBerry's Bluetooth radio:

1. Go to the Options application and scroll to the Bluetooth option.

2. Click the trackwheel to display the menu and choose the Options menu item. You will see two fields: a Device Name (used to identify your BlackBerry to other Bluetooth devices) and a Discoverable setting (when turned on, enables your BlackBerry to be discovered by other Bluetooth devices).

3. Turn off the Discoverable setting by selecting it and changing the option to No.

Backing Up and Restoring Your BlackBerry

As with any other type of computer that stores data — desktop, handheld, or otherwise — it is a very good idea to get in the habit of performing regular backups of your BlackBerry information. Yes, your e-mail, calendar, and contact information is probably synchronized with your desktop or enterprise server on a regular basis, but it can still be terribly inconvenient to lose data you've added since your last synchronization. As a simple example, if you travel for any extended period of time, it can be days or even weeks between synchronization sessions, and if you were to lose, drop, or damage your handheld at any point during that time, you would also potentially lose critically important data.

Aside from disaster protection, you should perform a safety backup of your BlackBerry prior to performing an installation of any BlackBerry system/firmware updates — just in case something goes wrong. It is also a good idea to do a backup before you install any additional application programs or software on your device.

Full Backups

BlackBerry devices do not support any kind of expansion memory card. To perform a full backup:

1. Connect your BlackBerry to your desktop PC using the supplied USB cable or cradle.

2. Run the BlackBerry Desktop Manager application on your PC, and double-click the Backup and Restore icon from the main screen. This brings up the Backup and Restore screen shown in Figure 8-4.

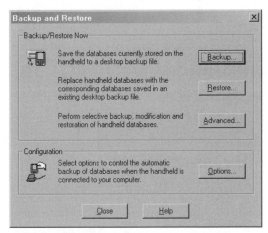

FIGURE 8-4: The Backup and Restore screen from Desktop Manager

3. From the Backup and Restore screen, click the Backup button, and choose a name and location for your backup file. Backup files use an .ipd extension, so a good convention might be to incorporate the backup date into the filename, such as 10-31-2005.ipd.

Caution Be sure to note the storage location of your backup file, as you will need to know it if you ever have to restore your BlackBerry!

The Desktop Manager now proceeds to back up all of the user data on your handheld.

Note   In case of a desktop computer crash, you should also have a good backup procedure for your desktop that incorporates backing up your .ipd BlackBerry backup files.

Selective Backups

Instead of backing up all of your handheld data, you can be more choosy about what gets backed up by using selective backup, which lets you choose exactly which application databases get backed up. So if, for example, you care only about backing up your Calendar data, you can speed up the backup by ignoring all of the other data on your handheld.

To perform a selective backup:

1. Connect your BlackBerry to your desktop PC using the supplied USB cable or cradle.

2. Run the BlackBerry Desktop Manager application on your PC, and double-click the Backup and Restore icon from the main screen. This brings up the Backup and Restore screen.

3. Click the Advanced button to see a list of available databases.

4. Check each database that you wish to back up.

5. Choose File Save As to begin the backup to a filename and location of your choosing.

Full Restores

To restore your BlackBerry data from a previous backup session:

1. Connect your BlackBerry to your desktop PC using the supplied USB cable or cradle.

2. Run Desktop Manager and double-click Backup and Restore. This brings up the Backup and Restore screen.

3. Click the Restore button.

4. Navigate to the location where your backup .ipd file is stored, select the file, and click Open.

5. At the prompt, click Yes to restore all of your original BlackBerry data from the specified backup file.

Selective Restores

As with the backup function, you can choose to perform a selective restore on one or more specific databases, rather than choosing to restore all of your BlackBerry data. This option is useful if one of your application databases has been damaged or deleted or if you are moving to a different BlackBerry handheld and you want to move only certain data over from your old handheld.

To perform a selective restore:

1. Connect your BlackBerry to your desktop PC using the supplied USB cable or cradle.

2. Run the BlackBerry Desktop Manager application on your PC, and double-click the Backup and Restore icon from the main screen. This brings up the Backup and Restore screen.

3. Click the Advanced button.

4. Choose the file to restore from by clicking File Open.

5. Navigate to the .ipd file you want to use and then click Open to select the databases you wish to restore from the Desktop File Databases section.

Note You can perform a selective restore from either a full backup or a selective backup.

Automatic Backups

Remembering to perform a regular backup can be a challenge. To ensure regular backups, you can configure the Desktop Manager to perform automatic backups of your BlackBerry according to a schedule. You can schedule a backup to occur as often as every day or, if you prefer, you can choose a longer interval.

To set up an automatic backup:

1. Connect your BlackBerry to your desktop PC using the supplied USB cable or cradle.

2. Run the BlackBerry Desktop Manager application on your PC, and double-click the Backup and Restore icon from the main screen. This brings up the Backup and Restore screen.

3. In the Configuration section at the bottom, click the Options button. This brings up the Backup and Restore Options screen, which includes the Automatic Backup setting, as shown in Figure 8-5.

4. Select the checkbox under Automatic Backup to enable the backup interval input field. You can directly enter the number of days, or you can use the up and down arrows to increase or decrease the number of days to use as the interval between backups. As part of the Automatic Backup options, you can also direct Desktop Manager to back up all of your handheld data from all applications, or you can choose to exclude selected types of data from the backup. You may choose to exclude e-mail messages from your backup, or you may choose to exclude the built-in BlackBerry Calendar, Address, Task, and Memo application databases (described on this screen as "PIM application data," where PIM stands for Personal Information Manager, a common term used to describe these four applications).

FIGURE 8-5: Configuring for an automatic backup

Automated backups will occur either on the days set by you in the Backup options or, if that day has passed, the first time you connect your handheld after the originally scheduled backup date.

Resetting Your BlackBerry

You most likely know that you can reboot your BlackBerry by opening up the back and removing the battery. But did you know that you can perform a soft reset of your BlackBerry device by pressing ALT+CAP+DEL? As with the battery removal option, this is a safe reset of your device — no data is lost.

But what if you are giving your BlackBerry to someone else to use? Or what if you are returning your BlackBerry for repair or a replacement? You probably don't want a perfect stranger to be able to read your e-mail and other personal information. In this case, you *want* the data to be lost.

To erase your BlackBerry so that it is clean of all data:

1. Open the Options application, scroll down to the Security option, and click the trackwheel. This takes you to the Security screen.

2. Click the trackwheel again, and you will see in the menu an option called Wipe Handheld.

Caution

Proceeding at this point will wipe your BlackBerry clean of all application data, including all your e-mails, contacts, calendar information, and other settings. So proceed only if you are absolutely sure that this is what you want to do!

3. Click Wipe Handheld, and then click Continue to erase your BlackBerry data.

You can take this one step further and completely restore your BlackBerry to its initial pristine state by not only removing any data, but also deleting any applications or settings that have been installed on your device. This is a very serious step and you should be aware that you will lose all data *and* applications if you proceed!

To completely wipe out your device, you must first assign a password to your device. Once you have a password:

1. Go to the Options application, and choose the Security option.

2. Enter the wrong password 10 consecutive times. Your device will completely reset, losing all applications and data.

Extending Your Battery Life

The biggest drain on BlackBerry battery life comes from wireless access and the screen display (especially the backlight). The screen generally turns off after inactivity, but persistent use of the backlight can adversely affect the battery.

If you know that your device is out of range, you can save battery life by turning off wireless access (go to the Applications screen and scroll to the Wireless On/Off icon) until you are back in a good coverage area.

With Bluetooth-enabled devices (such as the 7290), you can save power by turning off Bluetooth if you do not plan to use Bluetooth capabilities.

Securely Storing Your Personal Information

Your BlackBerry's built-in password system will help you feel comfortable about the safety of your e-mail and PIM data. But what about other personal data such as passwords, credit card numbers, bank accounts, and PINs? In today's world, there are so many of these bits of information to keep track of. Wouldn't it be great if there were a way to keep all this data on your BlackBerry so that you could access it whenever and wherever you needed it?

You could, of course, store some of this information in a memo or perhaps make use of the user-defined fields in your own Address Book entry fields. There are, however, several drawbacks to doing this. For one, your memos and addresses are synchronized with either your desktop or an enterprise server, and you may not want those extra copies of your personal data being transferred to other computers. Another drawback is that this kind of information is even more personal and sensitive than your e-mail and PIM information, so you may not feel totally comfortable with using just the standard BlackBerry password security for protection.

Password Keeper

If you own a BlackBerry device running the newer BlackBerry OS 4.0 or later, you can find a built-in program called Password Keeper in the Applications folder that offers a simple utility for storing and tracking passwords and other data of a personal nature. Password Keeper, pictured in Figure 8-6, is not terribly full-featured, but it does support the basic ability to store generic password information.

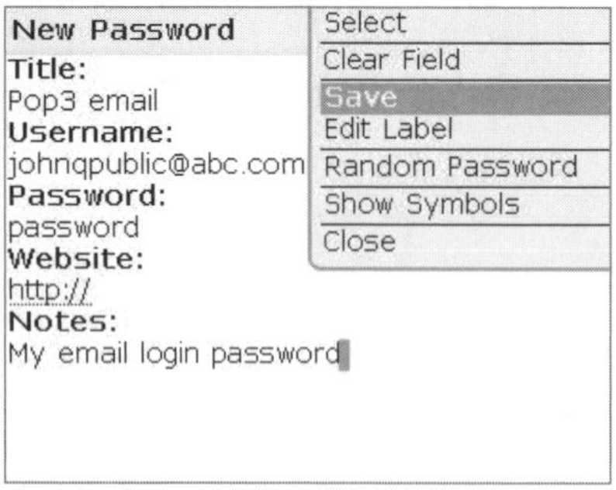

```
New Password        Select
Title:              Clear Field
Pop3 email          Save
Username:           Edit Label
johnqpublic@abc.com Random Password
Password:           Show Symbols
password            Close
Website:
http://
Notes:
My email login password
```

FIGURE 8-6: Adding a POP3 e-mail
password entry in Password Keeper

With Password Keeper, you create one entry for each password you want to track. For each password, you can store a title, a username/login (if applicable), your password, a website (if applicable), and additional notes about the password. Figure 8-6 shows a Password Keeper entry for a fictional POP3 e-mail account, but Password Keeper can just as easily store passwords for web sites, online shopping carts, bank PIN numbers, and more.

Access to the information you store in Password Keeper is itself protected by a password that you create the very first time you use the program. Thereafter, anytime you access Password Keeper, you are prompted to enter this password.

You may find Password Keeper to be insufficient for your needs. One obvious drawback I found was that every type of password you store uses the same cookie-cutter set of five fields, regardless of whether the fields make sense for the password you are entering. For example, the website and username fields offer little value when entering a simple PIN code for a bank account. It would be great if Password Keeper offered form templates customized for different kinds of personal data such as PINs, e-mail accounts, frequent flyer programs, and more.

If you are looking for more in a password-tracking program, you should read on to the next section, which presents a number of third-party add-on programs.

Third-Party Password Programs

If you have an older BlackBerry device (running versions older than OS 4.0), a number of available third-party software applications offer the ability to safely and securely store personal data such as passwords. This section provides a capsule overview of a few of these programs.

Note Even if you have a newer BlackBerry with Password Keeper, you may wish to investigate these alternative programs for their more extensive feature sets or friendlier user interfaces.

All three programs reviewed in the following sections test out well and serve as fine solutions for safely storing your personal information. All of them provide good password protection, data encryption, and a system for storing items of different types. Which one you choose to use depends on your experience and your preference for entering free-form versus structured personal data.

Note All of these programs are available for you to check out yourself at either www.blackberry.com or www.handango.com.

CryptMagic

CryptMagic by www.software-for-blackberry.com (see Figure 8-7) uses a category system to allow you to file your bits of personal information in Business, Private, or Unfiled categories. It also has a number of predefined templates, which are specially created to support data entry forms and fields for recording and storing bank, credit card, e-mail account, insurance, inventory, membership, software, and web login information.

FIGURE 8-7: The CryptMagic main screen

Getting started with CryptMagic is easy. A free trial download is available on the Web that lets you play with the program before you decide whether to buy it. Installation is pretty simple and straightforward. (See Chapter 2 for more information on how to add downloaded third-party software applications to your BlackBerry.)

Once you have downloaded and installed CryptMagic, you can launch it just as you would any of the built-in BlackBerry application icons on the home screen. You will be prompted to create a password specifically to protect the information stored inside of CryptMagic. (Don't get confused — this password is separate and distinct from the password you use to protect your BlackBerry.) Enter a password of your own choosing, and you are presented with the CryptMagic main screen.

By default, CryptMagic displays only the Unfiled category, although in practice you can also make use of Business and Personal categories. These categories are automatically displayed as you start adding new entries to either category. To start entering your own personal information:

1. Use the trackwheel to pop up the CryptMagic menu, and select the New menu option.

2. On the New Entry form, select a category (Business, Personal, or Unfiled) and a template that represents the kind of data you are about to record (bank, e-mail, and so on).

3. Once you have done this, the form fields will change to match the template you've selected, and you can start entering your data.

As you create more entries in CryptMagic, the main screen will start filling up with your items, automatically organized by category and template. You can even choose from a host of different icons to help visually distinguish your entries from one another at a glance.

| Tip | For more information on CryptMagic, visit the Handango Store for BlackBerry at www.blackberry.com. |

MySafe+ by Sprite Interactive Limited

Another alternative for tracking your personal information is an application called MySafe+ by Sprite Interactive Limited (see Figure 8-8). MySafe+ offers encrypted storage of account information, e-mail accounts, passwords, and the like.

FIGURE 8-8: The Main Menu in MySafe+

The user interface for MySafe+ is a bit different than CryptMagic and DataVault (see the following section) in that you create a new item with a name, and then it is up to you to associate as many fields as you wish with that new item. This turns out to be not quite as elegant as having predefined entry types such as "Bank Account" that automatically include all the necessary fields, but the MySafe+ approach could potentially be more flexible in that you can elect to store as little as one field of information or as many fields as you like.

At the time of this writing, MySafe is available at the Handango store at www.handango.com for $27.

DataVault by Ascendo

The third and last program I recommend for tracking your personal information is an application program called DataVault by Ascendo, Inc. DataVault, like MySafe+ and CryptMagic, is available as a free trial download from the Handango Store for BlackBerry at www.blackberry.com.

DataVault (see Figure 8-9) is an interesting middle ground between MySafe+ and CryptMagic. It offers both the flexibility of being able to enter unstructured items of personal data and a well-thought-out list of predefined item types. This list is richer than the items were in CryptMagic and includes types such as insurance, driver's license, frequent flyer, prescription information, and other important (but hard to remember) personal information categories.

FIGURE 8-9: The Item Type selection screen in DataVault

Summary

This chapter delved deeply into the issue of security and safety for the data stored on your BlackBerry device. As you've seen, data security is not achieved by implementing any single method. Rather, you need to incorporate a variety of techniques, including properly identifying your device in case of loss, enabling password security, implementing a regular schedule of backups to your desktop, and potentially investing in a solid third-party personal data storage solution.

As anyone who has ever lost his or her data on a desktop, laptop, or handheld can attest, losing your work is no fun. When it comes to losing personal or other sensitive information, it can be not only annoying, but also downright scary — and even damaging to your business or personal life. I hope that while it is fresh in your mind, you will now take the most important actions of all, which are to evaluate your own exposure to loss of data and use the information provided in this chapter to implement the security measures that make sense for you and your BlackBerry.

Getting Down to Business: Productivity Tools

The BlackBerry first came to the attention of the general public when it began to be seen in the hands of financial analysts, stock traders, brokers, and portfolio managers. These people were the perfect "early adopters" for the BlackBerry, given their fast-paced working environment and their need to be in constant communication with colleagues and customers worldwide.

Today, years after the device first gained recognition, it is of course common to see everyone from Hollywood celebrities to teenagers working their thumbs on their BlackBerrys. Even so, the product has become even more entrenched as a serious business tool and is now seen as standard equipment for just about anyone working in business.

Obviously, the biggest draw of the BlackBerry is its wireless messaging capability, but through the addition of some excellent add-on software, your BlackBerry can help you be more productive in other areas of your working life. In this chapter. I show you ways to enhance your BlackBerry to be able to work with office documents, track your hours and expenses, and make your business travel more productive and pleasant.

Helpful Utilities for the Frequent Traveler

BlackBerry is a great device for people who are on-the-go, and the opportunities for enhancing your BlackBerry with features that make traveling easier and more productive are practically limitless. With the right add-on software, you can access maps, driving directions, flight schedules, traffic alerts, and even the location of the nearest Starbucks! This section presents a sampling of software programs that provide essential services for the frequent traveler.

Google Local for Mobile

If you have ever tried using Google Maps at `maps.google.com`, you know that this web service offers a fantastic combination of street maps, satellite maps, driving directions, and a business finder, all wrapped up in an easy-to-use web page. The folks at Google have now created a special BlackBerry version of this wonderful functionality, and named it "Google Local for Mobile." Remarkably, Google has not only enabled the BlackBerry version with the same great features as those found on `maps.google.com`, but it has also thought through how to adapt the user interface so that it is quite usable on a small screen with a BlackBerry keypad.

In contrast to `maps.google.com`, Google Local for Mobile runs not as a web page, but as a downloadable standalone software application that installs on your BlackBerry. You can download the Google Local for Mobile by entering `www.google.com/glm` in your BlackBerry web browser. After confirming your device type, Google Local for Mobile downloads directly to your BlackBerry. Once downloaded, Google appears as an application icon on your BlackBerry home screen.

The main screen for Google is a Map view, which starts out as a map of the United States by default. To change the map view to show a specific location, click the trackwheel menu, choose "Search," and enter the desired location. Figure 9-1 shows a street map view of Manhattan after I entered "New York, NY."

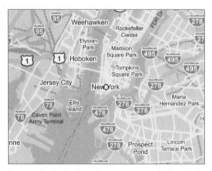

FIGURE 9-1: A street map view of Manhattan

After the map renders on the BlackBerry screen, you can pan up, down, left, or right by using the trackwheel. You can also zoom in a level at a time by pressing the I key (the minus key), and you can zoom out by pressing the O key (the plus key).

If you prefer a satellite map view, you can click the trackwheel and choose Satellite View instead of Map View. This will present you with a satellite image of your selected location, as shown in Figure 9-2.

As with Google Maps, Google Local for Mobile will let you zoom down to a remarkable level of detail. For example, after zooming in several times on the Manhattan map, it is quite easy to see close-up snapshots of familiar New York City landmarks such as Central Park and the Statue of Liberty, all shown in great detail.

FIGURE 9-2: A satellite map view of Manhattan

In terms of business productivity, the greatest benefits of using Google Local for Mobile lie in its wonderful ability to provide you with a method to quickly search for local businesses, as well as driving directions from point A to point B.

To locate a business, click the trackwheel and choose the Search menu. Instead of a location, enter a business name or even a type of business that you are looking for. As an example, Figure 9-3 shows the results of my search for "pizza in downtown Chicago."

FIGURE 9-3: My search for Chicago deep dish pizza shows promise.

As you can see, Google Local for Mobile plots the location of the nearest nine matching results for my pizza search. Now some of the thoughtfulness of the BlackBerry application's design comes into play. Because you don't have the luxury of using a mouse to point at the matching location you want to go to, Google assigns the numbers 1 through 9 to the first nine matching results. By simply pressing the BlackBerry keypad number corresponding to the matching result you want, you can view details for that location.

Even better is Google's mobile support for getting driving directions to a location. You can either enter in your own starting and ending locations or use a search result (such as the preceding pizza search) as either the start or end point for your directions. Google then creates a route for you, complete with turn-by-turn directions, as shown in Figure 9-4.

FIGURE 9-4: Turn-by-turn directions to get me to my favorite pizza place.

Note at the bottom of the screen how I can use the number keys on my BlackBerry to move forward or backward through the individual segments of my route. As I move forward, the map changes to illustrate the route segment I am on, and moves me forward toward my destination (which is, of course, a nice slice of deep dish pizza!).

I cannot recommend Google Local for Mobile highly enough. It is an extremely useful application to have on your BlackBerry, and it's free!

Traffic Edge

A company called MAQ Software has produced a very unique software program called Traffic Edge, which will be of interest to anyone who commutes to a job. Traffic Edge offers real-time camera images and traffic maps for a sizeable number of cities and locations in the United States and even worldwide.

When you install and run Traffic Edge on your BlackBerry, you are asked to choose a city or region, after which you can choose from among a number of traffic locations available within that area. You are then given a list of specific roads where either a traffic map or camera image is available. Choose a road or map, and after a brief pause, you are rewarded with a real-time picture of the traffic situation at that location! Figure 9-5 shows an example camera image from Traffic Edge.

FIGURE 9-5: Traffic seems to be running smoothly at this location.

While I suppose a still camera image is open to interpretation as an accurate measurement of how good or bad traffic is on a road, it is still quite remarkable to be able to gather this information wirelessly anytime, anywhere, and it can truly save you time and aggravation if it helps you avoid a traffic jam even once or twice.

At the time of this writing, Traffic Edge is available for a one-time cost of $9.99, which is a pretty amazing value. For more information you can visit MAQ Software's website at www.edgeq.com.

WorldMate

WorldMate, by MobiMate, is a very popular application, having carved out a niche by offering a unified collection of handy information and utilities, which together meet the needs of the busy business traveler.

WorldMate is sold as a subscription product and installs as a standard BlackBerry application icon on your home screen. When launched, WorldMate's elegant and polished user interface (shown in Figure 9-6) presents a set of vertical tabs for world clock, flight schedules, maps, weather, currency conversion, and travel information.

FIGURE 9-6: WorldMate's World Clock tab provides current time for up to five different world locations.

You can navigate among the different tabbed views by using the trackwheel (pressing the ALT key while scrolling makes the selection easier). Each tab has its own unique configuration options. World Clock lets you configure which cities to display, Flight Schedules lets you select your departure and arrival airport, and so on. All of the tab views are very professionally presented and formatted, and the configuration process for each is very easy and intuitive to follow. For example, I was able to quickly and easily bring up a weekly schedule of flights from Newark's Liberty Airport to Los Angeles (shown in Figure 9-7) almost effortlessly.

Depending on your own personal preferences, each WorldMate tab may offer more or less value to you as a user. While I will admit that none of the individual tabs represents an earth-shakingly powerful function, when they are all put together in as eye-catching a package as the folks at MobiMate have managed to create, it becomes quite an attractive package.

Car.	From	To	Dep.	Arr.	Dur.
UA	EWR	LAX	6:40	9:55	6:15
US	EWR	LAX	6:40	9:55	6:15
OZ	EWR	LAX	6:40	9:55	6:15
CO	EWR	LAX	7:00	10:07	6:07
AA	EWR	LAX	8:05	11:15	6:10
QF	EWR	LAX	8:05	11:15	6:10
AS	EWR	LAX	8:05	11:15	6:10
CO	EWR	LAX	8:50	11:57	6:07
CO	EWR	LAX	13:25	16:19	5:54
CO	EWR	LAX	15:30	18:39	6:09

EWR – LAX 7/03/2006
Last update: 8/03/2006

FIGURE 9-7: The WorldMate Flight Schedule display

Check out MobiMate's home page, www.mobimate.com, for more information on WorldMate and other mobile software applications, as well as a free trial download. WorldMate Standard Edition is priced at $34.95 for a one year subscription, while the Professional Edition adds wireless access to flight schedules and goes for $49.95.

Caffeine Finder

I've heard it said that sleep is just a symptom of caffeine deprivation. Indeed, for some people, quickly locating a place to get a caffeine fix is a quest of the highest importance. While researching this book, I had the good fortune to come upon a great little BlackBerry software application called Caffeine Finder, written by a company called Greystripe. Now, you might wonder why I've included a program whose sole purpose is to locate coffee shops in a chapter about business productivity, but I can personally vouch for how being in a highly caffeinated state many late evenings made it possible to write this book!

Caffeine Finder downloads onto your BlackBerry and, once installed, will let you locate the nearest coffee shop based on an address, a city and state, or even a location from your contact list. The main screen for Caffeine Finder is shown in Figure 9-8.

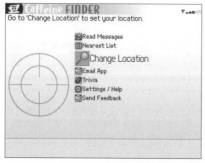

FIGURE 9-8: The Caffeine Finder main screen

Once you have selected your location, Caffeine Finder displays for you the name of the nearest coffee shop and a map showing the locations of the nearest shops. Caffeine Finder also gives you access to a list of the coffee shops nearest your chosen location. From this list, you can select a shop and view the basic address and phone number (see Figure 9-9).

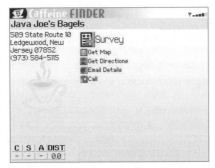

FIGURE 9-9: Caffeine Finder finds the nearest coffee shop.

Caffeine Finder will even give you directions to the selected coffee shop, using your location as a starting point, complete with a street map showing you where your cup of coffee is awaiting your arrival, as shown in Figure 9-10.

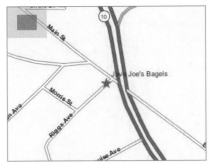

FIGURE 9-10: A map shows me the fastest way to my coffee!

Caffeine Finder has other nice features, including the ability to automatically dial the shop from your BlackBerry phone, a small "coffee trivia" section, and the ability to fine-tune settings such as the maximum radius to search in. The program is not infallible — it did not list one or two coffee shops in my area that I know of. But it did find most of them, and I suspect it is only as good as the source from which it is obtaining its coffee shop listings.

All in all, I found Caffeine Finder to be a very nice program. Given how useful it is as well as the obvious effort Greystripe put into making the program work so well, I simply could not believe that it is available for free. I recommend you get it while it's still free, at www.greystripe.com.

Beiks Dictionaries and Phrasebooks for BlackBerry

The Beiks dictionary series has long provided language translation dictionaries for handheld users, and now there are BlackBerry editions of its popular dictionaries. Available in many different languages, the Beiks dictionaries offer word translation between English and non-English languages (or vice versa) on mobile devices.

To use the Beiks dictionary, simply download and install the version you wish to use (for example, English-German) to your BlackBerry. Once on your device, just launch the dictionary, and enter a word that you wish to translate, as shown in Figure 9-11.

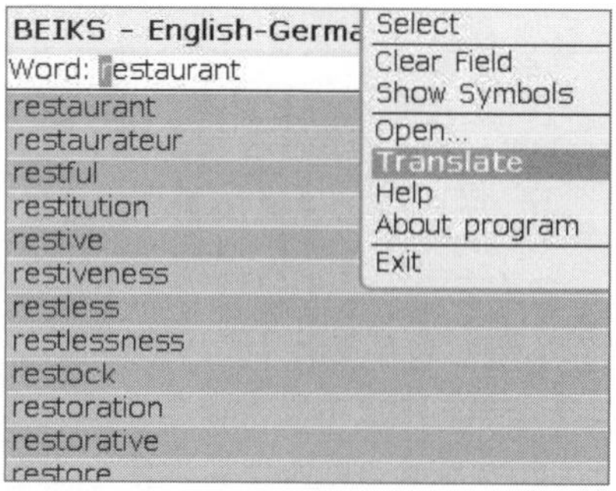

FIGURE 9-11: Beiks English-to-German
dictionary in action

In addition to dictionaries, Beiks also offers a series of phrasebooks that offer translation of common phrases from one language into another. For devices capable of audio output (see the Beiks website for compatibility information) the application will even play an audio clip demonstrating how to pronounce the phrase in your target language. The Beiks English-German phrasebook is pictured in Figure 9-12.

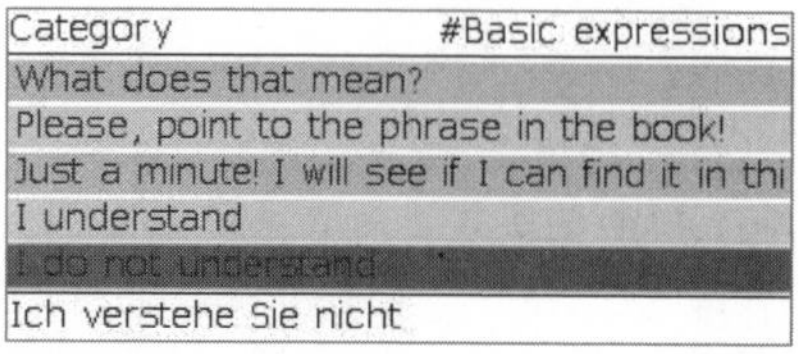

FIGURE 9-12: The Beiks English-to-German
phrasebook

The Beiks dictionaries and phrasebooks are available at www.handango.com or www.beiks.com.

Working with Office Documents and Databases

Besides e-mail, Office files such as those in Word, Excel, and Access are arguably the most important kind of data people work with at their jobs. Just think of all of the documents created, edited, viewed, or shared in a single working day! While BlackBerry has not yet embraced the idea of having a built-in office software suite, business users who need to work with document attachments and databases can choose from a number of excellent programs that can help fill this gap.

E-mail Attachments

Chapter 3 presented several third-party software applications that offer more advanced attachment handling than that offered by the built-in BlackBerry Attachment service. Repligo and DocHawk both offer better attachment handling and viewing, while eOffice by DynoPlex takes a more comprehensive approach and goes beyond viewing, offering local document editing on your BlackBerry device itself. See Chapter 3 for more information on these applications.

BlackBerry Database Viewer Plus

Cellica Software Services is the developer of a product called BlackBerry Database Viewer Plus. What this product does is unique in that it allows you to download and view databases from Microsoft Access, Oracle, dBase, Excel, and other formats to your BlackBerry. The program comes with both desktop and handheld components, and these components coordinate transfers of your database files over your USB cable connection.

I was able to take a simple Excel spreadsheet and transfer it successfully from my desktop to my BlackBerry, as shown in Figure 9-13.

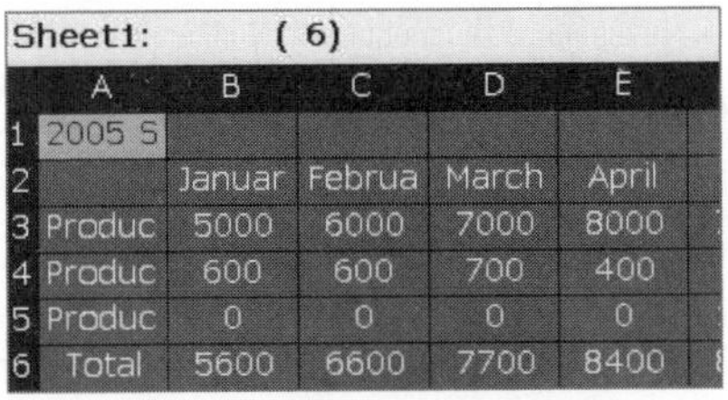

FIGURE 9-13: A sample spreadsheet
displayed in Database Viewer Plus

The program's main strength is in the file formats it supports. No other BlackBerry program I've seen can handle the database formats that Cellica does. However, the device-side viewer component itself is somewhat limited in functionality and offers only basic viewing of row-column tabular data. You can edit fields and have those changes sent back to the desktop, but the changes are not reflected back in the device file in terms of formula calculations.

For more information on Database Viewer Plus and other applications from Cellica, visit their website at www.cellica.com.

Keeping Track of Yourself

A good part of our lives is spent keeping track of things. We keep track of our expenditures, we log the hours we spend at work, and we chart our progress in so many areas of our work and personal lives. Although in some cases we do all this tracking out of idle interest, in some kinds of businesses (such as a law firm), keeping track of hours worked on a project or case is simply a requirement of the job.

If you are like most BlackBerry owners, you probably don't go anywhere without your handy little communicator. The fact that BlackBerry is constantly with you means that, effectively, you have a computer that can potentially be a great "electronic tracker" to help you record all of those bits of information.

This section explores a sampling of BlackBerry programs that help you track a variety of things, including mileage driven, business expenses, and billable time.

Tracking Your Mileage with My Mileage Tracker

Many people who use their personal vehicle for business purposes often need to track their trips, when they traveled, and how many miles they drove, so that they can either be reimbursed by their employers or document their use for accounting purposes. Others need to document and track their driven mileage for other reasons. Regardless of the reason, mileage tracking is another area where the BlackBerry can shine, with the addition of some clever add-on software.

My Mileage Tracker, by Sprite Interactive Ltd., is an excellent program for documenting your miles traveled. The program installs on your BlackBerry as a standard application icon and when launched presents an easy-to-navigate main window, shown in Figure 9-14.

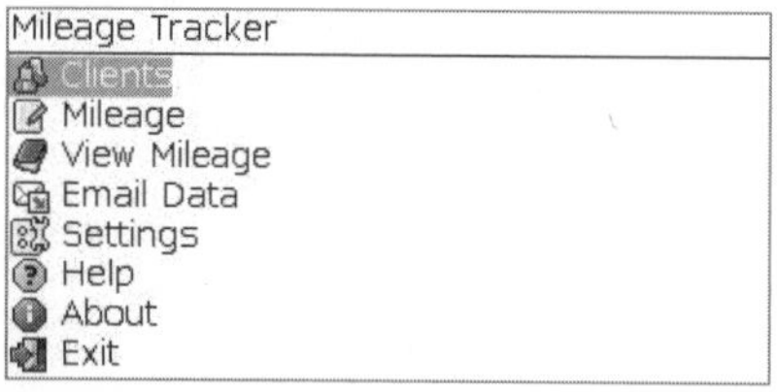

```
Mileage Tracker
 Clients
 Mileage
 View Mileage
 Email Data
 Settings
 Help
 About
 Exit
```

FIGURE 9-14: The main screen in My Mileage Tracker

My Mileage Tracker's main screen lets you enter your mileage traveled, view reports, and even send reports to your desktop via e-mail. In My Mileage Tracker, your mileage data is organized by which business client you are traveling for. Accordingly, the first thing you need to do is to create at least one client, using the Clients item on the main screen.

Once you've created a client, you can start entering mileage records, representing the miles traveled for that client. This is done by selecting the Mileage item on the main screen with the trackwheel. You are then prompted to select your client, which then brings up a form in which you can enter your mileage information, as shown in Figure 9-15.

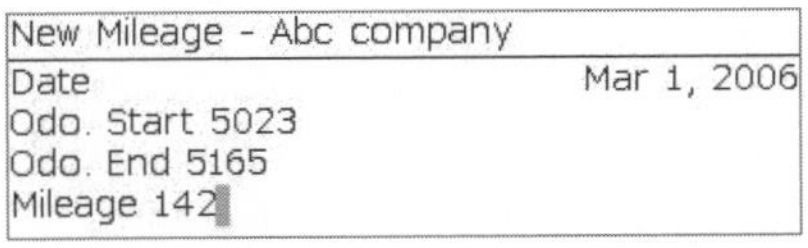

```
New Mileage - Abc company
Date                          Mar 1, 2006
Odo. Start 5023
Odo. End 5165
Mileage 142
```

FIGURE 9-15: Entering a new mileage record for "Abc company"

Each mileage record has a date and a starting and ending odometer reading. My Mileage Tracker automatically calculates the miles traveled for you based on this information. When you save your record, My Mileage Tracker will store your mileage in a database of mileage records associated with the specified business client.

Tracking your mileage with no way to report it to anyone would be rather pointless, so My Mileage Tracker enables you to choose from a number of different pre-defined reports you can run on your mileage records, as shown in Figure 9-16.

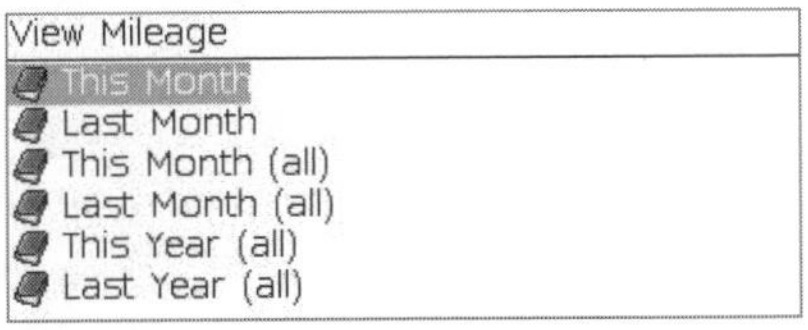

```
View Mileage
  This Month
  Last Month
  This Month (all)
  Last Month (all)
  This Year (all)
  Last Year (all)
```

FIGURE 9-16: Reporting Options for My Mileage Tracker

Once you've selected a type of report, My Mileage Tracker prompts you to select a client, and then produces a viewable report on your BlackBerry, listing the mileage records and totals that match your reporting criteria, as shown in Figure 9-17.

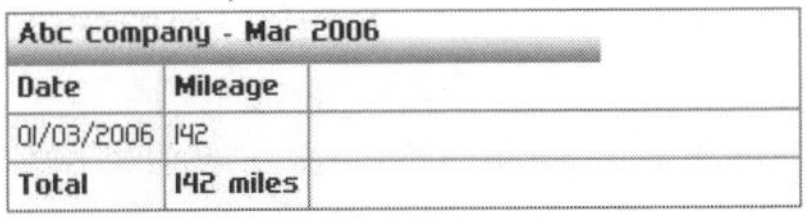

Abc company - Mar 2006		
Date	Mileage	
01/03/2006	142	
Total	142 miles	

FIGURE 9-17: A mileage report

Among other features, My Mileage Tracker offers a simple method of e-mailing your mileage records to yourself (or to another e-mail address) as an attachment, at which point you can print a report or integrate it into your own desktop-based reports. The program also offers some custom settings, such as using miles or kilometers.

My Mileage Tracker is available for a free trial download from www.handango.com or from Sprite at www.sprite.net, along with a number of other business applications. The program costs $30 to purchase.

Expenses

Writing up expense reports is a necessary evil for thousands of sales professionals who must report on how much they spend, on what, and when. Tracking expenses can be fairly painless if good records are recorded at the time of the expense and kept on file. Then it becomes a simple matter of gathering them up periodically for a report. Unfortunately, keeping good records requires discipline, and people do not always stay in the habit of recording expenses at the time they are incurred, which means coming up with an accurate expense report is going to require a lot more time and effort.

As with other "tracking" functions, expense tracking is a natural fit for the BlackBerry because your device is always with you, giving you the ability to quickly and accurately record expenses right on the spot. Given how widespread the need for expense tracking is, many applications have been developed for the purpose. Now take a close look at one of them, trackIT: Expense Edition, by Javatek Media.

trackIT: Expense Edition installs as a standard BlackBerry application icon on your home screen. Running the application on your device produces a somewhat out of the ordinary main screen that uses a graphical workstation as the main menu for the program's features, shown in Figure 9-18. (Presumably the program's designers felt this was clever, although I imagine some users would prefer a more straightforward list of functions.)

FIGURE 9-18: The trackIT main screen

Rolling the trackwheel over the various parts of the main screen image reveals the various program functions: Expenses, Accounts, Merchants, Categories, and more.

I liked the fact that trackIT let me get right to the task of entering my expenses without requiring a lot of up front configuration of accounts and categories. Choosing Expenses from the main screen lets you create a new expense right away, which I did, as you can see in Figure 9-19.

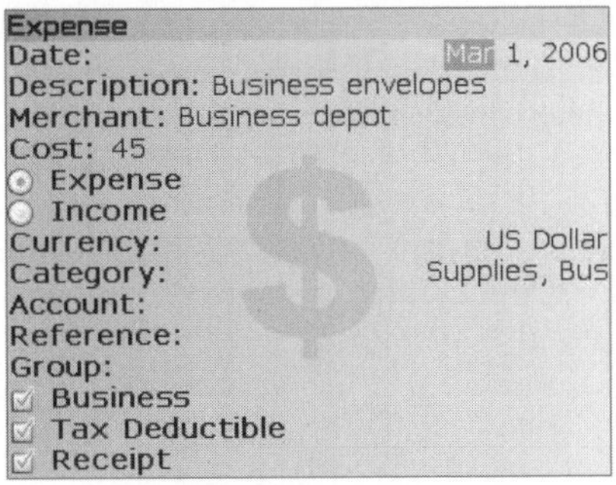

FIGURE 9-19: Entering a new expense

As you enter more expenses, trackIT builds up your list of expenses for the month and lets you view them in the main Expenses screen (shown in Figure 9-20). This screen enables you to navigate to other months, duplicate or edit your expense items, and filter or sort your expenses by type or category.

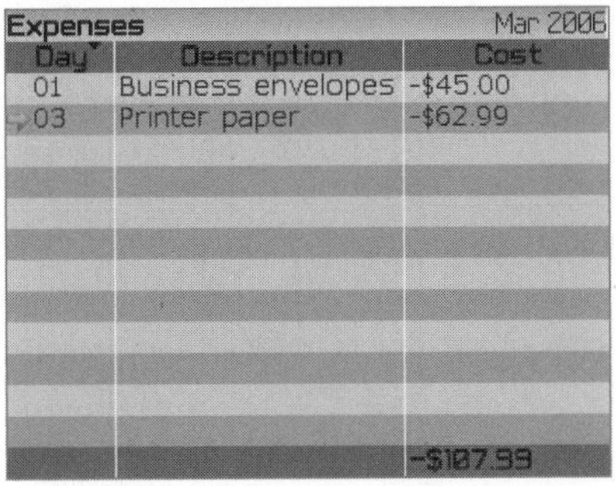

FIGURE 9-20: The monthly expense list screen

Additional features are available from this screen, including nice looking graphs showing daily expense levels.

When it comes time to creating your monthly expense reports, trackIT offers a rich set of exporting options. In addition to the commonly offered e-mail export option, the program is one of the few I have seen that offers its own desktop component, allowing you to use your BlackBerry USB cable to transfer your expense report from your BlackBerry directly to your PC. Many other export options are available, including formats such as CSV, HTML, and even Quicken and QuickBooks.

trackIT: Expense Edition is a very attractive and useful program and is available for a free trial download from www.handango.com as well as from Javatek's website www.javatekmedia.com. trackIT: Expense Edition costs $24.95, quite a value considering the wealth of features and polish that come with the program.

Note Given how widespread the need for expense tracking is, many applications have been developed for the purpose, including Expense Report Wizard, Expense Tracker, and ExpenseLog Pro, all of which can easily be found in the Handango store at www.handango.com by searching on the keyword "expense."

Tracking Your Time with BizTrackIt

For many professionals, from attorneys to contractors, time tracking is an essential part of their daily workday. Anybody who bills her time by the hour or the day or who is responsible for documenting the time that she spends on a particular task falls into this category. Any number of time and billing solutions are out there for desktop computer users. Not surprisingly, I was able to locate a few programs that had been written specifically for use on BlackBerry devices. For a mobile professional, the advantage of being able to use a time tracking tool on a BlackBerry is obvious — you can record your time and billing information on-the-spot, wherever and whenever you may need to, rather than waiting until you return to your desk.

BizTrackIt, by a company called Shrunken Head Software, is a project-oriented time-tracking tool that makes it easy to record and track the time you spend on any number of tasks or projects.

BizTrackIt installs as a BlackBerry software application as an icon on your home screen. When you launch BizTrackIt, the first thing you need to do is create a project, which will serve to organize your time and billing. Figure 9-21 shows the New Project screen, filled out with an example project I created.

```
New Project
Name: hacking blackberry
Billing Code: 0123
Description: Book
Client Name: wiley publishing
Client Billing Code: 9999
Round Up Interval:                    None
```

FIGURE 9-21: Creating a project in BizTrackIt

After saving a project description, all you need to do is select the In button to start the clock for a task you are going to work on for that project. While you work, the timer continues tracking your time, as shown in Figure 9-22.

When you are done with your work, click the Out button to stop the clock, at which point you are prompted to provide a description and add notes, which will be recorded in your time record. Once saved, your time record is stored in a database along with your other time and billing information for this and any other projects you create in BizTrackIt.

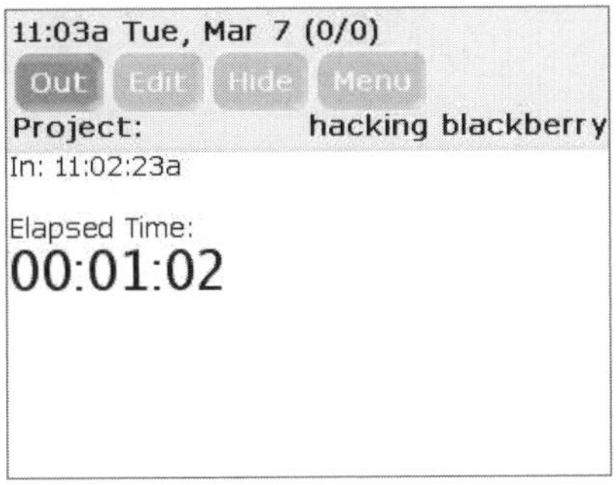

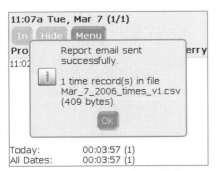

FIGURE 9-22: The BizTrackIt clock display

Getting information off of your BlackBerry and onto your desktop is a challenge that many BlackBerry users face, and BizTrackIt takes the common approach of allowing you to send your records wirelessly to an e-mail address, where you can then save them or import them into another time tracking tool. BizTrackIt gives you a flexible report creation screen that allows you to specify which projects to include and which date ranges to draw records from. Your time records are then e-mailed to the address you provide. Figure 9-23 shows BizTrackIt e-mailing a report.

FIGURE 9-23: Sending a time and billing report from the BlackBerry to an e-mail address.

More information on BizTrackIt is available at www.shrunkenhead.biz, including a free trial download that will provide you with up to five free uses of the software. The software is available for purchase at a one-time cost of $34.99.

Summary

The vast majority of BlackBerry users in the business arena have no idea that their device can do anything beyond handle e-mail and phone calls. Proving that add-on software is not just about fun and games, this chapter presents BlackBerry applications that can seriously raise your level of productivity. The next time you are lost in an unfamiliar city, Google Local for Mobile can show you the way. Stuck in traffic in Silicon Valley? Check your BlackBerry to see where the tie-ups are. Need to document the hours and miles you've spent on a project? Track it all on your BlackBerry.

The applications presented here are just a sample of what is available. Check out www.handango.com and the BlackBerry Software store to learn about more software applications for your device.

Beyond BrickBreaker: Fun, Games, and Entertainment

While BlackBerry has a solid reputation as being a serious business tool, even the busiest executive needs some downtime sooner or later. Whether they confess to it or not, almost everyone who has a BlackBerry has given the built-in BrickBreaker game at least one try. But BrickBreaker is not the final word on fun and games for your BlackBerry. A number of third-party add-on applications have now been developed and are available for download and purchase. These titles range from card games such as Texas Hold 'em to puzzle games, golf scorecards, and even health and fitness programs.

In this chapter, you take a look at a number of representative software programs from different categories. Their subject matter may not be terribly serious, but there is no doubt that some high quality programs are out there if you are willing to take a break from time to time.

Card Games

Poker games such as Texas Hold 'em have achieved unprecedented popularity these days, thanks in part to popular TV shows covering the World Poker Tour and celebrity tournaments. If you have played it, you know that the game itself is remarkably simple. It is played like regular poker but with community cards that are revealed in stages. The real excitement in Hold 'em is the betting. Few moments are as dramatic to watch as when a player pushes his chips to the center of the table and calls "all in."

In addition to poker games, card games in the Solitaire family have been popular for ages and have been the basis for many computer-based versions on desktops and mobile handsets alike.

This section reviews a couple of available card game software titles that are available for BlackBerry devices.

Aces Texas Hold 'em No Limit

Aces Texas Hold 'em No Limit, a BlackBerry software program created by a company called Concrete Software (www.concretesoftware.com), is a remarkably addictive version of the popular Hold 'em poker game adapted specifically for BlackBerry devices.

Aces Texas Hold 'em starts with a main screen as shown in Figure 10-1, letting you either begin a new game right away or change game play settings.

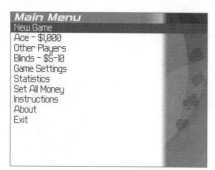

FIGURE 10-1: The Aces Texas Hold 'em main screen

When you begin a new game, you are dealt into a new Hold 'em game with five other computer-based players. These players quickly each take their turn and either fold or place bets until your turn comes up, as shown in Figure 10-2.

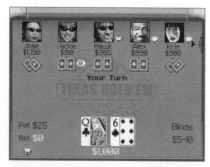

FIGURE 10-2: Okay, it's my turn. What to do?

In the example game shown, I decide to stay in the game and use the trackwheel menu to call the bet. Subsequently, the "flop" happens and three community cards are turned over in the center of the table, as shown in Figure 10-3.

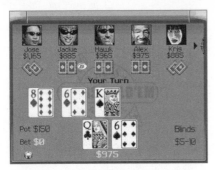

FIGURE 10-3: A pair of sixes is flopped — not as good as I had hoped.

Although I had been hoping to see some cards that matched up with my queen, I decide to stay in a bit longer. Two more cards are turned in the center, one at a time, and as you can see in Figure 10-4, I wind up with a fairly ho-hum hand (two pairs, 8's and 6's), and only two of the other players have folded (Jose and Kris).

FIGURE 10-4: Two pair. This can't be good enough to win, can it?

Still, it's just play money, so I decide to stick around and see what happens. I "check" and the others do as well, so the hands are revealed, as shown in Figure 10-5. Amazingly enough, I almost have the winning hand with two pairs. I am just barely edged out by Jackie, who has 9's and 8's, which beats my 8's and 6's by a hair!

Game over. Time to deal a new hand!

Aces Texas Hold 'em, just like the real thing, is an addictive game that keeps you coming back for more. Concrete Software's game is a great way to brush up on your Hold 'em skills and gain some experience without losing your shirt. If you like the game, there are an amazing number of books and videos that teach you to "know when to hold 'em and know when to fold 'em" so you can bluff and outwit your opponents.

FIGURE 10-5: Beaten, but just barely!

Aces Texas Hold 'em No Limit is available for purchase online at Concrete Software's website (www.concretesoftware.com), as well as from www.handango.com and the www.blackberry.com software store for $14.99. A free trial evaluation is also available.

Sol Mania

Another classic card game that has been adapted for BlackBerry handhelds is Solitaire. What most people think of when they hear Solitaire is the familiar game played with seven piles across, four "home" stacks that start with an ace, and a draw pile. This game is technically called Klondike and is, in reality, just one of many different one-player card games that are part of the Solitaire family of games.

One of the best examples illustrating the sheer variety of Solitaire games that have been invented is the BlackBerry program SolMania, developed by Gera. SolMania installs as a standard BlackBerry program icon on your device and gives you 24 Solitaire variations you can play, from the classic Klondike to other popular games such as Free Cell, Spider, Canfield, and Pyramid.

When you run SolMania, the main screen gives you access to each game variation via the trackwheel menu, as shown in Figure 10-6. You can scroll up or down through the list to access any of the 24 available games, or you can change game settings or access help.

FIGURE 10-6: The list of Solitaire games in SolMania

After choosing a game (I am choosing the classic Klondike as an example), SolMania sets up your game by dealing and displaying cards in an easy-to-read graphical screen, as shown in Figure 10-7.

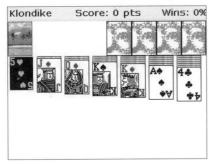

FIGURE 10-7: SolMania's Solitaire layout, ready to play

To begin playing, use the scrollwheel to move around the stacks of cards and press the spacebar to select a card to move from one stack to another. Press the spacebar again to drop the card on the new stack. To draw new cards from the draw pile, you can press the D key on the BlackBerry keyboard. Similarly, if you select a card with the spacebar, you can use the H key as a shortcut to send to one of the four "home" piles.

Within each Solitaire variation are custom settings you can apply to govern how scoring is done, as well as options such as three-card or one-card draw. Games can also be saved and resumed at a later point.

SolMania is available from www.handango.com for $9.99 and is also available as a free trial download.

Software for the Mobile Golfer

Golf-related software programs for handhelds usually fall into one of two categories: golf scorecards and arcade-style golf games.

Keeping Score with BlackBerry Software

The traditional way on the course of keeping your golf score is to scrawl the number of strokes for each hole on a piece of cardboard with a stubby little pencil. It seems golfers have done it this way since the dawn of time. But just because cavemen golfers played that way doesn't mean you have to!

Nowadays there are many electronic alternatives to paper and pencil for keeping track of your golf strokes. Golf scorecard software and golfing are a great match. Many players already have their BlackBerry with them on the course anyway, and golf is an inherently mobile game. Add in the obsessive factor, which touches so many of those who play, and you have an excellent opportunity to put a useful accessory in the hands of the golfer.

Benefits of Scorecard Programs

Being a casual golfer myself, I can testify that there are many benefits to using an electronic scorecard instead of the old paper-based method. An electronic scorecard can automatically do the math that shows you how much under (or in my case, well over) par you are at any given moment. And if you are willing to enter a little more information, these programs can total your putts, track the accuracy of your shots, and even automatically track the results of a variety of "friendly wagers" you might be playing with your foursome. Best of all, if you use a scorecard program over the course of many rounds, you can view statistics and graphs that show you your progress (let's hope!) in different areas of your game.

mScorecard

Several scorecard programs are out there for golfers, including Links Scorecast by Concrete Software (www.concretesoftware.com). One of the best scorecard programs I've seen for BlackBerry handhelds is mScorecard, by Velocor (www.mscorecard.com). mScorecard is a very user-friendly program that at its most basic provides an electronic version of the paper-based scorecard you would normally use. But that's where the similarity ends.

mScorecard goes far beyond what a paper scorecard gives you, and lets you track more details about your strokes, such as the number of putts, whether you hit the fairway or were left, right, short or long, up and down or sand saves, penalties, and club selection. Along the way, it tells you your total score so far and where you stand vs. par. You can score for just yourself, or for everyone in your foursome, and if your group is so inclined, you can even use mScorecard to keep score of a number of different "sidegame" variations.

Even more impressive, mScorecard helps you share completed scorecards by letting you send completed rounds to yourself or your friends via e-mail. Velocor also offers a website to registered mScorecard customers where you can electronically post your rounds, review your history, track your handicap, and view statistics about your play.

Using mScorecard to Score a Golf Round

Getting started with mScorecard is pretty simple. The software program installs on your BlackBerry and appears as a standard BlackBerry application icon on your device. When you run the program for the first time, you will need to first select the course you will be playing and enter the players in your group.

Velocor offers a web page with downloadable course scorecards on its website, but that page is available only to users who have purchased the program. If you are just trying out the program, you can alternatively take a minute or two and access the Courses menu to manually enter the par, handicap, yardage, and other information for each of the holes on the course you will be playing, as shown in Figure 10-8.

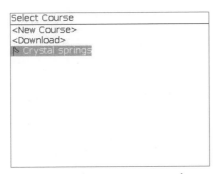

Hole	Par	Hcp	Lpar	Lhcp
1	4	13	=	=
2	4	11	=	=
3	5	3	=	=
4	3	17	=	=
5	5	5	=	=
6	3	15	=	=
7	4	1	=	=
8	4	7	=	=
9	4	9	=	=
10	5	12	=	=
11	3	18	=	=
12	4	14	=	=
13	4	8	=	=

FIGURE 10-8: Manually entering course information in mScorecard

Once you have entered (or downloaded) the course you will be playing, it appears in the course selection screen whenever you start a new round. Figure 10-9 shows mScorecard's course selection screen after entering a course scorecard for Crystal Springs.

```
Select Course
<New Course>
<Download>
Crystal springs
```

FIGURE 10-9: Selecting a course to play

Once you have selected a course, you need to select the players you wish to score in this round. You can add as little or as much information about your partners as you wish. Once a player has been entered, you don't need to keep adding them for future rounds, as their profiles are stored in the mScorecard database. Figure 10-10 shows the player selection screen in action.

You are now ready to tee off! mScorecard starts by presenting you with a scoring form for the first hole, as shown in Figure 10-11, and thereafter moves from hole to hole as you progress through your round. Entering scores is simple. Just use the trackwheel to navigate to the cell entry where you wish to record information and either type in a value or choose a value from the menu.

Note   You can always go back and view or even revise your scores at any time during the round, which is nice.

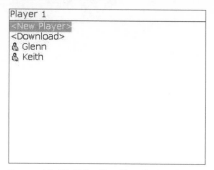

FIGURE 10-10: Selecting the players in your group

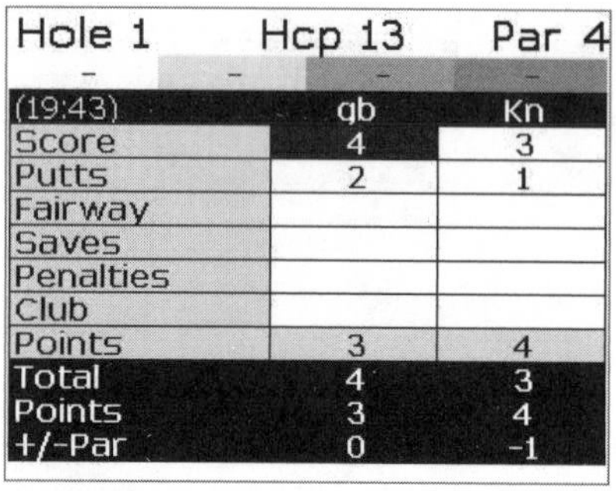

Hole 1	Hcp 13	Par 4
-	-	-
(19:43)	qb	Kn
Score	4	3
Putts	2	1
Fairway		
Saves		
Penalties		
Club		
Points	3	4
Total	4	3
Points	3	4
+/-Par	0	-1

FIGURE 10-11: Entering scores for the first hole

When you have completed your round, mScorecard shows you your completed scorecard as shown in Figure 10-12. You can scroll up or down to see your overall scoring over the 18 holes, as well as the total against par at the bottom. You can also use the trackwheel to show a variety of statistics (see Figure 10-13) for the round, including net score vs. handicap, holes won, number of putts, eagles, birdies, pars, bogeys, and more. Think of how much arguing mScorecard will save you and your buddies as you review a just-played round at the "19th hole"!

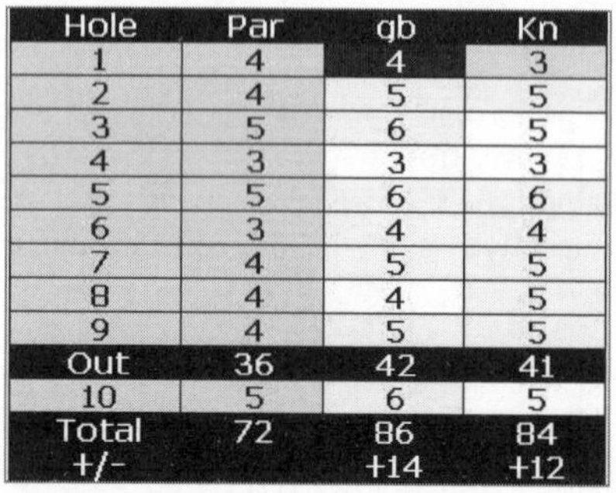

Hole	Par	qb	Kn
1	4	4	3
2	4	5	5
3	5	6	5
4	3	3	3
5	5	6	6
6	3	4	4
7	4	5	5
8	4	4	5
9	4	5	5
Out	36	42	41
10	5	6	5
Total	72	86	84
+/-		+14	+12

FIGURE 10-12: The final scorecard for our round

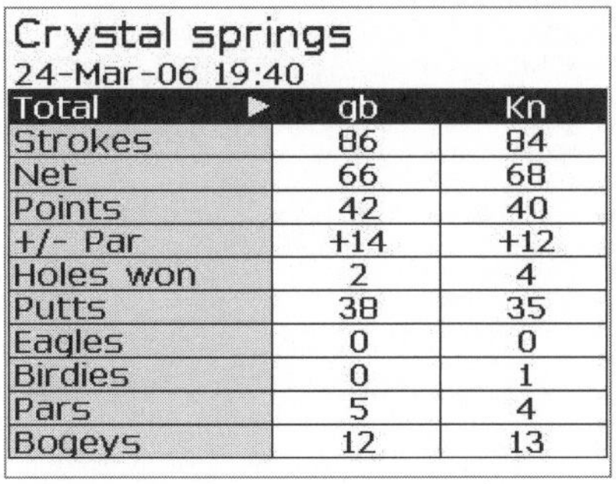

Crystal springs 24-Mar-06 19:40		
Total ▶	gb	Kn
Strokes	86	84
Net	66	68
Points	42	40
+/- Par	+14	+12
Holes won	2	4
Putts	38	35
Eagles	0	0
Birdies	0	1
Pars	5	4
Bogeys	12	13

FIGURE 10-13: The mScorecard Statistics screen

Sharing Rounds with mScorecard

As I mentioned earlier, one of the great added-value features of mScorecard is the ability to send your scorecards from your BlackBerry to yourself, your friends, and even to the mScorecast website where they will be stored along with other rounds you play.

After you have completed a round, simply choose the Send command from the trackwheel menu, and you can choose to send the round either to the mScorecard website or to one or more e-mail recipients. If you choose to send the round to the mScorecard website, the website will automatically recalculate and update the handicaps for any players you have entered.

mScorecard is a great accessory for BlackBerry-carrying golfers, and as I can attest, once you start using an electronic scoring program, the ability to view and analyze your play is so addictive, there is no turning back! mScorecard is available from www.handango.com or directly from www.mscorecard.com. A free trial is available for download, and the program can be purchased for $19.95.

Playing Golf on the BlackBerry

For me, things don't get much better than a beautiful summer day on one of my favorite golf courses. But life does not always cooperate with my golfing plans. If you are itching to play a round of golf but can't get out to the course, why not play a round on your BlackBerry?

With add-on software programs such as Par 3 Golf from RESETgame (www.resetgame.com) you can play a full round of arcade-style golf, complete with surprisingly realistic graphics, right on your BlackBerry handheld. Best of all, in contrast to the real game, you can play a round in minutes vs. hours, in the middle of winter, at night, whenever and wherever the mood strikes you!

Par 3 Golf is a golf "simulation" game that installs and runs on your BlackBerry device. If you have ever played one of the popular golf arcade machines or one of the many PC or game system golf simulations, Par 3 Golf should be fairly familiar to you. Just like those other golf simulations, Par 3 Golf delivers reasonable 3D graphics showing hills, water, fairways, sand traps, and greens. Wind and other factors are taken into account to determine ball direction and behavior. When preparing your shot, you can even choose between the standard view (from behind the golfer) or an overhead view with zoom in and zoom out as well as panning functionality.

Game play commences just like in real golf, at the first hole, pictured in Figure 10-14.

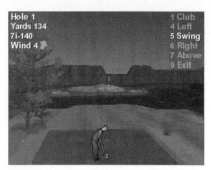

FIGURE **10-14: Teeing up on the first hole of Par 3 Golf**

You are given a default club selection that is appropriate for your distance, but you can change the club selection if you wish to experiment. Based on wind conditions or the slope of the green, you can also adjust your aim to the left or right of the target, or keep it centered right at the target. Prior to each shot, the yardage, club selection and wind speed/direction are displayed at the upper right.

To make a shot, Par 3 Golf uses the familiar golf arcade technique of displaying a vertical bar that represents how much of a backswing you wish to use, which affects how far the ball will travel. To start your swing, press the spacebar once (alternatively, you can click the trackwheel menu and choose Swing). You will see the vertical meter begin rising higher, representing a gradually increasing backswing. If you let the meter rise to the top, you are taking a full backswing. If you wish to use a shorter backswing for more control, press the spacebar at the point in the meter where you want to stop, and the golf swing will change from a backswing to a forward swing, striking the ball and following through. Figure 10-15 illustrates the golf swing process in Par 3 Golf.

FIGURE **10-15: The golf swing meter on Par 3 Golf**

Precise swing control can be tricky, but once you get the hang of it, you can really start to control how hard you hit the ball, and thus the distance.

Once you've hit your first shot, play proceeds as you would expect. You can see how your shot unfolds as the ball arcs to its landing spot. The screen then updates so you can set up to take your next shot, whether it landed in the fairway, the rough, a sand trap, or (ugh!) a water hazard. Figure 10-16 uses the overhead view to show the results of one of my better shots.

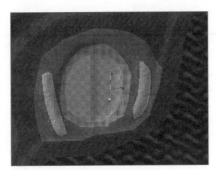

FIGURE **10-16: I'm on the green!**

As you complete each hole, Par 3 Golf displays your score, as shown in Figure 10-17. Play then advances to the next tee.

FIGURE **10-17: Darn it! Another three-putt.**

Although you can get around the course in far less time than it takes to play the real thing, game play includes the ability to pause a game and resume it later on.

Par 3 Golf is an entertaining golf arcade game and is available for purchase from www.resetgame.com or www.handango.com for $9.95. A free trial version that unlocks only the first hole for play is also available. (Once you purchase the full version, the remaining 17 holes are unlocked.)

Board Games

Board games may seem like an odd fit for a tiny handheld like a BlackBerry, but surprisingly enough, many of the most popular board games have been successfully adapted for handhelds. Monopoly, Scrabble, and Yahtzee have seen successful representations for Palm and Windows Mobile handsets. Unfortunately, no adaptations of these board games exist yet for BlackBerry, but I am sure someone is working on it.

Besides commercial board games, easily the most popular board game for handhelds is chess. The ability to play solo against a computer opponent or even wirelessly against a remote player makes chess an excellent game for BlackBerry, and indeed several chess games are now available.

Medieval Kings Chess

Magmic is a leader in wireless games and offers a slew of great games for BlackBerry users, including Medieval Kings Chess. Medieval Kings is a handsome, stylishly graphical take on the classic chess board game, optimized for the BlackBerry handheld. Medieval Kings runs as a standard BlackBerry application on your device. Upon launching and selecting a new game, you are presented with the New Game screen, shown in Figure 10-18.

FIGURE 10-18: New Game options in Medieval Kings

On the New Game screen, you can choose to play against either a real human (sharing your BlackBerry between the two of you) or a computer opponent at various skill levels. You can also choose the visual style for both the board as well as the playing pieces. You can also choose to play over the network against another BlackBerry user by choosing Network Play for up to 15 active games at once. In Network Play, each move made by you or your opponent is sent over the wireless network and reflected in each player's screen.

When you are happy with your game settings, scroll down and choose Begin Game, which displays the chess board and pieces in the standard starting position, white vs. black, as shown in Figure 10-19.

Making moves in Medieval Kings is pretty straightforward. Scrolling the trackwheel moves a piece selector around the board. When you are on the square with the chess piece you wish to move, press the trackwheel (or the spacebar), and then use the trackwheel to scroll to the square where you wish to move to the piece. Medieval Kings is smart enough to show you only valid spaces where your piece can move. If you change your mind, press the Back button to cancel the move and select a different piece.

FIGURE 10-19: The Medieval Kings game board, ready to play

If you are playing against the computer, the opponent quickly makes a move right after you have completed yours. The game proceeds as fast or as slow as you wish, until ultimately you (or in my case, the computer!) finally put your opponent in checkmate. (Take a look at Figure 10-20 for an example of my poor performance against the Medieval Kings computer!)

FIGURE 10-20: Beaten again!

At any time you can save a game in progress and recall it at a later point to continue playing. Medieval Kings is available for only $8.95 from www.handango.com or directly from Magmic at www.magmic.com. A trial version is available that lets you play for a couple of days before buying. It is a great chess game for your BlackBerry and is perhaps the most compact way ever to take the wonderful game of chess with you anywhere you go!

Puzzle Games

Puzzle games are more popular than ever. Crossword puzzles continue to be a mainstay in the daily newspaper. Word games and memory games are fun for kids and grownups alike. But the most recent boost to the popularity of puzzle games is the Sudoku phenomenon.

Mobile Sudoku

According to some, the puzzle game called Sudoku has origins as far back as the eighth century, when it was derived from a similar game called Magic Squares played by the Chinese and passed to the Arab and European world. Although it has been played for hundreds of years around the world, the first puzzle wasn't published in New York until 1979. Even then, Sudoku became a daily fixture in daily newspapers and the general media only when the *London Times* started publishing Sudoku puzzles in 2004. From there it was picked up by other papers and eventually spread across the Atlantic to the United States, where it now enjoys tremendous popularity, spawning websites, clubs, books, and videos.

The rules for playing Sudoku are pretty simple. The usual configuration of the puzzle grid is that of a 9 × 9 grid of squares, forming 9 rows and 9 columns. In addition, the grid is subdivided into nine 3 × 3 subgrids. Grids come with selected cells already filled in for you, and the object of the game is for you to fill in the missing cells of the grid using only the digits 1 through 9, such that each number appears only once in each row and column. So, for example, the number 4 can appear only once in any given row or column (meaning it will have exactly 9 appearances in the overall puzzle when completed). Further, each digit can appear only once in the smaller 3 × 3 subgrids. Traditionally, there is only one possible solution for any given puzzle.

The last time I checked, I counted more than ten Sudoku games on www.handango.com, evidence that the availability of Sudoku on handheld devices has helped fuel its growing popularity. In this section you look at Mobile Sudoku by Icenta, Inc. (www.icenta.com/mobile).

Mobile Sudoku enables you to play Sudoku games on your BlackBerry handheld. Game grids can be downloaded wirelessly or entered manually by you. Four new puzzles are made available for download each day as part of the application. Downloading a new game is as simple as choosing Get New Game from the main menu. It takes only a second or two to download.

Mobile Sudoku presents a new game, complete with a set of already-entered values, to get you started. Your job is to fill in the remaining cells so that only one of each of the digits 1–9 appears in each row. Figure 10-21 shows a new Sudoku game, ready to play.

To move around the grid, use the trackwheel. When you want to enter a value, just use the BlackBerry numeric keyboard. If you need to clear a cell value, use the 0 key.

There are (as expected) endless websites and other resources dedicated to discussing Sudoku puzzles and strategies for solving. Two basic strategies are:

- Look at the rows and columns, and fill in the blanks by looking at the numbers that are already present in a given row or column. If only one blank cell remains in a given row or column, then just fill in the one and only number that can satisfy the row or column. If there are two or three missing cells, try a couple of different combinations until you get one that works.

■ Look at the 3 × 3 boxes and you can eliminate many possibilities because a given digit can appear only once in each 3 × 3 box.

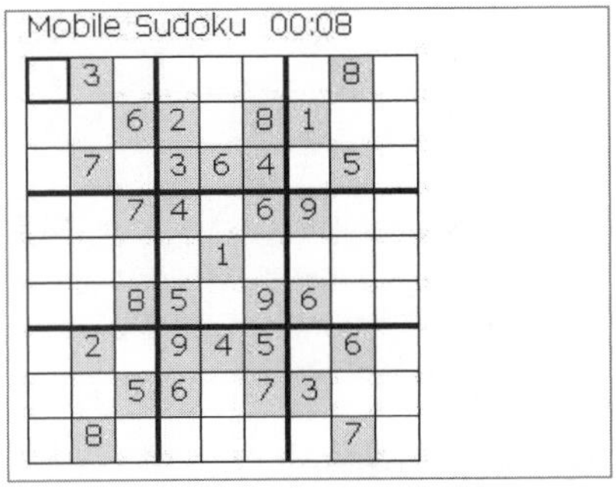

FIGURE 10-21: A new Mobile Sudoku game, ready to play.

Using each of these strategies (as well as in combination) doesn't necessarily quickly solve the puzzle, but it at least gives you a starting point. Naturally, as you start filling in the cells, some of the other rows and columns in the puzzle can become easier to solve because fewer valid digit choices will remain that will fit.

For example, in Figure 10-21, I start by looking at the sixth column because it has only three empty cells. I can tell that the remaining three cell values cannot be a 9, 8, 7, 6, 5, or 4, because those digits are already present in the sixth column. Focusing on the top-most empty cell, I also can see that the top-center 3 × 3 grid already has a 2 and a 3 in it. So for this cell, there is only one possible value, 1, which I enter in Figure 10-22. Whew, only 49 more cells to go!

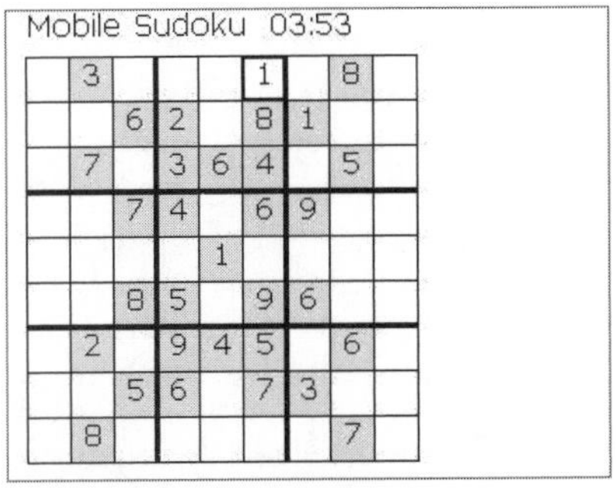

FIGURE 10-22: I've figured out that 1 is the only possible value in the top-most cell of the fifth column

Mobile Sudoku provides a handy Validate menu option, which you can use to check your puzzle and see if the cell values you have entered thus far will result in a solved puzzle.

More information on Mobile Sudoku is available from the Icenta website at www.icenta.com/mobile, and the game can be purchased at the Handango online store at www.handango.com for $8.99. A trial version is also available.

Going Beyond Games

Besides pure game diversions, there are indeed more practical applications for your BlackBerry that still fall firmly on the "non-business" side of the fence. Your handheld is, of course, always with you, so it's a great opportunity to carry databases of recipes and other handy reference information.

Shaken, Not Stirred: BlackBerry the Bartender

If you are looking to impress people with your vast knowledge of drinks at the next big bash, Mobile Bartender by Mobatech (www.mobatech.com) will make you look like a pro. Mobile Bartender is a BlackBerry program that includes almost 200 drink recipes, including cocktails, shots, and other concoctions. While not the most high-tech piece of software you'll ever run into, Mobile Bartender is quite adept at suggesting and serving up drink recipes from the familiar to the obscure.

When you run Mobile Bartender, you are greeted with a simple main menu, shown in Figure 10-23.

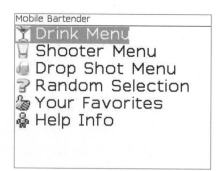

FIGURE 10-23: The Mobile Bartender main menu

From this screen, you can browse and search three categories of mixology: drinks, shooters, and drop shots. You can also have Mobile Bartender find a random drink recipe for you or access a favorites list where you can maintain a growing list of the drinks that you find yourself serving up again and again.

To find a drink recipe, just choose the category and then choose Search By Liquor or Search By First Letter. If you know one of the main liquors in a drink recipe or simply want to browse through a list of vodka drinks, Search By Liquor is your best bet. If you know the name of the drink you want (for example, Bloody Mary), just enter the first letter of the drink name and then scroll down the list until you find the drink you are looking for. Figure 10-24 shows the Search By First Letter option in action.

FIGURE 10-24: Searching by drink name in Mobile Bartender

Once you've found a drink recipe, just use the trackwheel to click and open it, and you are presented with a screen showing the ingredients for the selected drink, as shown in Figure 10-25.

FIGURE 10-25: A drink recipe displayed in Mobile Bartender

If you would like to add a drink to your personal Favorites list, just click the trackwheel and choose the Favorite Menu.

The Shooters database also has a handy Category search method, with which you can find a shooter using categories such as Candy, Sexy, or Fruity. (Certainly you can get yourself in a good bit of trouble in this part of the program!)

Overall, Mobile Bartender is a fun program to take with you if you are looking to expand your knowledge of drink recipes, surprise your friends, or even stump the bartender. Mobile Bartender is available for purchase from the Mobatech website at www.mobatech.com, as well as the Handango online store at www.handango.com, for $9.95.

Fitness: "Running" Your BlackBerry

After examining the fairly hedonistic world of BlackBerry bartending, let's take a trip in the totally opposite direction and look at a program that's actually nice and healthy for you: Running Log for BlackBerry.

Millions of people run, jog, or walk as part of their regular fitness regimen. Running as an amateur sport went through an explosion of popularity back in the 1970s and continues to gain new and enthusiastic followers each year. Running events such as the New York City Marathon number participants in the tens of thousands and have to actually turn away applicants to keep things manageable.

For runners who are pursuing a goal, such as competing in an event, losing weight, or even just achieving general fitness, many experts advocate the use of a log. A running log is designed to keep notes on when you run, for how long you run, what route you take, and how you feel each time you go out. A runner's log doesn't have to be fancy. It can be as simple as a cheap calendar on which you scribble some basic notes about each run. Over time, these logs can provide very valuable data that helps you note your progress toward your fitness goals, as well as provide ongoing inspiration for your next scheduled run.

Of course, it should come as no surprise that someone has figured out how to create a way to keep a running log on a BlackBerry. Sure enough, a number of fitness-oriented programs for BlackBerry devices have appeared over time. I found Running Log for BlackBerry by Mobiteq (www.mobiteq.com) to be a nice program for this purpose.

Running Log for BlackBerry is designed to act as a basic log, providing a simple form for you to enter some notes each time you complete a run. The program, which installs as an icon on your BlackBerry Applications screen, is very easy to use, and you can get started right away by adding a log entry, as shown in Figure 10-26.

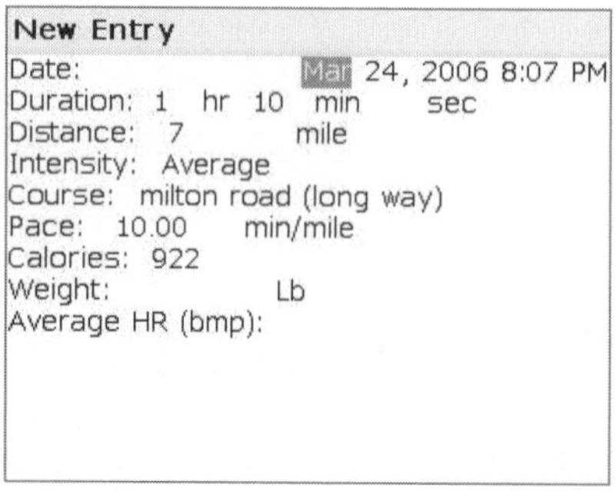

New Entry
Date: Mar 24, 2006 8:07 PM
Duration: 1 hr 10 min   sec
Distance: 7   mile
Intensity: Average
Course: milton road (long way)
Pace: 10.00   min/mile
Calories: 922
Weight: Lb
Average HR (bmp):

FIGURE 10-26: Entering a new entry in Running Log

You can choose to fill in as little or as much information on this screen as you wish, although obviously the more details you enter, the more historical information you will accumulate over time.

After you have entered your running notes and saved them, your entry is stored in the Runner's Log database and subsequently shows up on the main Running Log list, as shown in Figure 10-27.

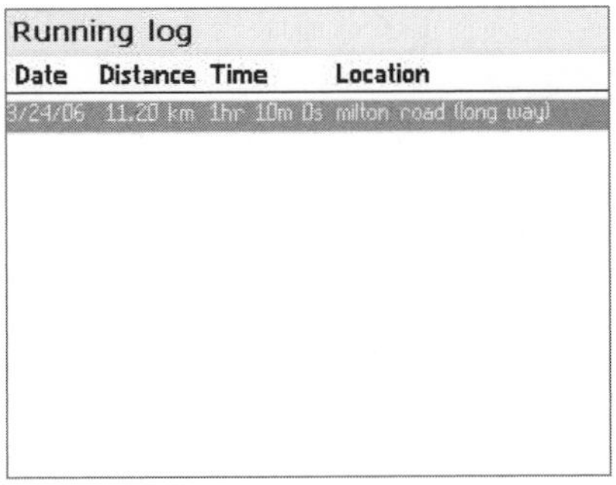

Running log

Date	Distance	Time	Location
3/24/06	11.20 km	1hr 10m 0s	milton road (long way)

FIGURE 10-27: The Running Log list

Most runners tend to use a couple of well-known routes that they have mapped out in their neighborhood or other runner-friendly locations. Running Log lets you create *courses*, which are simply named routes that you can then reference each time you add a new log entry. In the example shown in Figure 10-28, I have added two of my own common running routes.

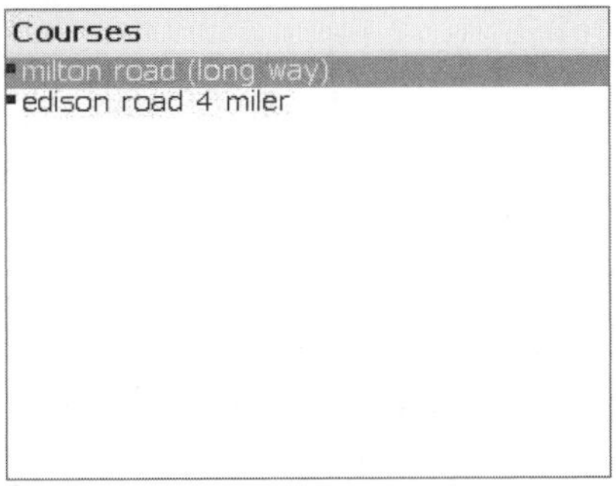

Courses
- milton road (long way)
- edison road 4 miler

FIGURE 10-28: The Courses list in Running Log

Once you have built up a number of log entries, Running Log becomes a rich tool for viewing statistics and graphs on your progress in a number of areas, as shown in Figure 10-29. You can choose to view graphs that chart your progress according to duration, distance, calories, heart rate, pace, or weight, shown over a period of time. Use Running Log's statistics to find your longest run, farthest run, fastest pace, or other key statistics.

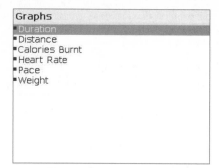

FIGURE 10-29: Graphs supported in Running Log

Running Log also provides a way to get your log entries off your BlackBerry and onto your desktop using a simple e-mail export feature. Choose the Export option, and Running Log prompts you for an e-mail address, as well as a date range encompassing the log entries you wish to export. Running Log e-mails a text file to the designated e-mail account. You can then choose to save this to your PC, print it, or import it into a database or other program of your choosing.

Running Log costs $14.49 at the time of this writing and can be purchased at the Mobiteq website, www.mobiteq.com, or the Handango store at www.handango.com. A trial version is also available. If you are a biking enthusiast, you may be interested to know that Mobiteq also offers a similar program called Cyclist's Log for BlackBerry.

Summary

This chapter has presented a number of representative software titles that are available to help you have a bit more fun with your BlackBerry, help you stay fit and trim, or even just waste a little time here or there, maybe at the airport or on the train. The programs reviewed here are among the most popular, but there are many more titles available in these and other categories, and new applications are being developed and published all the time.

As mentioned in other parts of this book, a great place to find these programs is at Handango at www.handango.com or the BlackBerry software store at www.blackberry.com. After a slow start, the BlackBerry add-on software selection is now growing rapidly, so it's a safe bet you will find many programs that match your interests!

Advanced BlackBerry Hacks: Put Your BlackBerry to Fun and Wacky Uses with Creative Software Projects

part

Developing Your Own BlackBerry Applications

chapter

11

Now that you know what your BlackBerry is capable of straight from the box, you can start to think about adding to its capabilities. This chapter focuses on working with Java application program interfaces (APIs) to create BlackBerry-specific software for your handheld.

After you learn how to build the simple BlackBerry program in this chapter, you will be equipped to create programs that can perform a wide range of tasks — serious *and* frivolous — on your BlackBerry.

However, if you have no interest in learning to program, you can safely skip this specific chapter. You don't have to be a BlackBerry programmer in order to have fun with the projects in the rest of this book.

Java and BlackBerry

If you are not familiar with Java, think of it as a special program that runs on a wide variety of computer operating systems. Computers that use Microsoft Windows, Apple's Mac OS, Linux, and UNIX are all capable of running the Java environment.

Tip Some operating systems come with built-in Java support. If yours doesn't, you can download Java from java.sun.com. This website is not only an excellent place to learn more about Java, but it is also *the* website for finding and downloading the latest Java platform and tools.

When RIM created the BlackBerry device, the developers decided that it was important for the devices to be based on the Java platform. That's why Java, an optional environment on Windows, is the *only* environment on the BlackBerry device. If you wish to create native software programs for your BlackBerry, you need to make sure that your programs work with Java.

In addition to being a software environment, Java is also the name of the programming language used to create software programs that run on the Java platform. The Java programming language is similar in concept to other modern programming languages. As with C++, Visual Basic, or Pascal, you can use the Java language as a set of instructions that, when put together with Java tools, can run on the Java platform and make the host computer perform useful tasks.

Java is often described as an "object-oriented" language, which (in a nutshell) means that Java programs are composed of a number of classes that interact with each other as your program runs. Classes represent an elegant way to organize your program functionality around the actual objects that your program uses.

Java was created in part to provide a software environment that would allow programs written in the Java language to run on any computer that supports the Java platform. Not only that, but once you learn to program in Java, you will have acquired the basic knowledge required in order to write programs that will run on Windows, Mac OS, Linux, and even web servers.

The theory behind Java is that a software program can be written in the Java language and run unmodified on any computer that supports the Java platform. This may sound wonderful but, in reality, the more fully you want to take advantage of the host computer's features, the more likely it is that you will need to write code using programming commands or techniques that will run on only that type of computer. This is the case for BlackBerry devices.

 Cross-Reference If you do not wish to program applications in Java, you can still create very interesting applications using the wireless web browsing capabilities in the BlackBerry device. To do this, you must have access to a website that you can use to post your own web content. You also need some basic knowledge of how to create web content using WML or HTML. I talk about web access on BlackBerry devices in Chapter 4 and describe some interesting ways to make use of that functionality.

The BlackBerry Platform and Profile

Because the BlackBerry device was to have relatively minimal computing capabilities, the designers chose to base the device on a smaller subset of the Java platform than the one that runs on your desktop computer. This subset is called the Java 2 Micro Edition and is commonly referred to as J2ME. The Java 2 Standard Edition (J2SE) runs on more powerful computers, but most of the differences between it and J2ME boil down to assumptions about the host computer's processing power, available memory, and network connectivity.

Note that J2ME is not software. Rather, the term "J2ME" is used to describe a general Java environment running on a small mobile device, such as a BlackBerry. By using the term "J2ME," you can be sure that you are talking about a constrained computer environment, such as that found on PDAs and smartphones. Within J2ME, a number of profiles have been defined, each of which addresses even more specific target environments and which make different assumptions about the capabilities of the target device.

The profile currently used for BlackBerry devices is the Mobile Information Device Profile (MIDP). MIDP is based on a specific Java configuration called the Connected Limited Device Configuration (CLDC). The designers at RIM chose MIDP 2.0 and CLDC 1.1 for the BlackBerry because the assumptions of MIDP match up well to the actual characteristics of the device itself. This means that software programs written for MIDP stand an excellent chance of running well on a BlackBerry device.

As a software programmer, you can write a pure MIDP application using the Java application program interfaces (commonly referred to as APIs) defined in MIDP 2.0 and CLDC 1.1. Doing this will give your program the best chance of running not just on BlackBerry but also on other mobile devices that support the Java platform and the MIDP 2.0 Java profile.

The BlackBerry Application Program Interfaces

Despite the versatility of the Blackberry's platform, many of your Blackberry's most interesting capabilities are specific to the BlackBerry device. In fact, in order for your program to take full advantage of the fact that it is running on a BlackBerry, you need to use BlackBerry-specific application program interfaces (APIs) when writing the program.

The BlackBerry APIs give you functions that allow you to interact with the BlackBerry device itself. These include user interface, BlackBerry networking, menus, file storage, notifications, and built-in BlackBerry applications such as e-mail, contacts, and the web browser.

Because the BlackBerry APIs are not part of the Java MIDP 2.0 specification, using the BlackBerry APIs in your programs means that your programs will not work on any other Java platform. Unless you're running your application on the BlackBerry Device Simulator (a fantastic feature I discuss later in this chapter), you will not be able to run your programs on Windows, Mac, or other Java environments.

Although using the BlackBerry APIs breaks the "Java applications run everywhere" theory, it is simply the reality of choosing between writing a program that will run on any computer and writing a program that looks and works like a good BlackBerry software application. There is certainly room for both kinds of programs in the world, and the designers of the BlackBerry device let you make that choice yourself.

Tip Because this book is about pushing your BlackBerry device to its limits and taking full advantage of its unique capabilities, the programs I provide are all written using the BlackBerry APIs. If you are interested in learning more about MIDP and CLDC with the goal of writing more cross-platform applications, you can find a wealth of information on these topics at developer.sun.com/techtopics/mobility.

The BlackBerry Java Development Environment

The official toolset for creating BlackBerry programs is the Java Development Environment for BlackBerry, commonly referred to as the JDE. The JDE includes the tools and APIs used to develop a software application that will run on a BlackBerry handheld device.

The BlackBerry Java Development Environment is available free of charge to interested software developers on RIM's BlackBerry website. To find the developer tools, go to www.blackberry.com/developers, and then follow these steps to download the JDE:

1. Choose Downloads in the menu on the left side of your screen.

2. Choose BlackBerry Java Development Environment (JDE).

System Requirements

The BlackBerry JDE is intended for use with Windows computers and works with Windows 2000 and Windows XP, specifically. The JDE also assumes that you have the Java 2 platform installed on your desktop computer; it will not work with the older Java 1.0 or 1.5 versions. You probably already have Java 2 on your computer. If not, you can obtain the latest version from `sun.java.com`. You should complete the Java 2 installation before proceeding with the installation of the JDE.

3. After filling out the required forms, click to proceed with the download. Because the JDE is a fairly large download (version 4.0.2 is almost 100MB), you need a reliable broadband Internet connection in order to download it in a reasonable amount of time.

4. After the download is complete, double-click to run the installer and follow the prompts to complete your installation.

Note   When you download the JDE, you will see several different versions available, ranging from 3.6 through 4.1. These version numbers correspond to the BlackBerry OS version numbers. The basic rule of thumb is that if you create a program using a JDE version, your program will most likely run on devices with a BlackBerry OS of that version or higher. The development projects in this book use JDE 4.0.2 because it addresses significantly more devices than 4.1, which addresses only BlackBerry devices running BlackBerry OS 4.1.

The BlackBerry Integrated Development Environment

The most important and most visible part of the JDE is the Integrated Development Environment (IDE). Just as Microsoft Word is the primary tool for creating and editing documents, the IDE is your tool for creating and working with Java programming projects.

The main features of the IDE allow you to:

- Create and work with projects and workspaces
- Write and edit source code
- Build programs
- Test and debug programs

Essentially, you will use the IDE at each step of the BlackBerry programming process, from the first line of code you write to building, testing, and running your finished application. If you have experience with Microsoft's Visual C++ or Visual Basic tools, the general concepts presented in this section will be familiar to you.

To begin working with the IDE on your Windows PC, go to Start ➪ Research In Motion ➪ Java Development Environment ➪ JDE.

Tip

Creating a Windows shortcut will make it quicker to launch the IDE next time. To do this, open Windows Explorer and navigate to the C:\Program Files\Research In Motion\BlackBerry JDE\bin folder, right-click the file ide.bat, and drag it to your Windows desktop to create your shortcut.

The IDE is written in Java so, as with most Java applications, you may notice a short wait when you start the IDE while your computer loads the Java environment. Once it is loaded, you will see the main IDE screen, similar to the one shown in Figure 11-1.

The IDE screen is divided into three main panels:

- **Workspace:** Located in the upper-left corner of the IDE screen, this panel is devoted to displaying a hierarchical view of your currently open workspace, including any projects contained within your workspace. (I discuss projects and workspaces in the next section.) This panel works much like a folder system on your computer and serves to organize your work.

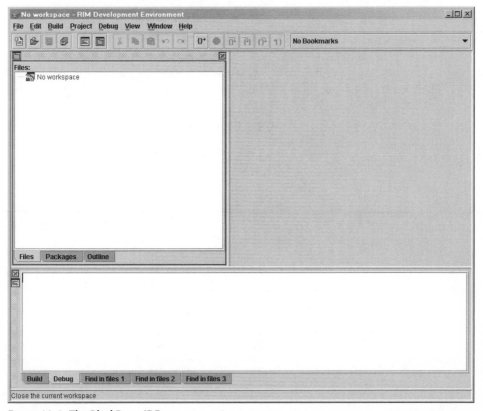

FIGURE 11-1: The BlackBerry IDE

- **Source Editor:** Located in the upper-right corner of the IDE screen, this panel contains one or more open source files within your project. You write and edit your Java code in this panel.

- **Output:** Located at the bottom of the IDE screen, this panel is reserved for displaying output from various operations you can perform in the IDE. For example, as you build your project, this panel displays the build progress and lists any errors or warnings it detects within your code.

Figure 11-2 shows an example of how the IDE and its three panels look when a BlackBerry project is open. This project (named HelloBlackBerry) is about the simplest BlackBerry program possible, but it illustrates nicely how the IDE works.

Later in this chapter, I use HelloBlackBerry as an example of how to create a simple BlackBerry application and how to work with projects within the BlackBerry IDE.

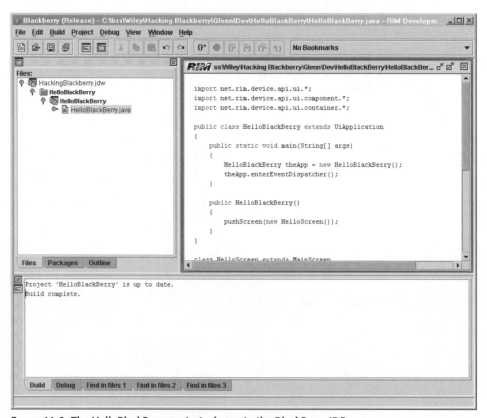

FIGURE 11-2: The HelloBlackBerry project, shown in the BlackBerry IDE

Setting Up Your Project

The BlackBerry IDE lets you organize your BlackBerry development into projects and workspaces.

- A *project* is a set of source code and other files that are used to create a single target (for example, an executable program). Think of a project as a recipe containing instructions for the creation of a BlackBerry program, and the individual project files as the ingredients needed to create the program. In the BlackBerry IDE, projects are stored as files with a .jdp extension.

- A *workspace* is really just a handy way to organize and work with one or more projects. A workspace doesn't have properties of its own (other than a name) — it is simply a container for multiple projects. If you take the recipe analogy a little further, a workspace can be thought of as a folder of recipes that are related in some way (such as a category for Italian dishes). Alternatively, a workspace can also be simply a collection of the projects you are currently working on. In the BlackBerry IDE, workspaces are stored as files with a .jdw extension.

The workspace I created for the programming projects used in the development of this book is named HackingBlackberry. As you will see in the next section, each program is represented by a different project within my workspace.

Now that you know what workspaces and projects are, you can get to work on your first BlackBerry programming project!

Creating a Workspace

Because this is your first step toward programming your BlackBerry, creating your first workspace might seem like a momentous decision. But it's really easy — as mentioned previously, all you really need to do to create a workspace is decide what to call it and where to store it.

To create a workspace:

1. Choose File ➪ New Workspace from the IDE's main menu.

 Note   You can have only one workspace open at a time. Therefore, if another workspace is already open and has any pending changes, the IDE prompts you to save your current workspace before creating your new workspace.

2. The Create workspace dialog box (see Figure 11-3) appears. Type your workspace name in the Workspace name field.

   If you plan to work on a series of related projects, give your workspace a name that will help you remember what the projects are collectively about. For this reason, I am using HackingBlackBerry as my workspace name.

3. Now choose a location to store your workspace file.

FIGURE 11-3: The Create workspace dialog box

By default, the IDE suggests the folder where you installed the JDE (typically a path like C:\Program Files\Research In Motion\BlackBerry JDE\). I strongly suggest that you choose an easy-to-find location that will make it more convenient to work on your programming projects (for example, C:\Development\HackingBlackBerry). Storing your projects in the \Program Files folder makes it harder to remember to back them up, which means that you may lose your work if you ever have a computer failure or if you need to move to a different computer. Your project files are also prone to being lost if you ever uninstall and reinstall the JDE, as this may wipe out the JDE folder in the \Program Files area.

Type in the path you want to use or click the Browse button to navigate to that path. If you want your workspace to live in its own subfolder (this is generally a good idea), go to the end of the path shown in the Create in this Directory field and add a forward slash, followed by the name of the folder you want to use. If the folder does not exist, the IDE will create it for you. As you can see, I am storing the HackingBlackBerry workspace in its own folder called /HackingBlackBerry.

4. To create your workspace file, click OK. The IDE automatically opens your new workspace, displaying it as an icon at the top of the Workspace panel of the main IDE window.

Creating a Project

Once you've created your workspace, you can populate it with one or more BlackBerry programming projects.

Note In the IDE, a Java project is not tied to any specific workspace. Rather, it becomes part of a workspace only when you specifically add it to your workspace. In fact, a project can be part of multiple workspaces. Think of it this way: A recipe for pasta primavera might be part of your Favorite All-Time Italian Dishes category, but it might also be part of your upcoming Holiday Dinner menu. In fact, you are likely to use that recipe in many culinary projects over time. Similarly, if you create enough BlackBerry programs, you will build up a number of projects and many of them may prove useful in multiple workspaces at different times.

To create a project:

1. Choose Project ➪ Create New Project from the IDE's main menu.

2. The Create new project dialog box (see Figure 11-4) appears. Type your project name in the Project name field.

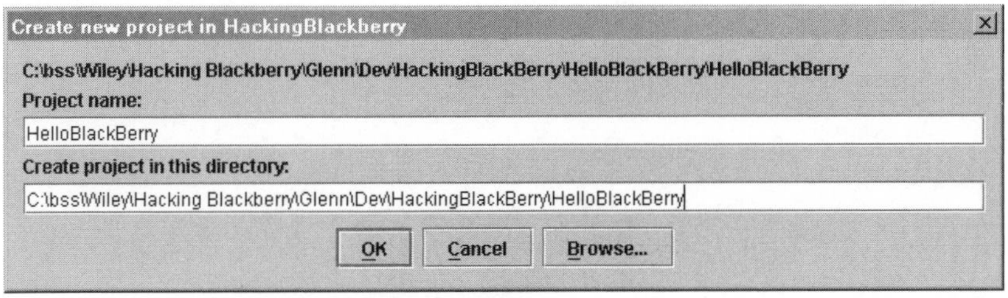

Create new project in HackingBlackberry

C:\bss\Wiley\Hacking Blackberry\Glenn\Dev\HackingBlackBerry\HelloBlackBerry\HelloBlackBerry

Project name:

HelloBlackBerry

Create project in this directory:

C:\bss\Wiley\Hacking Blackberry\Glenn\Dev\HackingBlackBerry\HelloBlackBerry

[OK]   [Cancel]   [Browse...]

FIGURE 11-4: The Create new project dialog box

Although this dialog box is visually similar to the Create workspace dialog box, the choice you make here is a bit more important. Your project name is tied to the name of the program you will be creating, and it has repercussions in terms of the names used in your Java source code. A good rule of thumb is to think about what you would like your *program* to be called, and use that as your *project* name. Accordingly, I am calling my project HelloBlackBerry.

3. Choose a location to store your project file.

As with workspaces, it is a good idea to carefully consider where on your computer you want your project and project source files to live. Although (unfortunately) the IDE does not enforce this concept, creating a separate folder for each project you work on is important; otherwise, all your project and source files will become hopelessly intermixed within the same folder. You can create a folder for each project under the main workspace folder but because projects aren't necessarily used in only one workspace, you are free to create project folders outside of the workspace folder.

I am storing my HelloBlackBerry project in a new folder within my HackingBlackBerry workspace folder. As with workspaces, you can force the IDE to create your folder for you by appending your new folder name to the end of the path shown in the dialog box.

4. To create your project file, click OK. The IDE creates your new project file with a .jdp extension in the folder you specified. If you already have a workspace open, the BlackBerry IDE will automatically add your new project to the currently open workspace. If you did not have a workspace open when you created your project, or if you wish to add an already existing project to a new workspace, choose Project ⇨ Add Project to Workspace from the IDE's main menu. Select the .jdp file representing the project you wish to add to your workspace and click OK to add it.

At this point, the IDE main screen should show your workspace and your first project in the Workspace panel, as shown in Figure 11-5.

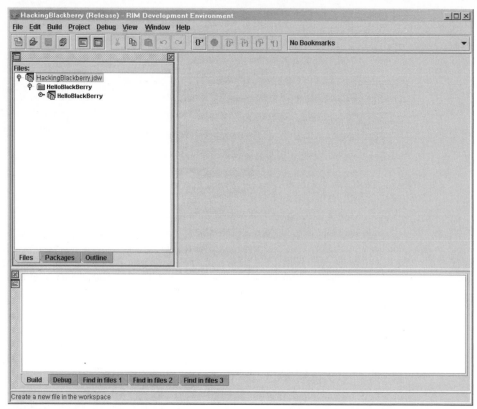

FIGURE 11-5: The HelloBlackBerry project, shown as part of the HackingBlackBerry workspace

Reviewing Your Project Properties

Before you begin coding your project, you need to review the project properties:

1. Select your project in the Workspace panel and right-click to pop up the context menu for the project.

2. Near the bottom of the popup, select the Properties menu item. The project Properties dialog box (see Figure 11-6) appears.

3. Under the Application tab, set the Project Type to be CLDC Application. This indicates that you will be building a native BlackBerry application program.

   Aside from this, you may wish to fill out a few of the descriptive fields in the General tab such as project name and version, but these are not essential for your project. If you do fill out the version, make sure you use a numeric designation such as 1.43 and avoid using letters. There are many other project properties, and for most of them the default settings are fine, especially for your first example project. Until you more fully understand what these settings do, it's best to not fiddle with them.

4. Click OK to exit the dialog box.

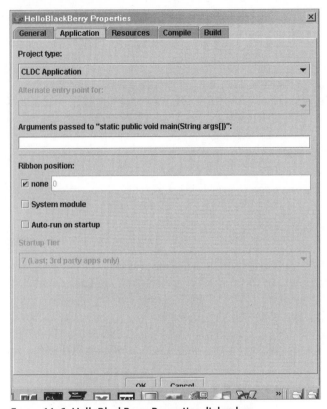

FIGURE 11-6: HelloBlackBerry Properties dialog box

Tip   For more information on the various settings, go to IDE Help.

Writing Your Source Code

By this point, you should have an open workspace with a new project defined, as shown in Figure 11-5. It is time to start writing the code that will form the instructions for how your program will work on a BlackBerry. You write Java code in the IDE by creating a new source file in your project, and then editing it using the Editor panel.

Creating a Source File

To create a new source file:

1. Choose Project ➪ Create New File In Project from the IDE's main menu.

2. The Create new source file dialog box (see Figure 11-7) will appear. Type your source file's name in the Source file name field.

FIGURE **11-7: Creating a new source file in the HelloBlackBerry project**

You should give your source file a meaningful name. In the HelloBlackBerry project, you will have only one source file, but larger projects often have multiple source files. The standard convention is to name your source file after the main class, which is defined in the file itself. Always use an extension of .java. For this project, I am using HelloBlackBerry.java as the name of the new source file.

3. In the "Create source file in this directory" field, enter the location where you wish to store your .java source file. (You don't have use the default project directory.) Large projects may store source files in many areas, but with this simple project you can store everything in one folder.

4. Click OK to create your new source file.

At this point, the IDE should look something like the screen shown in Figure 11-8. Note that the IDE has opened a new Java source file in the Editor panel. In addition, it has created a new file entry in the Workspace panel under your project node. Depending on your IDE settings, some basic skeleton code and comments may be created for you in the new source file.

Writing Your Source Code

I have great news: You finally get to write some code! If you are familiar with how to write Java programs, the Java code for your first BlackBerry application should look pretty familiar to you: HelloBlackBerry has the structure of a basic Java program:

```
import net.rim.device.api.ui.*;
import net.rim.device.api.ui.component.*;
import net.rim.device.api.ui.container.*;
public class HelloBlackBerry extends UiApplication
```

```
{
    public static void main(String[] args)
    {
        HelloBlackBerry theApp = new HelloBlackBerry();
        theApp.enterEventDispatcher();
    }
    public HelloBlackBerry()
    {
        pushScreen(new HelloScreen());
    }
}
class HelloScreen extends MainScreen
{
    public HelloScreen()
    {
        super();
        LabelField applicationTitle =
            new LabelField("Hello BlackBerry Title");

        setTitle(applicationTitle);
        RichTextField helloWorldTextField = new ↵
RichTextField("Hello BlackBerry!");
        add(helloWorldTextField);
    }
    public boolean onClose()
    {
        Dialog.alert("What? Leaving so soon?");
        System.exit(0);
        return true;
    }
}
```

 Note If you are new to Java, I explain the basic structure of this code later in this section. However, there are excellent books and online resources that will do a much more thorough job of teaching you how to write Java programs than I can in a few short pages. I recommend checking out the many resources at sun.java.com, which is a great starting point.

To write your program:

1. Delete any previous code that the IDE may have generated for you, and type the preceding code into the HelloBlackBerry.java window in the Editor panel.

 Tip The Editor panel works the way you might expect: Like NotePad and Word, it allows standard typing, deleting, and highlighting. The IDE editor also supports additional editing features, which you can learn about in the IDE Help.

2. Once you have typed or pasted in the code, save your work by going to File ➪ Save.

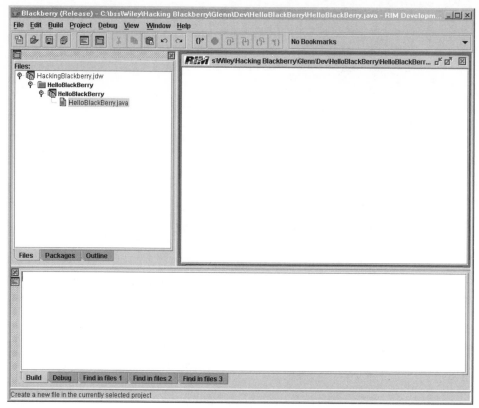

FIGURE 11-8: The HelloBlackBerry project after creating the new HelloBlackBerry.java source file

Note If you don't wish to type in all the code manually, the complete source code for this chapter's project is available on the Wiley web page at www.wiley.com/go/extremetech.

Now you can break it down by doing a simple top-to-bottom walk-through of the HelloBlackBerry program code you just wrote. Because the code references specific pieces of the BlackBerry APIs, it starts off with these three import lines:

```
import net.rim.device.api.ui.*;
import net.rim.device.api.ui.component.*;
import net.rim.device.api.ui.container.*;
```

In order for the IDE to build HelloBlackBerry, it needs to resolve any references to the BlackBerry API. The standard way to resolve these references is by using the import statement, which serves to tell the IDE where the relevant BlackBerry feature is defined in the SDK.

This code has only two tiny classes, but they do the remarkable job of starting up HelloBlackBerry as a real BlackBerry application. The first class in the HelloBlackBerry.java source file is the main application class. The main class is a standard part of every BlackBerry application. In this project, the main class is called `HelloBlackBerry`:

```
public class HelloBlackBerry extends UiApplication
{
    public static void main(String[] args)
    {
        HelloBlackBerry theApp = new HelloBlackBerry();
        theApp.enterEventDispatcher();
    }
    public HelloBlackBerry()
    {
        pushScreen(new HelloScreen());
    }
}
```

This section of code begins with the class declaration for `HelloBlackBerry`. Note that `HelloBlackBerry` extends a class called `UiApplication`. Any BlackBerry application that provides a user interface extends `UiApplication`, a BlackBerry class found in the `net.rim.device.api.ui` package (hence the first import statement). The `extends` keyword is basis for inheritance in Java. So essentially with this first line you are saying, "I am declaring a new class `HelloBlackBerry`, and I wish it to inherit all of the behaviors found in the `UiApplication` class."

All BlackBerry programs start at a special function called `main()`, so it stands to reason that the main program class `HelloBlackBerry` should have a `main()` method. The code `public static void main(String[] args)` signifies that the `HelloBlackBerry` class has a `main()` method and that the lines of code in `main()` will be executed at program startup. In this simple HelloBlackBerry program, `main()` does the bare minimum job of creating an instance of the `HelloBlackBerry` class and starting the necessary event-handling process by calling `enterEventDispatcher()`. Doing this allows a BlackBerry program to listen in on and participate in system events and messages and is a standard part of any BlackBerry application.

The other piece of your `HelloBlackBerry` class is the constructor. All classes have a constructor, which is the place where an instance of a class can perform any tasks that must be taken care of when the instance comes to life within a program. In the HelloBlackBerry program, the constructor does one thing: launches the user interface for itself by creating an instance of the `HelloScreen` class using the inherited `pushScreen` method of `UiApplication`.

The second class in the HelloBlackBerry.java source file is called `HelloScreen`:

```
class HelloScreen extends MainScreen
{
    public HelloScreen()
    {
        super();
        LabelField applicationTitle =
            new LabelField("Hello BlackBerry Title");
        setTitle(applicationTitle);
```

```
        RichTextField helloWorldTextField = new ↵
RichTextField("Hello BlackBerry!");
        add(helloWorldTextField);
    }

    public boolean onClose()
    {
        Dialog.alert("What? Leaving so soon?");
        System.exit(0);
        return true;
    }
}
```

The `HelloScreen` class is responsible for handling the (rather simplistic) HelloBlackBerry user interface by inheriting from the BlackBerry `MainScreen` class, which in turn inherits from the `Screen` class. All this inheritance means that the simple HelloBlackBerry program gets to enjoy some automatic menu handling, such as presenting a standard Close menu when the user presses the Esc key. It also gives the HelloBlackBerry program the ability to listen for `trackwheel` and `keyboard` events, which are notifications sent to your program when the user operates the TrackWheel or presses a key on the keyboard.

The constructor for `HelloScreen` is responsible for setting up the initial appearance and layout of the HelloBlackBerry program's main screen. The first thing `HelloScreen` does is invoke the constructor for its `MainScreen` parent by calling `super()`. Next, it sets contents of the application title bar to be "Hello BlackBerry Title" by calling `MainScreen`'s `setTitle` method. `HelloScreen` passes the title text into `setTitle` by creating a `LabelField` user interface and setting it with the desired text. Finally, it displays the message "Hello BlackBerry" on its screen by creating a `RichTextField` object and adding it to the screen layout.

Note Even HelloScreen's short constructor calls our attention to some new and unfamiliar concepts, such as `LabelField` and `RichTextField`, which are user interface classes that are part of the BlackBerry API and described in full in the JDE developer documentation. Many other interesting user interface classes useful for more complex programs than HelloBlackBerry are also described in the API. One of the nicest things about object-oriented programming, as well as the Java programming language and the BlackBerry API, is that you can begin to use some fairly complex system facilities with very little knowledge or effort. HelloBlackBerry is a fine illustration of that benefit.

The last portion of code is `HelloScreen`'s `onClose()` method. The `onClose()` method comes from `MainScreen` and is automatically called when `HelloScreen` closes. `HelloScreen` responds to this call by first showing an alert dialog box, and then asking the system to close the HelloBlackBerry application.

```
    public boolean onClose()
    {
        Dialog.alert("What? Leaving so soon?");
        System.exit(0);
        return true;
    }
```

That's it! You now have a perfectly legitimate BlackBerry application, comprised of barely 30 lines of code, complete with a user interface, a menu, and proper application startup and close handling. To bring HelloBlackBerry to life, however, you need to build a program out of it.

Building Your Program

In addition to providing a source code editor and a project organizer, one of the BlackBerry IDE's main jobs is to build programs out of Java source code. BlackBerry applications are stored as .cod files; the IDE's responsibility is to transform your project's .java source code into the .cod format so that it can be recognized and run in the BlackBerry environment.

To build HelloBlackBerry, choose Build ⇨ Build Selected from the IDE's main menu. This causes the IDE to begin examining and validating the Java code in your project files; if it determines that everything looks good, it proceeds to create, or "build," your program.

Figure 11-9 displays the IDE after building HelloBlackBerry.

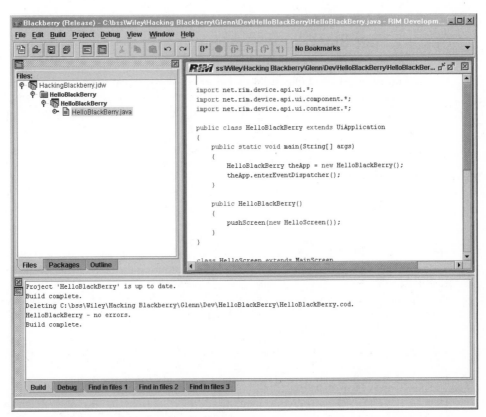

FIGURE 11-9: A successful build of HelloBlackBerry

As you can see in the IDE's Output panel, the IDE did not find any errors in HelloBlackBerry.java, so it proceeded to successfully create HelloBlackBerry.cod in the HelloBlackBerry project folder.

If the IDE finds errors in the .java file, it will describe each error in the Output panel and will not build the .cod file for your program. Because I supplied you with the correct code to HelloBlackBerry, there were no errors this time. But making mistakes or forgetting the proper Java syntax is extremely common when writing new code. Therefore, building a newly written BlackBerry program is usually an iterative process of writing code, building code, correcting errors in code, building code, correcting errors in code, and repeating until the build is successful.

Tip

If you are curious, you can see how the IDE handles Java coding errors by going in and "breaking" the program by intentionally writing bad Java code. For example, go to the first line of code and delete the semicolon after the line `import net.rim.device.api.ui.*;`. Now try to build. When an error is reported, you can usually double-click on the error in the Output panel and the Editor will automatically bring you to the line of code that caused the error.

Testing Your BlackBerry Program

As any experienced programmer will tell you, writing and building your application code is only half the battle. Much of the hard work in software development begins when the time comes to test your program and see if it actually does what you hope it will do. Although HelloBlackBerry is a pretty simple program, it is very easy for the smallest mistakes in your program code to cause a wide range of problems.

To help you test your BlackBerry programs, the BlackBerry JDE comes with the BlackBerry Device Simulator. As its name implies, the Simulator is designed to provide a simulation of a BlackBerry device on your desktop computer. Simply being able to experiment with the BlackBerry environment without having an actual device in your hands is a great feature. When you add in the fact that you can actually test and debug your own programs in the Simulator, you can see why the Simulator is an essential tool for any BlackBerry programmer.

Navigating on the Simulator

To launch the Simulator, choose Build ⇨ Build and Run from the IDE's main menu. The IDE attaches to the Simulator and transfers your program to the Simulator, where it will appear in the standard BlackBerry main Applications ribbon. Figure 11-10 shows the Simulator in action, with a HelloBlackBerry icon on the Applications ribbon.

To become familiar with the Simulator, navigate in and out of some of the standard BlackBerry applications and try out various keys and buttons until you feel comfortable with it. Getting around on the Simulator, especially scrolling and selecting using the trackwheel and the Escape button, can take a little getting used to.

Here are some basic moves: To scroll among the Application icons on the ribbon, simply use the up and down arrow keys on your computer keyboard. Because the Enter key on your keyboard is mapped to the Enter key on the device, once you select an application icon, you can launch it by pressing your Enter key. You can also position your mouse pointer above the trackwheel and click to simulate a push on the trackwheel. The same technique works for the Escape key if you want to close an application or go back to a previous screen.

FIGURE 11-10: HelloBlackBerry in the BlackBerry Device Simulator

Running Your Program in the Simulator

Now that you've spent a little time getting to know the Simulator, it's time to run HelloBlackBerry and see the results of your efforts in this chapter. To do this, use the Simulator to scroll to the HelloBlackBerry icon and hit the Enter key to launch the program. The main screen will show that the title bar and window text are set as programmed in your HelloScreen class (see Figure 11-11).

To close the Simulator, choose File ➪ Exit on the Simulator's menu. HelloBlackBerry responds to being closed by displaying an alert dialog box (see Figure 11-12).

FIGURE 11-11: HelloBlackBerry's main screen

FIGURE 11-12: HelloBlackBerry's onClose() handler in action

Tip

These figures show the Simulator looking and behaving like a BlackBerry 7290 device, but you can configure the Simulator to resemble other BlackBerry models as well. To do this, go to the Edit ⇨ Preferences menu option in the IDE, choose a different device in the General tab of the Preferences dialog box, and click OK. The next time you launch the Simulator, your selected device will be the model for that Simulator session.

Debugging with the Simulator

The IDE comes with an integrated debugger. Using the Simulator allows you to trace through and debug your BlackBerry application. This feature can be extremely useful for a couple reasons. First, you can learn a lot about BlackBerry programs by observing what happens on the device as you step through your program's source code. Second, when problems occur during program execution, you can quickly find and fix errors in your program code by seeing exactly where things go wrong.

To start a debugging session for your project:

1. Choose Debug ⇨ Go from the IDE's main menu. Just as when you selected Build and Run, the IDE launches the Simulator and transfers your program to the Simulator.

2. Now switch back to the IDE and move your cursor to the first line of code in HelloBlackBerry.java in the HelloScreen class constructor (the one that calls super()).

3. Press F9; a red circle appears to the left of the line of code. This red circle indicates a breakpoint, which is a tag you can apply to a line of code telling the debugger to freeze execution of your program when it reaches that statement in your program. Breakpoints are an essential part of debugging because they enable you to stop your program and observe what is happening in your program at a given moment.

Now go back to the Simulator and launch HelloBlackBerry. Almost immediately, control returns to the IDE; execution stops at the call to super(). If you arrange the IDE and the Simulator so that you can see both at the same time, you will note that the main screen for HelloBlackBerry has yet to appear.

1. To see the program execution advance to the next line of code, the one that creates the LabelField object, press F10. Nothing is on the Simulator screen yet.

2. Keep pressing F10 until you get to the end of the HelloScreen constructor function.

3. Press F10 again — you are now in the constructor for HelloBlackBerry, which makes sense because the constructor is where HelloScreen was created. Now press F10 again and you will find yourself in the main() function of HelloBlackBerry. After using F10 to go to the line where new HelloBlackBerry is called, you'll notice on the Simulator that HelloBlackBerry's main screen finally appears.

What just happened?

The entry point for a BlackBerry application is main(). The first thing main() does is call the constructor for the HelloBlackBerry class. The first thing the HelloBlackBerry constructor does is to invoke the constructor for the HelloScreen class. The HelloScreen constructor sets up the main screen's title and window text. Only after all this constructing is finished does the application's main screen appear on the device, and the user gains control of the application by virtue of the enterEventDispatcher call.

By putting HelloBlackberry under the microscope of the IDE debugger you are able to observe the startup sequence for HelloBlackBerry and learn some valuable information about how BlackBerry applications come into being on a device!

Tip

You may have noticed also that, while you were stepping through the code, a new panel opened up on the IDE main screen. This is a special panel that you can use to make observations of various aspects of your program while it is running. By default, this panel displays the Locals view, which tracks the values associated with any local program variables in the scope of the current program statement. By using the IDE View menu, you can add further types of views to the debugging panel. For more information on how to perform other debugging tasks, refer to IDE Help.

Installing Your Program to Your BlackBerry

When the time comes to try to run your program on a real BlackBerry device, you must perform a couple of extra steps. In Chapter 2 you learned that to install a BlackBerry program from your desktop computer to your BlackBerry, you connect your device to your computer with the standard BlackBerry USB cable. Once a connection is made, you can run the BlackBerry Desktop Manager to add applications.

Adding an application through the Desktop Manager requires that the application come with a special .alx file, which is a separate file from the .cod file which contains your application code. An .alx file doesn't contain any program code; rather, it is a special file that tells the Desktop Manager's application loader how to install a BlackBerry program.

When you built HelloBlackBerry in the IDE, the file HelloBlackBerry.java was built into a BlackBerry .cod program file. To generate an .alx file, you need to go the IDE menu and choose Project ➪ Generate ALX file. Then go and look in your project folder, and you should find that there is a small .alx file (in this case, HelloBlackBerry.alx).

You are now ready to install HelloBlackBerry onto your BlackBerry. This process is exactly the same as described in Chapter 2 when you learned how to install third-party applications. Just run the Desktop Manager's Application Loader, navigate to your HelloBlackBerry project folder, and select the file HelloBlackBerry.alx. The Application Loader then guides you through transferring your program to your BlackBerry.

Summary

Compared to what's known about more widespread environments such as Windows, there is simply not a great wealth of information available to the general public on BlackBerry programming. In some cases, the only way for you to learn how to do something is to try it for yourself.

If you are familiar with Java programming and would like to learn more about how to program for BlackBerry devices, I recommend that you continue working with the BlackBerry IDE. Learn as much as you can from IDE Help (the provided developer documentation) and the sample code that comes with the JDE. Additionally, many great resources are available to you on the BlackBerry developer website at www.blackberry.com/developers. You can also join online communities (check out the BlackBerry developer website or search Yahoo! or Google) to get connected with other developers.

If you have a programming background but are not familiar with Java, a good next step would be to visit the java.sun.com Java Developer website to learn about Java programming in general. If you know another programming language, especially C++, you will be surprised by how quickly you can pick up the basics of Java programming.

If you're just a brave soul who doesn't consider yourself to be a programmer but are nevertheless interested in learning how to create custom BlackBerry programs of your own, one of the best ways to learn is to experiment.

Because learning to program for a new computing device and operating system in the space of a single chapter is a challenge, the subsequent chapters in this part will build on the basics to help you create your own custom BlackBerry programs. Writing your own BlackBerry programs is the ultimate in hacking BlackBerry because you can do virtually anything you want!

A Classic Sketcher Application

chapter

12

On just about every kind of computer you can think of, desktop or mobile, big or small, you can find a graphics drawing program that lets you perform basic line drawing and other functions. On desktops, the availability of pointing devices (for instance, the mouse) makes this kind of program possible, while on mobile devices a touch screen and stylus supply similar support.

The BlackBerry device has no touch screen or pointing device, and there are currently no widely known or available drawing programs for BlackBerry devices. In considering the physical design of the BlackBerry, I was struck by an odd similarity to the classic Etch-A-Sketch children's drawing toy, and I quickly came up with the idea to create a BlackBerry program that mimics the Etch-A-Sketch both in terms of the drawings and the controls.

In this chapter, you will continue with another custom software project, which I have dubbed "SketchBerry." As you create SketchBerry, I cover such topics as how to capture user trackwheel events, how to draw graphics on the screen, and how to work with bitmaps.

Designing a BlackBerry Drawing Program

The classic Etch-A-Sketch children's drawing toy was first produced by a company called Ohio Arts almost 50 years ago. Fifty years and thousands of new toy products later, Etch-A-Sketch remains among the most memorable iconic toys from the pre-video game era. Even among the new generation of youngsters, the original Etch-A-Sketch is so undeniably retro that most kids will still recognize one and have fun playing with it if you place it in their hands.

One theory I have for why Etch-A-Sketch enjoys such an enduring legendary status is that like many of the very best products, it claims to do one thing and one thing only, and it is simple to understand and use (despite its surprisingly interesting and complex interior workings). Kids love to draw, and in an age before we all had three computers in our homes and game consoles and BlackBerry wireless e-mail, the idea that you could hold a screen on your lap and twiddle some knobs to draw a picture surely seemed

---

chapter 12

in this chapter

- ☑ Designing a drawing program
- ☑ Capturing trackwheel events
- ☑ The BlackBerry graphics interface
- ☑ Drawing on the screen

magical. In fact, to a young enough child, the product still must appear to be based on pure magic. Plus, no batteries or power cord are required, and it never runs out of juice. It can be discarded for months or years, picked up again, and still work just like new. Truly remarkable!

Because the goal for this chapter is to create a sketching program that is reminiscent of an Etch-A-Sketch, take a closer look what it is that you are trying to replicate. Admittedly, there's not much — a screen and two knobs. But digging a little deeper, you can see the Etch-A-Sketch's functional specifications as follows:

- The unit sports a rectangular screen and two control knobs (left and right).

- The screen renders line segments as they are drawn by the user.

- All rendered line segments are retained on the screen until erased by the user, thus letting the user see his or her drawing in progress.

- The left control knob draws a horizontal line in the left or right direction depending on whether it is turned counter-clockwise or clockwise.

- The right control knob draws a vertical line in the up or down direction depending on whether it is turned counter-clockwise or clockwise.

- The screen can be "erased" by turning the unit upside down or shaking it.

That's all there is to it from the Etch-A-Sketch user's perspective. With these features, the user is left with her own imagination, skill, and talent to produce whatever drawing she wishes. The product has one of the smallest feature sets you will ever encounter. No stylus or touch screen. No on/off switch. No user login. No security or firewall. And perhaps most disappointingly to millions of budding da Vincis, there is no way to save your drawing. Once it is erased, it is gone forever.

Creating a Design for SketchBerry

In designing the SketchBerry program, the main challenge is to decide how to best replicate the Etch-A-Sketch functionality described in the preceding section on a standard BlackBerry device. When you think about it, a BlackBerry device is actually not a bad piece of hardware to model an Etch-A-Sketch on. Consider the following:

- It has a rectangular display screen capable of rendering graphics.

- The screen is not touch sensitive, and there is no stylus.

- All user interaction and navigation is through the trackwheel or other hardware buttons.

So as it turns out, although it is a much more powerful and useful device, the BlackBerry shares some of the same qualities as an Etch-A-Sketch, which makes it easier to think about how the sketching program will work on a BlackBerry.

The main thing to consider is how to model the left and right control knobs for vertical and horizontal line drawing. Although you can, of course, make up whatever key press or button assignments you want, choosing something arbitrary such as ALT+SHIFT+U for up is probably not going to be intuitively obvious to a user of SketchBerry. It is usually best to go with what is already familiar to users of a given device. Accordingly, consider what action would be most familiar to BlackBerry users in terms of controlling up-down and left-right movement. The most common hardware button associated with vertical movement is the trackwheel and its control over vertical scrolling action in most BlackBerry programs. In many BlackBerry programs horizontal scrolling is controlled by holding down the ALT key while scrolling the trackwheel. Based on these considerations, it makes sense to have SketchBerry users use the trackwheel to draw lines up or down and use ALT+trackwheel to draw lines horizontally.

Besides planning how to draw, the other main design decision you have to make is how to start over with a new drawing. Since the original Etch-A-Sketch method of turning the unit upside down or shaking it simply will not work with a BlackBerry (not to mention the odd looks you would get from people as they saw you shaking your BlackBerry!), some other method is required for starting over. To keep things simple, you can have the user exit the program using the standard ESC button in order to erase his or her drawings. When SketchBerry is restarted, a clean slate is provided.

As you read through the implementation/programming part of this chapter, along the way you will consider other smaller design decisions. But decisions made here are the main ones because they affect the main user interface to the program.

The SketchBerry Project Plan

At this point you have most of the information you need in order to move ahead. You have a prototype for your program, which (as luck would have it) is a real-world product — the original Etch-A-Sketch. You also have a design concept that describes how the product features will work on an actual BlackBerry device.

It is time to organize your approach to writing the SketchBerry program. When you approach any software development project, you should try to break it down into sub-tasks so that the actual parts of the program are more easily understood. You can break down the SketchBerry development project into three main sub-tasks as follows:

1. Create the main SketchBerry application skeleton.

2. Implement the trackwheel handling.

3. Render the line segments to the screen as they are drawn.

As you will see, some of these tasks involve more than meets the eye, but this is a good enough plan to get started.

Developing the SketchBerry Program

SketchBerry is a software program that you will code in Java using the BlackBerry JDE. Accordingly, I will assume that you have at least a very basic knowledge of Java programming and an interest in working with the BlackBerry Java Development Environment (JDE) to write your own programs.

Note For an introduction to the BlackBerry JDE and BlackBerry programming, please refer to Chapter 11, as this chapter builds on the basic concepts presented there.

Note The SketchBerry code listing is short enough to present just about all of the code here in printed form, but please note that complete source code for the program described in this chapter is available for download on the Wiley website at `www.wiley.com/go/extremetech`.

This section walks you through the steps involved in coding the SketchBerry program as it follows the rough project breakdown and design presented in the previous section. The code listings are from a single Java source file called SketchBerry.java. As with HelloBlackBerry and the other software programming projects in this book, you need to create a new workspace and new project in the BlackBerry JDE in order to be able to build and run SketchBerry.

Creating the Main SketchBerry Application Skeleton

SketchBerry's basic code structure should look familiar to you if you understand the HelloBlackBerry program from Chapter 11. Most BlackBerry programs, even complicated ones, follow the same basic structure of having a `UiApplication` class that contains your `main()` method and handles program startup, as well as a `MainScreen` class that handles screen layout and display. SketchBerry's code skeleton follows the same model, and later you will see how you add to this structure to create the SketchBerry-specific functionality.

```
public class SketchBerry extends UiApplication
{
    public static void main(String[] args)
    {
        SketchBerry theApp = new SketchBerryBerry();
        theApp.enterEventDispatcher();
    }

    public SketchBerry()
    {
        pushScreen(new SketchBerryScreen());
    }

public class SketchBerryScreen extends MainScreen
{
    public SketchBerryScreen()
    {
    // this is a placeholder for now - more will happen
    // here later.
    }
}
}
```

There is one notable difference between the program skeleton for SketchBerry and the structure for HelloBlackBerry. In HelloBlackBerry, the `MainScreen` class lived in the code as a separate standalone class. In SketchBerry, the `SketchBerryScreen` class is inside of the `SketchBerry` application class.

Why the change? Well, strictly speaking you don't have to do it this way, but making the screen class be part of the application class is an easy technique for allowing the two classes to share access to the same program data in the form of data variables. The need for each of these classes to access each other's data will become apparent in a little bit, so for now, just bear with me.

So far, all you have is a general application skeleton. Now it's time to start doing some more interesting things with SketchBerry.

Intercepting Trackwheel Events

In Chapter 11, the simple HelloBlackBerry program you created was extremely short — about 15 lines of code. Yet HelloBlackBerry managed to exhibit many of the standard features of a BlackBerry software program, including a title bar, a screen display, and automatic handling of the BlackBerry trackwheel. Adding these features required no effort on your part; they simply came free for the ride because your program by default included the features found in the base `UiApplication` and `MainScreen` classes that are provided as part of the BlackBerry SDK.

The method for telling the BlackBerry OS that your program should include the default behaviors of another class is to add the `extends` keyword to the code for your close, like so:

```
public class HelloBlackBerry extends UiApplication
```

This declaration tells the BlackBerry OS that HelloBlackBerry should assume behavior consistent with that of the built-in `UiApplication` class, unless it is told otherwise.

But what if you wanted your program to act slightly differently than the base `UiApplication` class? Would you have to abandon `UiApplication` entirely and add all of that default behavior yourself, just because you want to change one or two things? Absolutely not. One of the best things about working with objects and classes in Java is that you can decide which behaviors you want to keep and which behaviors you want to override. If you don't like a specific behavior provided by a base class, all you need to do to change it is replace that one behavior with your own code that does things the way that you want it to. When you do this, what you are telling the BlackBerry OS in effect is "Gee, thanks for offering this great function, but I think I'll handle it myself."

All BlackBerry programs that extend `UiApplication` get some free trackwheel handling as part of the deal. As you saw with HelloBlackBerry, a `UiApplication`-based program automatically knows how to handle some trackwheel events for you. This includes the display of a Close menu when you press and release the ESC button and the display of context-specific menus when user interface elements such as fields are present on the screen.

Your design for SketchBerry calls for the use of the trackwheel as the "control knob" for positioning and drawing on the screen. This is definitely not standard `UiApplication` behavior, so you need to override the default trackwheel methods and provide your own functionality that does what you want. In order to do this, you need to add custom handlers for the built-in methods `trackwheelClick()` and `trackwheelRoll()`.

TrackwheelRoll Events and the TrackwheelListener

trackwheelClick and trackwheelRoll are Java methods that are part of the BlackBerry-specific TrackwheelListener interface, found in net.rim.device.api.system. The TrackwheelListener interface allows you to create a class that "listens" for trackwheel events. The events that you are allowed to listen for are click, unclick, and roll. A click event is sent when the trackwheel is pressed in. An unclick event is sent when the trackwheel is released. A roll event is sent when the trackwheel is rolled (up or down).

By default, your application never sees these events, and the system takes care of them on your behalf. But by making your class TrackwheelListener, you get the opportunity to see these events inside your application and even perform your own custom actions when the events occur. So how do you make your class TrackwheelListener? It's actually easy. All you have to do is add the syntax implements TrackwheelListener to the class declaration line, like so:

```
public class SketchBerry extends UiApplication implements
TrackwheelListener
```

This allows your class to add the special methods trackwheelClick, trackwheelUnclick, and trackwheelRoll. Note that you don't need to add all three methods. You can add one or two of them if that's all you need.

Most applications listen for trackwheel events so that they can create and display their custom menus at the appropriate time. In SketchBerry, you have a different purpose in mind, which is using the trackwheel to change the current drawing position on the screen. Take a look at some code that will process the trackwheelRoll event:

```java
public boolean trackwheelRoll(int amount, int status, int time)
{
    if ((status & TrackwheelListener.STATUS_ALT) == 1)
    {
        _horzPos += amount;
    }
    else
    {
        _vertPos += amount;
    }
    return false;
}
```

Once added to your code, the trackwheelRoll method will be called within your program each time the trackwheel is rolled up or down. If the trackwheel is rolled down, the amount parameter is positive, and if the trackwheel is rolled up, the amount parameter is negative.

What does the value of the amount parameter actually represent? Whatever you want it to represent. For an e-mail program that lists messages, it might make sense for this value to be the number of messages to scroll up or down in a list. In the MemoPad viewer it might be best to map this to the number of lines of text to scroll up or down. In SketchBerry you want to give the user a certain degree of precision with which to draw line segments, so you will interpret the amount parameter as the number of screen pixels to move the drawing cursor up or down. Different BlackBerry devices have varying screen dimensions, but my BlackBerry 8700 has a 320 × 320–pixel screen, so on my screen it would take 320 single rolls of the trackwheel to draw a vertical line from the top of the screen to the bottom of the screen.

Tracking the Current Drawing Position

The main reason you want to receive `trackwheelRoll` events is so that you can track the position of the SketchBerry drawing cursor as it moves around the screen. Ultimately, you will need to respond to these movements by drawing lines in the proper direction, but for now it will suffice to use a couple of program variables called `_newVertPos` and `_newHorzPos` to store the new x/y position of the drawing cursor on the screen. These variables are declared as private integers at the top of your main `SketchBerry` class:

```
private int _horzPos;
private int _vertPos;
```

By adding the value of the `amount` parameter to `_newVertPos`, you are able to track the movement of the SketchBerry cursor up or down the screen.

As mentioned in the earlier SketchBerry design section, horizontal drawing is enabled by pressing and holding down the ALT key. You can tell whether the ALT key is pressed by using the following piece of code:

```
if ((status & TrackwheelListener.STATUS_ALT) == 1)
```

So if the ALT key is pressed, your code applies the `amount` value to the horizontal position variable `_newHorzPos`; otherwise it is applied to the vertical position variable `_newVertPos`.

Starting and Stopping Drawing Mode with TrackwheelClick

Because SketchBerry will be tracking the drawing position based on `trackwheelRoll` events, where should the drawing position start when SketchBerry launches as an application? You can put it anywhere, but you can start by trying the cursor out at the upper-left corner of the screen, at x/y position (0,0). This, however, causes a little bit of a problem in that all drawings made with SketchBerry would start in the upper-left corner and consist of a single continuous line that winds around the screen. That could be restrictive, so add the concept of a drawing mode to the program. The initial drawing mode would be off, which allows the user to position the cursor wherever he wants before drawing starts. Furthermore, the drawing mode could be toggled on or off at any point, which in effect lets the user "lift their pen up," move it to a different location, and then place the pen back down to start drawing again.

The drawing mode state can be tracked with a simple Boolean variable `_drawing`, and `_drawing` can be flipped to `true` or `false` by trapping the `trackwheelClick` event, like so:

```
public boolean trackwheelClick( int status, int time )
{
    _drawing = !_drawing;
    return true;
}
```

Things are getting a little more interesting now that you can keep track of a drawing position as the user moves it horizontally and vertically around the screen with the trackwheel. But SketchBerry still doesn't really do anything useful yet. It's time to start drawing!

Understanding the BlackBerry Graphics Model

Drawing on the BlackBerry screen is accomplished by making use of the BlackBerry `Graphics` class, which is part of the `net.rim.device.api.ui` package. The main purpose of the `Graphics` class is to provide developers with a "surface" on which various kinds of drawing operations can be performed. Supported `Graphics` drawing operations include text, rectangles, bitmaps, and lines. The `Graphics` class also supports the capability to set background and foreground colors, as well as the current font used for text drawing.

How does a `Graphics` object get created, and when can you use it to draw on the screen? The BlackBerry `MainScreen` class (upon which you have based your `SketchBerryScreen` class) uses a "painting" model common to many other event-driven operating systems, including Windows. In this model, your code doesn't just draw on the screen whenever it feels like it. Rather, the screen is treated as a precious resource that may potentially need to be shared by many different parts of your code, or even multiple programs running at the same time. To maintain some kind of control over how and when the screen gets drawn, the BlackBerry `MainScreen` class includes a `paint()` method that is called whenever the `MainScreen` class determines that the screen needs to be painted. The `paint()` method represents a single point of control for drawing on the screen. The `paint()` method passes a single parameter, which just so happens to be a `Graphics` object, all set up and ready for you to use to draw on your screen.

So how does `MainScreen` get to the point where it thinks it needs to paint the screen? You can let the `MainScreen` class know that you want to paint the screen by invalidating either the whole screen or a region of the screen by using the `invalidate()` method. Thus the general flow of logic is:

1. Your code decides that program conditions require a change to the screen display.

2. Your code calls `MainScreen`'s `invalidate()` method, which tells the `MainScreen` that it needs to schedule a `paint()` operation the next chance it gets.

3. `MainScreen` calls the `paint()` method, passing it a `Graphics` object that can be used to draw on the screen.

4. The `paint()` method draws on the screen.

Drawing on the Screen with paint()

In order for a program to draw its own graphics, it needs to implement the `paint()` method in its screen class. Look at a simple version of a `paint()` method:

```
protected void paint(Graphics gr)
{
        gr.drawText("Hello There", 0, 0);
}
```

This `paint()` function draws the text string "Hello There" at x/y coordinate (0,0) on the screen, using the `Graphics` object passed to it as the `gr` parameter. Elsewhere in your code, whenever the situation calls for the screen to be redrawn, simply invoke the `invalidate()` method of your screen class, and the `paint()` method is called.

You can now apply this technique to SketchBerry and make use of the x/y drawing position you've been tracking by drawing lines as the user scrolls their way around the screen. To draw a line between two points on the screen is easy: just call the `drawLine()` method of the `Graphics` object, which takes four parameters. The first two parameters are the x/y coordinates of the starting point, and the next two parameters are the x/y coordinates of the end point. Here are some examples of using `drawLine` (assuming a 320 × 320 screen display):

```
// draw a horizontal line across the top of the screen
gr.drawLine (0, 0, 319, 0)
// draw a vertical line in the middle of the screen
gr.drawLine (160, 0, 160, 319)
```

A First Try at Sketching

Armed with knowledge of how to draw lines, along with the ability to trap and receive trackwheel events, you are ready to take a shot at implementing SketchBerry's line sketching functionality. Your goal is to make your `paint()` method draw line segments that correspond to the movement of the current drawing position from one point to the next, either vertically or horizontally. In order to accomplish this, you need to add a couple of enhancements to the SketchBerry code you have developed thus far.

Tracking a Starting and Ending Point

In the earlier section on `trackwheelRoll` handling, you used the `amount` parameter value to adjust the current drawing position. In order for you to be able to draw a new line each time the trackwheel is scrolled, you do need to know the new drawing position, but you also need to know where the origin of the new line starts. So, expand your x/y tracking variables to include both an "old" position and a "new" position, as follows:

```
private int _horzPosOld;
private int _vertPosOld;
private int _horzPosNew;
private int _vertPosNew;
```

In `trackwheelRoll()`, you now will use the `amount` parameter to update the New position variables:

```
if ((status & TrackwheelListener.STATUS_ALT) == 1)
{
    _horzPosNew += amount;
}
else
{
    _vertPosNew += amount;
}
```

Drawing a Line Segment in paint()

You can now use the old and new positions to draw a line segment in response to each track-wheel scroll. In the paint() method, you can draw a line as follows:

```
protected void paint(Graphics gr)
{
    gr.drawLine (_horzPosOld, _vertPosOld,
                 _horzPosNew, _vertPosNew);
```

As each paint() request is processed, you also need to make the end point the new starting point for the next line segment:

```
_horzPosOld = _horzPosNew;
_vertPosOld = _vertPosNew;
```

Finally, you need to be able to trigger a paint() call in response to each trackwheelRoll event by calling invalidate at the end of the trackwheelRoll() handler:

```
_mainScreen.invalidate();
```

Here is the source code listing for SketchBerry as it stands now:

```
public class SketchBerry extends UiApplication implements
TrackwheelListener
{
    private myScreen _mainScreen;
    private int _horzPosOld;
    private int _vertPosOld;
    private int _horzPosNew;
    private int _vertPosNew;
    private boolean _drawing;
    public class myScreen extends MainScreen
    {
        public myScreen()
        {
        }

        protected void paint(Graphics gr)
        {
            if (_drawing)
            {
                gr.drawLine (_horzPosOld, _vertPosOld,
                        _horzPosNew, _vertPosNew);
            }
            _horzPosOld = _horzPosNew;
            _vertPosOld = _vertPosNew;
        }
    };

    public static void main(String[] args)
```

```
    {
        SketchBerry theApp = new SketchBerry();
        theApp.enterEventDispatcher();
    }

    public SketchBerry()
    {
        _mainScreen = new myScreen();
        _horzPosOld = 0;
        _vertPosOld = 0;
        _horzPosNew = 0;
        _vertPosNew = 0;

        _drawing = false;
        _mainScreen.addTrackwheelListener(this);
        pushScreen(_mainScreen);
    }

    public boolean trackwheelClick( int status, int time )
    {
        _drawing = !_drawing;
        _mainScreen.invalidate();
        return true;
    }
    public boolean trackwheelRoll(int amount, int status, int time)
    {
        if ((status & TrackwheelListener.STATUS_ALT) == 1)
        {
            _horzPosNew += amount;
        }
        else
        {
            _vertPosNew += amount;
        }

        _mainScreen.invalidate();
        return false;
    }
}
```

Not Quite There Yet

If you compile and run this code, you will find that this version of SketchBerry will indeed draw line segments on the screen, as you scroll vertically and horizontally with the trackwheel. But there is a problem. Each time the invalidate() function is called, the screen is cleared. The net effect of this is that the only line segment you see on the screen is the current one. While it's kind of amusing to watch a little 1-pixel line segment snake its way around the screen, it falls short of SketchBerry's goal of producing Etch-A-Sketch–style drawings.

Note If you were to take the SketchBerry project and add a method for tracking all of the line segments painted thus far, you could fairly easily create a "snake" or "maze" game that could sense when the head of the current line collided with a previous line, or even other obstacles of your own design.

Another problem with the current code is that even if `invalidate()` did not erase the entire screen, other things could ruin the SketchBerry drawing. For example, the user could pop up a menu. When the menu went away there would be no way to go back and redraw the portion of the current sketch that was erased.

What SketchBerry needs is a way to not only draw new line segments as you move around the screen, but also a way to render the entire set of line segments drawn so far — the whole picture, on demand, anytime. The most common way to solve this problem is by using an off-screen bitmap. With this technique, you do not draw directly on the screen. Instead, you draw only to a bitmap that is the same size as the screen. Then, whenever you need to display your drawing, you simply copy your bitmap to the screen. Because nothing ever erases the contents of your bitmap, it always contains a perfect representation of the entire drawing.

In the next section, you see how to implement the off-screen bitmap technique, and you complete the SketchBerry program.

Working with Bitmaps

The BlackBerry SDK includes a `Bitmap` class that is suitable for displaying on a BlackBerry device. If you are not familiar with working with bitmaps and image file formats, don't worry. You don't need to know anything about bitmap formats. All you need to do is create a new bitmap like this:

```
myBitmap = new Bitmap( width, height);
```

Through the magic of the BlackBerry `Graphics` class, you will be able to draw lines on an off-screen bitmap without knowing anything about the actual memory format of the bitmap itself.

This small piece of sleight of hand is accomplished by creating your own `Graphics` object. So far, the `Graphics` object you have been working with is one that has been passed to you by the `paint()` method. But you are free to create your own `Graphics` object and draw into it for whatever reason. To construct a `Graphics` object for this purpose, you need to pass it a bitmap that will act as the drawing surface:

```
myGraphics = new Graphics( myBitmap );
```

So, to create an off-screen `Graphics` object that matches the dimensions of the BlackBerry screen and can be drawn to, you would use the following code:

```
// obtain the width and height of the screen
// and create a bitmap with those dimensions
myBitmap = new Bitmap( getWidth(), getHeight);
// create a graphics object which will use the bitmap as its
// drawing surface
myOffScreenGraphics = new Graphics( myBitmap );
```

This off-screen graphics object can be created once by placing it in an `onDisplay` handler in your `MainScreen` class:

```
protected void onDisplay()
{
    // Create an offscreen bitmap you can draw to
    _myOffScreenBitmap = new Bitmap( getWidth(),
getHeight());

    _myOffScreenGraphics = new Graphics(
_myOffScreenBitmap );

    //clear offscreen bitmap
    _myOffScreenGraphics.clear();
}
```

Now, in `paint()`, instead of drawing on the screen `Graphics` object, you can draw on this off-screen `Graphics` object:

```
myOffScreenGraphics.drawLine (_horzPosOld _vertPosOld,
                        _horzPosNew, _vertPosNew);
```

Okay, so you've created an off-screen `Graphics` object with a bitmap, and you can draw SketchBerry's line segments to it. You now have a perfect way to record all of SketchBerry's drawing actions by writing them to a bitmap that never gets erased.

But how do you get the contents of this bitmap to show on the BlackBerry display? You might be inclined to scan through the list of `Graphics` and `Bitmap` class methods in the BlackBerry developer documentation, looking for a helpful function with a name like `CopyBitmapToScreen` or `Copy(src, dest)`. Well, there is no such thing.

The method you want comes with the unlikely name of `rop()`, which stands for raster operation. A raster operation can be thought of as a manipulation of image bits in some manner. If you look at the API documentation for `rop()`, you'll note that it can perform quite a number of interesting and obscure operations on images. The reason for this is that any drawing function on BlackBerry, from text to bitmaps to lines to backgrounds, eventually resolves down to a raster operation.

For your purposes, you don't need any of the more exotic raster operation types. All you will use is `ROP_SRC_ALPHA`, which simply copies a source bitmap to the destination `Graphics` object. Thus, to copy your off-screen bitmap to the `Graphics` object passed to you by `paint()`, and of course the BlackBerry screen, the following code does the trick:

```
gr.rop(gr.ROP_SRC_ALPHA, 0, 0, getWidth(), getHeight(), myBitmap, 0,0 );
```

This piece of code says "Copy the contents of myBitmap, using the origin (0,0), to the screen `Graphics` object at coordinate (0,0)". Now revisit your `paint()` routine, and use the new off-screen bitmap technique:

```
protected void paint(Graphics gr)
{
    if (_drawing)
    {
```

```
            _myOffScreenGraphics.drawLine (_horzPosOld, ↵
_vertPosOld, _horzPosNew, _vertPosNew);
            }

            // make sure you always draw the last good screen ↵
bitmap from the off-screen bitmap
            gr.rop(gr.ROP_SRC_ALPHA, 0, 0, getWidth(),
getHeight(),
_myOffScreenBitmap, 0,0 );
            _horzPosOld = _horzPosNew;
            _vertPosOld = _vertPosNew;
        }
```

Your paint() routine now draws each new line segment into the off-screen bitmap and then slams the bitmap onto the screen using the super-fast rop() method. If you compile and run SketchBerry with this technique, you'll see that it works great.

Using SketchBerry

To compile, build, and run SketchBerry, you'll need the full source code for SketchBerry.java. You'll also need to have created a workspace and project for SketchBerry in the Java JDE. Once built, SketchBerry installs to your BlackBerry as a standard application, through the BlackBerry Desktop.

Running SketchBerry on a Device

To run SketchBerry on your device, go to the Applications folder and select the SketchBerry icon. When SketchBerry first loads, it will look like Figure 12-1.

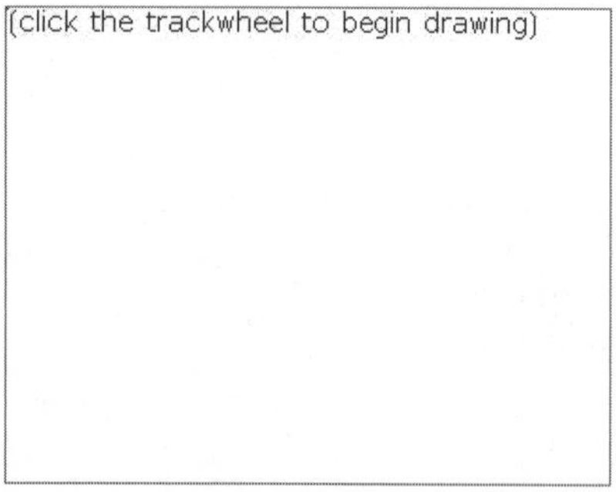

(click the trackwheel to begin drawing)

FIGURE 12-1: SketchBerry after launching

As explained earlier, SketchBerry does not start out in drawing mode, in order to give users a chance to reposition the drawing cursor to the screen location where they would like to start their drawing. As a courtesy to the user, when not in drawing mode, your `paint()` method displays the message "(click the trackwheel to begin drawing)" at the top of the screen.

To start drawing, click the trackwheel. At this point, anytime you roll the trackwheel up or down or use the ALT key with the trackwheel to move left or right, you create a line segment that continues until you change direction or pause drawing by clicking the trackwheel again. An example of a SketchBerry drawing session appears in Figure 12-2.

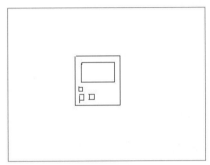

FIGURE 12-2: Hmm. This could take a long time to get good at . . .

As with the original Etch-A-Sketch, it takes quite a bit of patience and skill to create a drawing of any higher complexity than a rectangle, but you will see that the SketchBerry program is essentially true to the original model in its usage and results.

Running SketchBerry on the Simulator

If you wish to run SketchBerry in the BlackBerry Simulator, you will need to learn the keystrokes necessary to simulate both the trackwheel and the ALT key as follows:

- **Desktop up arrow:** Rolls the Simulator trackwheel up by one unit.

- **Desktop down arrow:** Rolls the Simulator trackwheel down by one unit.

- **Desktop CTRL key:** Presses the Simulator ALT key.

Note

Alternately you can use your mouse to click the onscreen simulator ALT key, but doing this while operating the arrow keys requires a bit of keyboard gymnastics.

For more information on the BlackBerry Simulator, please refer to Chapter 11.

Summary

In this chapter you saw how to take a simple do-nothing BlackBerry application skeleton and build it up to handle more sophisticated tasks such as trapping trackwheel events, drawing on the screen, and working with off-screen bitmaps. The result is a real, working sketch program for BlackBerry devices. SketchBerry is by no means a commercial-quality program but it's easy to see where additional features and capabilities would push it closer to that goal if you were up for doing further work. Some obvious areas where improvements can be made are:

- Ability to save your drawings as named bitmaps
- Ability to load saved drawings from memory
- Change color of the lines drawn
- An "erase" feature
- An "undo" feature
- Better controls for switching between horizontal and vertical direction

Beyond these, you can, of course, go well beyond the Etch-A-Sketch model and add more sophisticated drawing tools for text, shapes, and color. With the introduction provided in this chapter, these features should be within your reach.

Music to My Ears: A Toy Piano in the Palm of Your Hand

BlackBerry is not particularly known for its multimedia capabilities. In fact, a quick scan through the icons on the BlackBerry home screen reveals very little evidence of fun at all — the applications are all about business and productivity. While BlackBerry competitors such as Palm and Windows Mobile have long promoted the ability to play music, display photos, take pictures, and even work with digital video, RIM has kept the focus on work and not play within the BlackBerry product family.

In some cases the unfortunate lack of BlackBerry media features simply boils down to holes in the device hardware. For example, no BlackBerry device released to date has support for an expansion card slot. The lack of this slot means that users can put on their device only those files that will fit in the relatively small main device memory. This effectively eliminates the possibility of storing any realistic MP3 audio or digital video files, which generally require many megabytes of memory each. Until recently, the built-in processor of the BlackBerry was too feeble to be able to conjure up the horsepower necessary to handle music and video.

Yet the newest BlackBerry devices, the 8700 and 7130, have improved screen displays, stronger processors, and better system level audio capabilities. Ringtones available for these devices show that reasonable audio quality can be had. As a result, the main barriers to making a BlackBerry more multimedia-friendly would seem to be the lack of software applications that play audio and video.

In this chapter, I thought it would be fun to take a crack at exposing some of the BlackBerry's audio capabilities by creating a program that can play music. While playing MP3 audio is still problematic because of the lack of device memory storage, I wondered whether you could simply create your own music. So I decided to try to create a simple "piano" program that let you play different notes in a scale, just like the keys on a piano.

The techniques used in the "PianoBerry" custom software project build on the basic BlackBerry programming concepts you've already covered in the development project chapters. New areas I cover in this chapter include how to access the BlackBerry speaker through the system audio support, how to define musical tones that match the notes on a piano, and how to add BlackBerry keypad control.

Playing Audio with the BlackBerry Alert Interface

As with most software development projects, before you write a line of code it's a good idea to step back and think about any areas where you need to do some research. For PianoBerry, the most obvious unknown is how to coax a BlackBerry to play audio. It is of course readily apparent that BlackBerry can play sound. Evidence of this is found in the phone ringer, calendar appointment alarms, ringtones, and other miscellaneous beeps and chirps that can be emitted from the speaker. But how can a software program access this audio playing capability?

The answer actually depends on which BlackBerry device model you are talking about. Earlier BlackBerry models support only basic monotone sounds and buzzes. Later models support polyphonic sound, MIDI sound, and even MP3 playback. The BlackBerry `Alert` class, part of the BlackBerry SDK, provides an interface that software developers can use to determine what level of audio support a given device has; it also offers member functions that may be used to play different kinds of audio information. The `Alert` class, as per its name, is designed as a means for an application to alert the user when an event or scenario occurs that the application deems worthy of user notification. Alerts come in many forms, including vibrate and audio, but for your purposes in creating PianoBerry, audio is the only alert mechanism of interest.

The `Alert` class offers a set of `isSupported()` functions that can be used by a program to query device audio capabilities. The currently implemented set of functions in this family comprises `isAudioSupported()`, `isADPCMSupported()`, `isBuzzerSupported()`, `isVibrateSupported()`, and `isMIDISupported()`. Your focus will be on the audio capability that is found on all modern BlackBerry devices, so a call to determine if audio is supported looks like this:

```
boolean bAudio = Alert.isAudioSupported ();
```

It's always a good idea to check your assumptions about device capabilities instead of just going ahead and calling functions that may fail (or worse) because the support is not there.

 Note Using ADPCM or MIDI is beyond the scope of this chapter, but if you have an interest in producing more complex sounds, it will be useful to determine what level of sound support is found on a given device.

What's the Frequency: A Short Music Theory Detour

It is time to present a brief primer on the science of how musical notes are formed. My aim is not to panic you with flashbacks to high school physics class, so I'm just going to go over the basics needed in order to teach a BlackBerry how to play a specific note. I am certainly no expert in music theory, so if you are, just feel free to skip over this section. Personally, I found it was fairly easy even for a musical novice to find the information needed by Googling and a bit of research.

When a note is played on a piano (or any other musical instrument), the sound travels in a wave, which is measured as a frequency expressed in Hertz (usually written in shorthand as Hz). The frequency can also be described as the number of vibrations per second. An *octave* is made up of 12 such notes, each of which has a specific frequency. Later in this chapter, you will be using specific frequencies to play each note.

So given a music note, how do you know what the frequency is? In my research I found many web pages with this information, and it seemed that every website had a different formula for calculating frequency. One source I found stated that to calculate the frequency of any given note, you can use the following formula:

Frequency (in Hertz) = 6.875 × 2^((3 + MiddleC) / 12)

Here, MiddleC is a constant defined to be 60, according to the MIDI standard, which is commonly used in measuring frequency, especially for applications.

Thus the frequency for middle C can be calculated as:

6.875 × 2^((3 + 60)/12) = 261.6255

Here, middle C can be rounded up to 262. In fact, "middle C" is known to have a frequency of 262 Hz. Any other note in the scale can be calculated by adjusting the MiddleC value of 60 up or down by the number of notes your note is away from middle C. For example, the next note Db would be calculated using a value of 61, and so on.

The other standard frequency value that came up from my research was that A is commonly defined as a having frequency of 440. It is used as a common tuning standard across different musical instruments. Somewhat arbitrarily, I simply chose to start the 12-note scale used in PianoBerry at A, with a frequency of 440. Table 13-1 shows the frequency values for each note in the 12-note scale, starting at A (440) and going on up through Bb, B, C, Db, D, Eb, E, F, Gb, G, and finally ending at Ab at 831 Hz. The values in this table are readily available on the Web from many different sources (although if you are math-inclined, you will no doubt feel compelled to calculate them manually with your slide rule).

Table 13-1   Frequency Values for Music Notes (12-Note Scale)

Note	Frequency
A	440
Bb	466
B	494
C	523
Db	554
D	587
Eb	622
E	659
F	698

Table 13-1	Continued
Note	Frequency
Gb	740
G	784
Ab	831

Creating the Main PianoBerry Application Skeleton

Now that you've covered some of the basic techniques that will allow you to play music notes, it is time to put these concepts to the test in a real program. In the next few sections, you build PianoBerry, which is a standard BlackBerry application built using the JDE. If you have not yet read Chapter 11, which introduces how to create your own BlackBerry applications using the BlackBerry Java Development Environment (JDE), now would be a great time to do so before proceeding. The rest of this chapter assumes you have read Chapter 11 and have understood the basic Java program structure introduced in the HelloBlackBerry project.

As shown in the following code listing, PianoBerry uses the exact same basic program structure as you used in the HelloBlackBerry project in Chapter 11. Just like HelloBlackBerry, PianoBerry starts life with a UiApplication class that contains main() and handles basic program startup. In PianoBerry, the only real responsibility of the application class is to launch the MainScreen, which is called PianoBerryScreen. PianoBerryScreen, as shown in the following code, does not do anything other than display a title, but that will change soon enough as you add menu handling, the ability to play audio tones, and keypad handling.

```java
public class PianoBerry extends UiApplication
{
    public static void main(String[] args)
    {
        PianoBerry theApp = new PianoBerry();
        theApp.enterEventDispatcher();
    }
    public PianoBerry()
    {
        pushScreen(new PianoBerryScreen());
    }
}
class PianoBerryScreen extends MainScreen
{
    public PianoBerryScreen()
    {
        super();
        LabelField applicationTitle =
            new LabelField("PianoBerry");
        setTitle(applicationTitle);
    }
}
```

If you follow the same steps for creating a new BlackBerry workspace and project as I described in Chapter 11, you can enter the preceding code into a source file called PianoBerry.java, and it will indeed compile and run on the BlackBerry Simulator and on a real device. Unfortunately, the way it stands it is quite possibly the most boring program ever created, so it is better to move on and start adding some functionality.

Adding the PianoBerry Menu System

The first thing you will do to enhance PianoBerry is add a menu system. Although your ultimate goal is to play music notes using keys on the BlackBerry keypad, when developing a new program I always like to start out by hanging the main program functions I need off of a menu. As you'll see, besides providing an alternative way to select a note to play, creating your own menu offers additional benefits, such as a means for adding custom handling for application closing as well as a menu for detecting the device's audio capabilities.

To add a trackwheel menu to your MainScreen class, you will need to make several enhancements to PianoBerryScreen. I would like PianoBerry's menu to have three main functions:

- The ability to play any of the 12 notes in the scale
- A custom Close() handler for when you wish to quit
- A special menu that will query the device and tell you what audio capabilities are supported

The following code listing shows PianoBerryScreen, enhanced with the ability to capture a trackwheel click and assemble a menu with the items you want:

```
class PianoBerryScreen extends MainScreen implements
TrackwheelListener
{
    // this is a boilerplate makeMenu function which
    // will properly create your menu.
    protected void makeMenu(Menu menu, int instance)
    {
        Field focus = ↵
UiApplication.getUiApplication().getActiveScreen().getLeafFieldWit
hFocus();
        if(focus != null) {
            ContextMenu contextMenu = focus.getContextMenu();
            if( !contextMenu.isEmpty()) {
                menu.add(contextMenu);
                menu.addSeparator();
            }
        }
        // here you add your own items
        menu.add(AudioSupportItem);
        // these menu items will play the note indicated
        menu.add(AItem);
        menu.add(BbItem);
```

```
        menu.add(BItem);
        menu.add(CItem);
        menu.add(DbItem);
        menu.add(DItem);
        menu.add(EbItem);
        menu.add(EItem);
        menu.add(FItem);
        menu.add(GbItem);
        menu.add(GItem);
        menu.add(AbItem);
        menu.add(_closeItem);
    }
    public boolean trackwheelClick( int status, int time )
    {
        Menu menu = new Menu();
        makeMenu(menu, 0);
        menu.show();
        return true;
    }
    public boolean trackwheelUnclick( int status, int time )
    {
        return true;
    }
    public boolean trackwheelRoll(int amount, int status, int
time)
    {
        return false;
    }
```

Now you need to add menu handlers for each of the menu items that are added to the menu in `makeMenu()`.

First you add a simple `closeItem` handler, as shown here:

```
    private MenuItem _closeItem = new MenuItem("Close", 0, 0)
    {
        public void run()
        {
            Dialog.alert("What? Leaving so soon?");
            System.exit(0);
        }
    };
```

Now, all this menu handler does is pop up a dialog box alert prior to exiting, but you can, of course, enhance it to allow the user to cancel the closing operation or do anything else you want.

Next, you add a handler for the `AudioSupportItem` menu item. `AudioSupportItem` will use the `Alert` functions covered earlier in the chapter to query the system and find out what level of audio support is included on the device PianoBerry is running on. Regardless of any other supported audio interfaces, PianoBerry uses only basic audio, but the query is nonetheless useful to have available, particularly because you might want to customize the program in the future for other audio capabilities.

```
private MenuItem AudioSupportItem = new MenuItem("Audio Support", 0, 0)
    {
        public void run()
        {
            boolean bAudio = Alert.isAudioSupported();
            boolean bMIDI = Alert.isMIDISupported();
            boolean bADPCM = Alert.isADPCMSupported();

            if (bAudio)
            {
                Dialog.alert("Audio supported");
            }
            if (bMIDI)
            {
                Dialog.alert("MIDI supported");
            }
            if (bADPCM)
            {
                Dialog.alert("ADPCM supported");
            }
        }
    };
```

This menu handler uses the `Alert` class interface to query the system and see if the three main audio subsystems are supported: Audio, ADPCM, and MIDI. In your simple program, PianoBerry does nothing more with this information than to display a dialog box for each interface supported, but the program perhaps could be enhanced to make use of MIDI or ADPCM if they are present to provide richer sound.

Finally, you add menu handlers for each of the music notes you want to be able to play: A, Bb, B, C, Db, D, Eb, E, F, Gb, G, and Ab, as shown in the following code listing:

```
private MenuItem AItem = new MenuItem("A", 0, 0)
    {
        public void run()
        {
            // Play an A note
        }
    };
private MenuItem BbItem = new MenuItem("Bb", 1, 0)
    {
        public void run()
        {
            // Play a Bb note
        }
    };

private MenuItem BItem = new MenuItem("B", 2, 0)
```

```
    {
        public void run()
        {
            // Play a B note
        }
    };
private MenuItem CItem = new MenuItem("C", 2, 0)
    {
        public void run()
        {
            // Play a C note
        }
    };
private MenuItem DbItem = new MenuItem("Db", 2, 0)
    {
        public void run()
        {
            // Play a Db note
        }
    };
private MenuItem DItem = new MenuItem("D", 2, 0)
    {
        public void run()
        {
            // Play a D note
        }
    };
private MenuItem EbItem = new MenuItem("Eb", 2, 0)
    {
        public void run()
        {
            // Play an Eb note
        }
    };
private MenuItem EItem = new MenuItem("E", 2, 0)
    {
        public void run()
        {
            // Play an E note
        }
    };
private MenuItem FItem = new MenuItem("F", 2, 0)
    {
        public void run()
        {
            // Play an F note
        }
    };
private MenuItem GbItem = new MenuItem("Gb", 2, 0)
    {
        public void run()
        {
```

```
                      // Play a Gb note
          }
    };
    private MenuItem GItem = new MenuItem("G", 2, 0)
        {
            public void run()
            {
                // Play a G note
            }
    };
    private MenuItem AbItem = new MenuItem("Ab", 2, 0)
        {
            public void run()
            {
                // Play an Ab note
            }
    };
```

You'll note that in the run() code for each menu handler, I have not yet added the actual code to play the corresponding note. For that, you need to define a "tune" structure for each note, as well as call the Alert.startAudio() function to play the note.

Playing Notes Using Alert.startAudio

In order to have your PianoBerry menu items actually play their corresponding note, you need to call the BlackBerry function Alert.startAudio(). Alert.startAudio takes two parameters, one that represents the "tune" to be played and another that represents the percent volume you want to play the tune at. The tune parameter is actually an array of integer pairs that use the following format: {frequency, duration}. Each pair thus plays a note of a given frequency for the length of time you specify. In this pair of integers, the frequency is expressed in MHz, while the duration is expressed as milliseconds.

Although the tune parameter is an array and can contain an actual sequence of notes to be played, for the purposes of PianoBerry you are interested in playing only a single note at a time. So what you need to do is to figure out the frequency value for each of the 12 notes in your scale, and then create pairs of integers that define the note and duration.

Earlier in the chapter you determined frequency values for each of the notes in your scale. Your scale starts arbitrarily at A with a value of 440, and proceeds higher up the scale until you reach the highest note, Ab, which has a defined value of 831. I suppose you could be lazy and simply type in the frequency number wherever you call Alert.startAudio(), but it is cleaner and makes your code easier to read if instead you create named variables that represent the notes you want to play.

So, to express these values properly in the PianoBerry Java code, you simply define a set of named short integers as data members within the PianoBerryScreen class, as follows:

```
    // these represent the frequencies for your scale
    private static final short A = 440; // 440.00
```

```
private static final short Bb = 466; // 466.16
private static final short B = 494; // 493.88
private static final short C = 523; // 523.25
private static final short Db = 554; // 554.36
private static final short D = 587; // 587.32
private static final short Eb = 622; // 622.25
private static final short E = 659; // 659.25
private static final short F = 698; // 698.45
private static final short Gb = 740; // 739.98
private static final short G = 784; // 783.99
private static final short Ab = 831; // 830.60
```

Once you've done this, anywhere you want to play a G note, you simply reference it by the variable name G instead of having to always remember that the frequency of G is 784. Similarly, rather than hard-coding a duration value for the note everywhere you call startAudio, you can predefine another data member called duration1sec that will have a value of 1000 (milliseconds).

```
private static final short duration1sec = 1000;
```

This makes it easier to see what your code is doing. Instead of specifying a G note that plays for 1 second as {784, 1000}, I think you will agree that it is nicer to write {G, duration1sec}.

You can also pre-define a volume level you want to use for the same reason:

```
private static final int VOLUME = 100; // Percentage volume.
```

Now, because startAudio() requires that you pass both the frequency and the duration as an integer array, the final little code-cleanliness thing you want to do is pre-define a set of named two-integer arrays, which you can then directly pass into the startAudio() call whenever you want to play a note. So, you write up 12 additional class data members, with names such as TUNEA, TUNEBb, TUNEC, and so on. These two-integer arrays are coded as follows:

```
// pre-defined tune arrays for use with the startAudio function
private static final short[] TUNEA = new short[] {A, duration1sec};
private static final short[] TUNEBb = new short[] {Bb, duration1sec};
private static final short[] TUNEB = new short[] {B, duration1sec};
private static final short[] TUNEC = new short[] {C, duration1sec};
private static final short[] TUNEDb = new short[] {Db, duration1sec};
private static final short[] TUNED = new short[] {D, duration1sec};
private static final short[] TUNEEb = new short[] {Eb, duration1sec};
private static final short[] TUNEE = new short[] {E, duration1sec};
private static final short[] TUNEF = new short[] {F, duration1sec};
private static final short[] TUNEGb = new short[] {Gb, duration1sec};
private static final short[] TUNEG = new short[] {G, duration1sec};
private static final short[] TUNEAb = new short[] {Ab, duration1sec};
```

Now you've set yourself up perfectly so that whenever you need to play a tune, you just call Alert.startAudio() as follows:

```
Alert.startAudio(TUNEAb, VOLUME);
```

You can now fill in your menu handlers with calls to `startAudio`, as follows:

```
private MenuItem AItem = new MenuItem("A", 0, 0)
    {
        public void run()
        {
            // Play an A note for 1 second
                            Alert.startAudio (TUNEA, VOLUME)
        }
    };
```

The remaining 11 menu handlers for the notes in your scale are coded in a similar fashion.

At this point, if you've entered all the pieces of code correctly, you can actually test out PianoBerry using the menu system on either the BlackBerry Simulator or an actual device. When you run PianoBerry, you will see a blank screen with a simple title, "PianoBerry." To play a note, click the trackwheel menu and choose one of the menu items corresponding to a note, as shown in Figure 13-1.

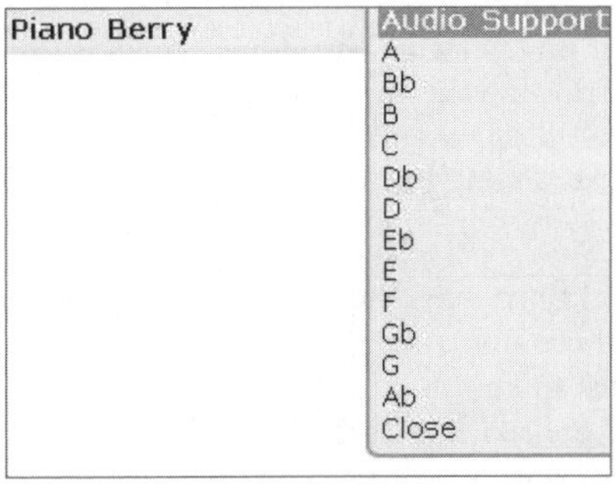

FIGURE **13-1**: PianoBerry's main menu lists the notes you can play.

Drum roll, please. When you click the menu item for a note in the scale, you should hear the note through either your computer speaker or the BlackBerry speaker. That first note sounds so sweet!

Capturing Keypad Events

At this point the hard work is done. You've coaxed your BlackBerry into playing 12 different notes from a piano scale. The only problem is that every time you want to play a note you have to click the menu to choose a note. That's kind of tedious, right? If this was how a real piano worked, Beethoven might very well have decided to take up gardening! Obviously you need to have a more intuitive way to play notes if you want to convince anyone to compose a piano sonata on their BlackBerry.

A quick glance at a BlackBerry yields the clear solution: PianoBerry should assign each note to a key on the BlackBerry keypad, so that when you press a key, a note plays, just like the keys on a real piano. To be sure, the BlackBerry QWERTY keypad layout is not a perfect match for a piano keyboard, but with a little creative thinking in terms of mapping keys to notes, you should be able to make it work.

You now have a plan, but you also have a challenge: How does a BlackBerry application become aware that the user pressed a key on the keypad? Certainly it must be possible to do so because numerous BlackBerry applications let you type text using the keypad and even assign special functions to different keys.

In the development projects you've covered thus far, you have not needed to catch keystrokes, but you have had to trap a different kind of hardware event, the trackwheel. In each of the chapter examples, you've generally implemented the `TrackwheelListener` interface in order to receive `trackwheelClick` events and display a menu. What if there were a similar mechanism for trapping keypad events?

Sure enough, there is. The `KeyListener` interface is typically added to a `MainScreen` class that wants to "listen" in on keypad events. With `TrackwheelListener`, you needed to add handlers for `trackwheelClick`, `trackwheelRoll`, and `trackwheelUnclick`. These handlers acted as an override to the built-in `MainScreen` trackwheel handling. Similarly, with `KeyListener` the member functions you can override in your `MainScreen` class are `keyChar`, `keyDown`, `keyUp`, `keyStatus`, and `keyRepeat`. `keyDown`, `keyUp`, `keyStatus`, and `keyRepeat` let you have pretty granular control over specific key actions, but `keyChar` is the one you want to focus on now.

The `keyChar()` function notifies you when BlackBerry has determined that the user has formed a character with a single key press or a valid combination of a key with modifier keys such as ALT, SHIFT, or CAPS LOCK. In contrast to `keyChar()`, `keyDown` and `keyUp` are lower-level handlers that just detect when a key is pressed or released. The job of figuring out that the user meant to type a capital *A* is up to you. With `keyChar()`, the handler does all the interpretation for you, so you don't have to worry about `keyUp()` or `keyDown()`.

The `keyChar()` function looks like this:

```
public boolean keyChar(char key, int status, int time)
```

Although `keyChar` passes your class three parameters, the main piece of information is the `key` parameter. The others are simply extra information in case you want to know if any modifier keys were pressed or what the exact time was when the key was pressed. The `key` parameter represents the actual character that was generated by the keyboard event.

On other kinds of computers, figuring out what character was entered often means you have to learn ASCII codes and hexadecimal numbers. BlackBerry has simplified things for programmers by offering a special Java class called `Characters` that contains a named value representing every possible character that can be generated by the keypad. So a capital *A* is represented by the constant `Characters.LATIN_CAPITAL_LETTER_A`, a lowercase *c* is represented by the constant `Characters.LATIN_SMALL_LETTER_C`, and so on.

Armed with this information you can now test for specific characters that were pressed like so:

```
public boolean keyChar(char key, int status, int time)
{
    switch (key)
    {
        case Characters.LATIN_CAPITAL_LETTER_A:
        {
            // a capital "A" was pressed - do something
            return true;
        }
        // add other case statements here for each character
        // you want to handle
    }
    return false;
}
```

Mapping BlackBerry Keys to Piano Keys

Now that you know how to capture keypad events and trap when specific characters are entered, you have an interesting decision to make. Which BlackBerry keys should play which music notes?

Given the QWERTY keyboard layout and how different it is from a standard piano keyboard, plus the lack of anything close to the white key/black key piano keyboard arrangement, how you map BlackBerry keys to piano notes is really kind of arbitrary. There is no "right" way to do it. One possibility to consider is to assign each full note to its corresponding letter on the keypad (an A note would play if you pressed the A key, and so on). But what about flatted notes such as Ab? Conceivably that could be handled by using a modifier key such as ALT or SHIFT, but ultimately that seems awkward. Besides, the whole point of this exercise is to make it easier to play notes than it is by using the trackwheel menu; adding special keystrokes is at odds with that goal.

A simpler solution is to take the 12 keys that run across the top of the BlackBerry keypad and map them sequentially, starting at the low A and ending in the high Ab at the top of the scale. To accomplish this, you can use the mapping shown in Table 13-2.

Table 13-2 PianoBerry Key Mappings

BlackBerry Key	Piano Note
A	A
Q	Bb
W	B
E	C

Table 13-2 *Continued*	
BlackBerry Key	**Piano Note**
R	Db
T	D
Y	Eb
U	E
I	F
O	Gb
P	G
L	Ab

If you ignore for a moment that the letters on the keys don't match up at all with the letters of the notes, it actually sort of makes sense in that keys are laid out in the same sequence left to right as they would be on a real piano. Don't worry. If you hate the layout, just come up with a better idea and change the code! Speaking of the code, the following code illustrates how to implement this keypad mapping using your keyChar() handler:

```
public boolean keyChar(char key, int status, int time)
{
    super.keyChar(key, status, time);
    switch (key)
    {
        case Characters.LATIN_CAPITAL_LETTER_A:
        case Characters.LATIN_SMALL_LETTER_A:
        {
            Alert.startAudio(TUNEA, VOLUME);
            return true;
        }
        case Characters.LATIN_CAPITAL_LETTER_Q:
        case Characters.LATIN_SMALL_LETTER_Q:
        {
            Alert.startAudio(TUNEBb, VOLUME);
            return true;
        }
        case Characters.LATIN_CAPITAL_LETTER_W:
        case Characters.LATIN_SMALL_LETTER_W:
        {
            Alert.startAudio(TUNEB, VOLUME);
            return true;
        }
        case Characters.LATIN_CAPITAL_LETTER_E:
        case Characters.LATIN_SMALL_LETTER_E:
        {
            Alert.startAudio(TUNEC, VOLUME);
            return true;
        }
```

```
        case Characters.LATIN_CAPITAL_LETTER_R:
        case Characters.LATIN_SMALL_LETTER_R:
        {
            Alert.startAudio(TUNEDb, VOLUME);
            return true;
        }
        case Characters.LATIN_CAPITAL_LETTER_T:
        case Characters.LATIN_SMALL_LETTER_T:
        {
            Alert.startAudio(TUNED, VOLUME);
            return true;
        }
        case Characters.LATIN_CAPITAL_LETTER_Y:
        case Characters.LATIN_SMALL_LETTER_Y:
        {
            Alert.startAudio(TUNEEb, VOLUME);
            return true;
        }
        case Characters.LATIN_CAPITAL_LETTER_U:
        case Characters.LATIN_SMALL_LETTER_U:
        {
            Alert.startAudio(TUNEE, VOLUME);
            return true;
        }
        case Characters.LATIN_CAPITAL_LETTER_I:
        case Characters.LATIN_SMALL_LETTER_I:
        {
            Alert.startAudio(TUNEF, VOLUME);
            return true;
        }
        case Characters.LATIN_CAPITAL_LETTER_O:
        case Characters.LATIN_SMALL_LETTER_O:
        {
            Alert.startAudio(TUNEGb, VOLUME);
            return true;
        }
        case Characters.LATIN_CAPITAL_LETTER_P:
        case Characters.LATIN_SMALL_LETTER_P:
        {
            Alert.startAudio(TUNEG, VOLUME);
            return true;
        }
        case Characters.LATIN_CAPITAL_LETTER_L:
        case Characters.LATIN_SMALL_LETTER_L:
        {
            Alert.startAudio(TUNEAb, VOLUME);
            return true;
        }
return false;
}
```

The preceding code is pretty straightforward. It traps each keypad letter in your layout, and it plays the appropriate music note using `Alert.startAudio()`.

PianoBerry: Putting It All Together

You did it! You now have a working program that can play 12 notes on the BlackBerry keypad. The keyboard layout is a bit strange, and the audio quality is a far cry from a baby grand, but it works nonetheless.

Here is the complete source code listing for PianoBerry. (The full source code and the JDE project are also available on the Wiley website at www.wiley.com/go/extremetech.) If you build this source in the BlackBerry JDE, you will wind up with a PianoBerry program that can be installed to your BlackBerry through the BlackBerry Desktop Application Loader feature.

```
/**
 * PianoBerry
 */
import net.rim.device.api.ui.*;
import net.rim.device.api.ui.component.*;
import net.rim.device.api.ui.container.*;
import net.rim.device.api.system.*;
import java.util.*;
public class PianoBerry extends UiApplication
{
    public static void main(String[] args)
    {
        PianoBerry theApp = new PianoBerry();
        theApp.enterEventDispatcher();
    }

    public PianoBerry()
    {
        pushScreen(new PianoBerryScreen());
    }

}
class PianoBerryScreen extends MainScreen implements KeyListener, ↵
TrackwheelListener
{
    // these represent the frequencies for your scale
    private static final short A = 440; // 440.00
    private static final short Bb = 466; // 466.16
    private static final short B = 494; // 493.88
    private static final short C = 523; // 523.25
    private static final short Db = 554; // 554.36
    private static final short D = 587; // 587.32
    private static final short Eb = 622; // 622.25
    private static final short E = 659; // 659.25
    private static final short F = 698; // 698.45
    private static final short Gb = 740; // 739.98
    private static final short G = 784; // 783.99
    private static final short Ab = 831; // 830.60

    // how long each note will play for (in milliseconds)
    private static final short duration1sec = 1000;
```

```
// pre-defined tune arrays for use with the startAudio function
private static final short[] TUNEA = new short[] {A, duration1sec};
private static final short[] TUNEBb = new short[] {Bb, duration1sec};
private static final short[] TUNEB = new short[] {B, duration1sec};
private static final short[] TUNEC = new short[] {C, duration1sec};
private static final short[] TUNEDb = new short[] {Db, duration1sec};
private static final short[] TUNED = new short[] {D, duration1sec};
private static final short[] TUNEEb = new short[] {Eb, duration1sec};
private static final short[] TUNEE = new short[] {E, duration1sec};
private static final short[] TUNEF = new short[] {F, duration1sec};
private static final short[] TUNEGb = new short[] {Gb, duration1sec};
private static final short[] TUNEG = new short[] {G, duration1sec};
private static final short[] TUNEAb = new short[] {Ab, duration1sec};
private static final int VOLUME = 100; // Percentage volume.
// some menu items you will add to your menu
private MenuItem _closeItem = new MenuItem("Close", 0, 0)
    {
        public void run()
        {
            onClose();
        }
    };
// this menu is useful to show what audio capabilities ↵
are supported on a device
private MenuItem AudioSupportItem = new MenuItem("Audio Support", 0, 0)
    {
        public void run()
        {
            boolean bAudio = Alert.isAudioSupported();
            boolean bBuzzer = Alert.isBuzzerSupported();
            boolean bVibrate = Alert.isVibrateSupported();
            boolean bMIDI = Alert.isMIDISupported();
            boolean bADPCM = Alert.isADPCMSupported();

            if (bAudio)
            {
                Dialog.alert("Audio supported");
            }
            if (bMIDI)
            {
                Dialog.alert("MIDI supported");
            }
            if (bADPCM)
            {
                Dialog.alert("ADPCM supported");
            }

            // shows how to set the volume
            Alert.setVolume (100);

        }
    };
```

```java
    // these are all menu items just as alternative means for selecting a
note.
    private MenuItem AItem = new MenuItem("A", 0, 0)
    {
        public void run()
        {
            Alert.startAudio(TUNEA, VOLUME);
        }
    };
    private MenuItem BbItem = new MenuItem("Bb", 1, 0)
    {
        public void run()
        {
            Alert.startAudio(TUNEBb, VOLUME);
        }
    };

    private MenuItem BItem = new MenuItem("B", 2, 0)
    {
        public void run()
        {
            Alert.startAudio(TUNEB, VOLUME);
        }
    };
    private MenuItem CItem = new MenuItem("C", 2, 0)
    {
        public void run()
        {
            Alert.startAudio(TUNEC, VOLUME);
        }
    };
    private MenuItem DbItem = new MenuItem("Db", 2, 0)
    {
        public void run()
        {
            Alert.startAudio(TUNEDb, VOLUME);
        }
    };
    private MenuItem DItem = new MenuItem("D", 2, 0)
    {
        public void run()
        {
            Alert.startAudio(TUNED, VOLUME);
        }
    };
    private MenuItem EbItem = new MenuItem("Eb", 2, 0)
    {
        public void run()
        {
            Alert.startAudio(TUNEEb, VOLUME);
        }
```

```
        };
private MenuItem EItem = new MenuItem("E", 2, 0)
    {
        public void run()
        {
            Alert.startAudio(TUNEE, VOLUME);
        }
    };
private MenuItem FItem = new MenuItem("F", 2, 0)
    {
        public void run()
        {
            Alert.startAudio(TUNEF, VOLUME);
        }
    };
private MenuItem GbItem = new MenuItem("Gb", 2, 0)
    {
        public void run()
        {
            Alert.startAudio(TUNEGb, VOLUME);
        }
    };
private MenuItem GItem = new MenuItem("G", 2, 0)
    {
        public void run()
        {
            Alert.startAudio(TUNEG, VOLUME);
        }
    };
private MenuItem AbItem = new MenuItem("Ab", 2, 0)
    {
        public void run()
        {
            Alert.startAudio(TUNEAb, VOLUME);
        }
    };

public PianoBerryScreen()
{
    super();
    LabelField applicationTitle =
        new LabelField("Piano Berry");
    setTitle(applicationTitle);
}
public boolean onClose()
{
    Dialog.alert("What? Leaving so soon?");
    System.exit(0);
    return true;
}
```

```
        // overrides MainScreen's standard keypad handling by ↵
associating the top row of keys to the notes of the scale
        // Starting from the left side of the keyboard, the mappings are:
        // Key  Note
        // A    A
        // Q    Bb
        // W    B
        // E    C
        // R    Db
        // T    D
        // Y    Eb
        // U    E
        // I    F
        // O    Gb
        // P    G
        // L    A
        public boolean keyChar(char key, int status, int time)
        {
            super.keyChar(key, status, time);
            switch (key)
            {
                case Characters.LATIN_CAPITAL_LETTER_A:
                case Characters.LATIN_SMALL_LETTER_A:
                {
                    Alert.startAudio(TUNEA, VOLUME);
                    return true;
                }
                case Characters.LATIN_CAPITAL_LETTER_Q:
                case Characters.LATIN_SMALL_LETTER_Q:
                {
                    Alert.startAudio(TUNEBb, VOLUME);
                    return true;
                }
                case Characters.LATIN_CAPITAL_LETTER_W:
                case Characters.LATIN_SMALL_LETTER_W:
                {
                    Alert.startAudio(TUNEB, VOLUME);
                    return true;
                }
                case Characters.LATIN_CAPITAL_LETTER_E:
                case Characters.LATIN_SMALL_LETTER_E:
                {
                    Alert.startAudio(TUNEC, VOLUME);
                    return true;
                }
                case Characters.LATIN_CAPITAL_LETTER_R:
                case Characters.LATIN_SMALL_LETTER_R:
                {
                    Alert.startAudio(TUNEDb, VOLUME);
                    return true;
```

```
        }
        case Characters.LATIN_CAPITAL_LETTER_T:
        case Characters.LATIN_SMALL_LETTER_T:
        {
            Alert.startAudio(TUNED, VOLUME);
            return true;
        }
        case Characters.LATIN_CAPITAL_LETTER_Y:
        case Characters.LATIN_SMALL_LETTER_Y:
        {
            Alert.startAudio(TUNEEb, VOLUME);
            return true;
        }
        case Characters.LATIN_CAPITAL_LETTER_U:
        case Characters.LATIN_SMALL_LETTER_U:
        {
            Alert.startAudio(TUNEE, VOLUME);
            return true;
        }
        case Characters.LATIN_CAPITAL_LETTER_I:
        case Characters.LATIN_SMALL_LETTER_I:
        {
            Alert.startAudio(TUNEF, VOLUME);
            return true;
        }
        case Characters.LATIN_CAPITAL_LETTER_O:
        case Characters.LATIN_SMALL_LETTER_O:
        {
            Alert.startAudio(TUNEGb, VOLUME);
            return true;
        }
        case Characters.LATIN_CAPITAL_LETTER_P:
        case Characters.LATIN_SMALL_LETTER_P:
        {
            Alert.startAudio(TUNEG, VOLUME);
            return true;
        }
        case Characters.LATIN_CAPITAL_LETTER_L:
        case Characters.LATIN_SMALL_LETTER_L:
        {
            Alert.startAudio(TUNEAb, VOLUME);
            return true;
        }

         // intercept the ESC key - exit the app on its receipt
        case Characters.ESCAPE:
        {
            if (Dialog.YES == Dialog.ask(Dialog.D_YES_NO, ↵
"Are you sure you want to exit?", Dialog.YES ))
            {
                OnClose ();
```

```
                    }
                    else
                    {
                        return true;
                    }
                    break;
                }
            }
            return false;
        }
    public boolean keyDown(int keycode, int time)
    {
        return false;
    }
    public boolean keyRepeat(int keycode, int time)
    {
        return false;
    }
    public boolean keyStatus(int keycode, int time)
    {
        return false;
    }
    public boolean keyUp(int keycode, int time)
    {
        return false;
    }
    // this overrides makeMenu in UIApplication, and gives you ↵
full control over your menu
    protected void makeMenu(Menu menu, int instance)
    {
        // this attempts to see if there are any context menus added, ↵
and makes sure that they are retained
        Field focus = ↵
UiApplication.getUiApplication().getActiveScreen().getLeafFieldWithFocus();
        if(focus != null) {
            ContextMenu contextMenu = focus.getContextMenu();
            if( !contextMenu.isEmpty()) {
                menu.add(contextMenu);
                menu.addSeparator();
            }
        }
        // here you add your own items
        menu.add(AudioSupportItem);
        menu.add(AItem);
        menu.add(BbItem);
        menu.add(BItem);
        menu.add(CItem);
        menu.add(DbItem);
        menu.add(DItem);
        menu.add(EbItem);
        menu.add(EItem);
        menu.add(FItem);
        menu.add(GbItem);
```

```
        menu.add(GItem);
        menu.add(AbItem);
        menu.add(_closeItem);
    }

    public boolean trackwheelClick( int status, int time )
    {
        Menu menu = new Menu();

        makeMenu(menu, 0);

        menu.show();

        return true;
    }

    public boolean trackwheelUnclick( int status, int time )
    {

        return true;
    }

    public boolean trackwheelRoll(int amount, int status, int time)
    {
        return false;
    }

}
```

Summary

In this chapter you were able to take a standard BlackBerry and turn it into a tiny little piano. Along the way I showed you how to play audio using the BlackBerry `Alert` interface and how to trap BlackBerry keypad events.

PianoBerry is far from perfect, and if you are up for a challenge, consider enhancing the following areas:

- Using the ADPCM or MIDI interface to play richer audio
- Storing the notes played in a file for later playback
- Volume control
- Visual display of the notes played
- Using varying note durations (half-notes, quarter-notes, and so on)

If you want to try to implement these features, most of the information you will need is scattered throughout the BlackBerry developer guides, the BlackBerry online knowledge base, and the example programs that come with the BlackBerry JDE.

Meet BlackBerry, Your Personal Masseuse

I n the preceding chapter you worked on a programming project that turns a BlackBerry into a toy piano. If you followed the example code, you saw that it made use of the BlackBerry `Alert` interface to force the BlackBerry to play audio through the BlackBerry speaker. If you were paying close attention, you may have even noticed that you could do other things with the `Alert` interface than play audio. The `Alert` interface can be used to directly control the standard BlackBerry vibrate mode.

Vibrate mode is, of course, a standard feature on BlackBerry devices (and for that matter, just about every other handheld and smartphone device) and is used as a means for alerting you when an event of significance has occurred. Examples of this would be an incoming phone call, the arrival of a new e-mail or voice mail message, or an appointment reminder. Vibrate mode is most useful in situations when it would be inconvenient (or downright rude) to have your device play audible sounds — for example, in a movie theater. If you must carry your phone into the theater, it is polite to set it for vibrate mode. That way, only you are able to tell if your phone is ringing. (Now if only you could make it so that talkative movie-goers had their voices set to vibrate!)

BlackBerry users have some control over the use of vibrate mode on their devices. The BlackBerry Profiles icon lets you manage several different profiles that govern how your device will behave when different kinds of events and notifications occur. Within each profile are settings for each kind of alert: Calendar, Messages, Phone, and so on. The idea is that you can define a set of behaviors for different situations you might be in. A set of pre-defined profiles are provided, including Loud, Vibrate, Quiet, Normal, Phone Only, and Off. Although these should be sufficient, you have the ability to create new custom profiles of your own choosing. If you are entering a movie theater, simply switch your device to the Vibrate profile. When you come out, switch it to Normal. If you are on a loud city street or at an outdoor sporting event, you might want to use Loud. And so on.

Figure 14-1 shows how to use BlackBerry Profiles to edit your vibrate settings.

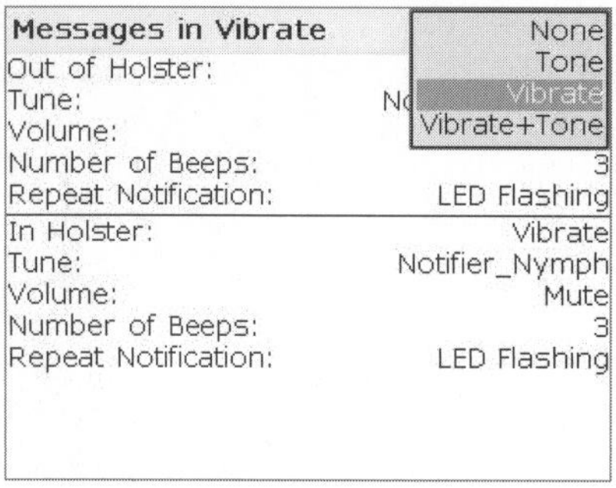

FIGURE **14-1: Configuring vibrate mode with BlackBerry Profiles**

All this is very nice for your average user who is satisfied with basic control of vibrate mode. But if you are reading this book, you are not your average BlackBerry user, are you? I didn't think so! The BlackBerry SDK makes available a function that is accessible from an application program which can directly control vibrate mode. Naturally I could not resist the temptation to figure out some way to use it more creatively.

What I came up with was a program that would turn a BlackBerry into a handheld masseuse. Rather than wait for a phone call or reminder to start vibrate mode, Masseuse lets you turn vibrate on or off with a click of the BlackBerry trackwheel. Once turned on, Masseuse forces your BlackBerry to vibrate until you turn it off.

Read on to learn more about how you can create Masseuse with just some basic programming steps.

Vibrate Mode and the BlackBerry Alert Interface

In the previous chapter you took a look at the BlackBerry SDK `Alert` class. The `Alert` class offers a number of different mechanisms for notifying BlackBerry users of interesting events that have occurred, such as incoming phone calls and appointment reminders. Because your main goal for the PianoBerry project was to coax a BlackBerry into playing musical notes over the device speaker, you focused on the `Alert` interface's audio-related functionality, specifically `startAudio()`, `isAudioSupported()`, and `setVolume()`.

If you opened up the API help in the BlackBerry JDE and read the description for the `Alert` class closely, you may have noticed that there were a couple of interesting-looking functions that looked like they might control the BlackBerry vibration mode. In fact, two functions in particular, called `startBuzzer()` and `startVibrate()`, are related to controlling the BlackBerry vibrate feature. `startBuzzer()` is the older of the two functions and provides the ability to start and stop a vibrate-like effect on older BlackBerry device models.

The most current information on the BlackBerry Developer knowledge base advises that `startBuzzer()` has been replaced by the `startVibrate()` function, and that your program should make use of `startVibrate()` instead of `startBuzzer()` when running on newer devices. To manage this change, the SDK offers the functions isBuzzerSupported() and isVibrateSupported() to help your program decide which is the best function to use on the device it is running on. To detect whether to use the buzzer or vibrate function, you can add the following lines to your BlackBerry program:

```
boolean bBuzzer = Alert.isBuzzerSupported ();
boolean bVibrate = Alert.isVibrateSupported ();
```

If bBuzzer returns true, then the Buzzer interface is supported. If bVibrate returns true, then the Vibrate interface is supported. It is possible on relatively recent devices that both interfaces are supported, in which case you should just use the vibrate mode. In my tests on a modern 8700 device, only isVibrateSupported() returns true. Although you could certainly support both, given that Vibrate has been supported for some time now, you will assume the Vibrate interface for this project.

Creating the Masseuse Application Skeleton

Masseuse will be created as a standard BlackBerry application that is built using the JDE. If you have not yet read Chapter 11, which introduces how to create your own BlackBerry applications using the BlackBerry Java Development Environment (JDE), you should take the opportunity to do so now because the rest of this chapter assumes you know how to create and build a simple BlackBerry program in Java using the JDE. Also, although not required, reading the previous chapter and working the PianoBerry project will make the concepts in this chapter seem simple because both programs rely on the Alert interface.

In the following code listing, you start Masseuse with the same basic program structure as you used in the beginning of the PianoBerry project, which in turn was originally based on the HelloBlackBerry project in Chapter 11. Masseuse has a standard UiApplication class that contains main() and handles basic program startup. The real action moving forward is contained in MasseuseScreen, which is derived from the BlackBerry MainScreen class. You use the following code skeleton as the starting point for the rest of Masseuse.

```
public class Masseuse extends UiApplication
{
    public static void main(String[] args)
    {
        Masseuse theApp = new Masseuse();
        theApp.enterEventDispatcher();
    }

    public Masseuse()
    {
        MasseuseScreen myScreen = new MasseuseScreen();
        pushScreen(myScreen);

    }

}
class MasseuseScreen extends MainScreen
```

```
{
    public MasseuseScreen()
    {
        super();
        LabelField applicationTitle =
            new LabelField("Masseuse");
        setTitle(applicationTitle);
    }
}
```

To build Masseuse, you need to follow the same steps for creating a new BlackBerry workspace and project as described in Chapter 11. The preceding code should be entered in a text file called Masseuse.java, and included in the Masseuse project. If you have avoided any typing errors, Masseuse.java will compile and run on the BlackBerry Simulator and on a real device.

Adding a Trackwheel Menu to Masseuse

As per the requirements described earlier for Masseuse, there needs to be a way to manually start and stop Masseuse from vibrating. The easiest way to do this is to add a menu system with Start and Stop menu items on it.

To add a trackwheel menu to the MainScreen class, you just need to add the following code:

```
class MasseuseScreen extends MainScreen implements ↵
TrackwheelListener
{
    // some menu items you will add to the menu
    private MenuItem closeItem = new MenuItem("Close", 0, 0)
        {
            public void run()
            {
                onExit();
            }
        };
    private MenuItem supportItem = new MenuItem("Support", 0, 0)
        {
            public void run()
            {
                boolean bBuzzer = Alert.isBuzzerSupported();
                boolean bVibrate = Alert.isVibrateSupported();
                if (bBuzzer)
                {
                    Dialog.alert("Buzzer supported");
                }
                if (bVibrate)
                {
                    Dialog.alert("Vibrate supported");
                }
            }
        };
```

```
    private MenuItem startItem = new MenuItem("Start", 0, 0)
        {
            public void run()
            {
                // start vibrating
            }
        };

    private MenuItem stopItem = new MenuItem("Stop", 1, 0)
        {
            public void run()
            {
                // stop vibrating
            }
        };

    public MasseuseScreen()
    {
        super();
        LabelField applicationTitle =
            new LabelField("Masseuse");
        setTitle(applicationTitle);
    }
    public boolean onClose()
    {
        Dialog.alert("What? Leaving so soon?");
        System.exit(0);
        return true;
    }

    protected void makeMenu(Menu menu, int instance)
    {
        // this attempts to see if there are any context ↵
menus added, and makes sure that they are retained
        Field focus = ↵
UiApplication.getUiApplication().getActiveScreen()↵
.getLeafFieldWithFocus();
        if(focus != null) {
            ContextMenu contextMenu = focus.getContextMenu();
            if( !contextMenu.isEmpty()) {
                menu.add(contextMenu);
                menu.addSeparator();
            }
        }
        // here you add your own items
        menu.add(supportItem);
        menu.add(startItem);
        menu.add(stopItem);
        menu.add(closeItem);
    }

    public boolean trackwheelClick( int status, int time )
    {
        Menu menu = new Menu();
```

```
        makeMenu(menu, 0);

        menu.show();

        return true;
    }

    public boolean trackwheelUnclick( int status, int time )
    {
        return true;
    }

    public boolean trackwheelRoll↵
(int amount, int status, int time)
    {
        return false;
    }
```

This is fairly standard menu code for a BlackBerry application, and it uses the same techniques as are used in the other programming projects in this book. First, you modified the MasseuseScreen class to extend TrackwheelListener, to give the class the ability to capture trackwheel events. Next, you added a boilerplate makeMenu function, which constructs the menu and menu items. Finally, you add a set of menu handlers for Close, Support, Start, and Stop.

For the moment, the menu handlers don't do anything, so you are now at the point where you need to implement Start and Stop by using Alert.startVibrate().

Forcing Vibrate Mode Using Alert.startVibrate()

To start a vibrate alert manually from within a BlackBerry program, you need to call Alert.startVibrate, which is part of the Alert interface and looks like this:

```
    public static void startVibrate (int duration)
```

Interestingly, startVibrate takes a parameter that specifies how long the vibration should last. This parameter is expressed in milliseconds, so to start a vibration that is one second long, you would pass a value of 1000 like so:

```
Alert.startVibrate (1000); // vibrate for 1 second
```

To try it out, just add this line of code to the Start menu handler in Masseuse, as follows:

```
    private MenuItem startItem = new MenuItem("Start", 0, 0)
        {
            public void run()
            {
                Alert.startVibrate (1000); // vibrate for 1 second
            }
        };
```

If you build Masseuse with this code change and then click the trackwheel menu and choose Start, your BlackBerry vibrates for one second. Pretty cool!

Note
If you want to try running Masseuse in the BlackBerry Simulator on your desktop computer, you may be surprised to find that vibration mode is indeed supported. But instead of causing your entire computer to vibrate until it breaks into a million pieces (a bad thing, I would think), those clever folks at Research In Motion designed it so that the BlackBerry Simulator will simulate vibration mode by visually "shaking" the image of the device on the display.

At this point you might be thinking, "But wait! It lasts only one second!" You noticed that, did you? I realize that if you had paid for a real massage and the masseuse stopped after just one second, you'd probably feel a bit cheated. Well, with `startVibrate`, you can extend the duration to last a little bit longer. But according to the BlackBerry API documentation for `startVibrate`, the maximum value you can pass is 25500, or 25 seconds. This is a little better than 1 second, but still not quite the luxurious long-lasting massage you were hoping for. You need a way to make the vibration go on indefinitely, until the Stop menu item is selected.

Speaking of stop, how do you stop vibration mode? Read on.

Handling vibrateDone with AlertListener

It is not surprising that BlackBerry does not provide a simple way to make a vibration last indefinitely. There's no real justifiable business use for such a feature and, of course, if you let the vibration go on long enough it will drain the BlackBerry battery. (How long it actually takes to drain the battery will vary, depending on the specific BlackBerry model.) But there is a way to get it done.

If you read the description for `Alert.startVibrate` closely, it states that "When the Alert is completed, the AlertListener.buzzerDone (int) method is invoked on the event thread." While this statement doesn't exactly explain things in plain-speak, it does indicate that you should take a look at the `AlertListener` class. The `AlertListener` class, like `TrackwheelListener` and `KeyListener`, allows your class to receive events and even trap them with custom handling if you want. In the case of `AlertListener`, the events you can trap include notifications that a vibration initiated from `Alert.startVibrate` has completed. When a vibration is complete, `AlertListener` calls your `vibrateDone()` method if you provide one.

If Masseuse can get notified whenever a vibration stops, theoretically it should just be a simple matter of restarting it again, right? What you have to do is add `AlertListener` to the top of the `MasseuseScreen` class, as follows:

```
class MasseuseScreen extends MainScreen implements ↵
TrackwheelListener, AlertListener
```

This signals the BlackBerry OS that it should notify `MasseuseScreen` whenever a vibration initiated from `Alert.startVibrate()` completes. To handle the notification, you need to add an override to the `stopVibrate` method of `AlertListener` in the class, like so:

```
public void vibrateDone(int reason)
{
    // restart the vibration!
    Alert.startVibrate(1000);
    return;
}
```

Finally, you need to do one more thing and that is to explicitly add `MasseuseScreen` to the list of classes that implement `AlertListener`. This is done by adding a call to `addAlertListener` to the main `UiApplication` class. This call can be made in the constructor, so now the main class looks like this:

```
public class Masseuse extends UiApplication
{
    //private myScreen _mainScreen;

    public static void main(String[] args)
    {
        Masseuse theApp = new Masseuse();
        theApp.enterEventDispatcher();
    }

    public Masseuse()
    {
        MasseuseScreen myScreen = new MasseuseScreen();
        pushScreen(myScreen);
        // add MasseuseScreen to the list of listening classes
        addAlertListener(myScreen);
    }

}
```

Note It is somewhat strange that `AlertListener` requires an explicit call like this, whereas `KeyListener` and `TrackwheelListener` do not, but that's the way it works.

Now that you can use `vibrateDone()` to "catch" whenever the `startVibrate()` duration has ended, all you need to do is restart it. Here is how it is done:

```
    public void vibrateDone(int reason)
    {
        // if the vibration ended because the duration was over
        // just restart it. Let it stop for all other reasons
        if (reason == REASON_COMPLETED)
        {
            Alert.startVibrate(1000);
        }
        return;
    }
```

In `vibrateDone()`, you are passed a `reason` for why the vibration ended. This reason can be REASON_COMPLETED, REASON_STOP_CALLED, or REASON_KEY_PRESSED. If the `reason` code indicates that the vibration stopped simply because the duration ran out, you can restart the vibration with another call to `startVibrate()`. This cycle continues until either you explicitly call `stopVibrate()` (from the trackwheel menu) or the user presses any key.

Masseuse: Putting It All Together

Here is the complete source code listing for Masseuse (as with all of the book programming projects, the full source code and the JDE project for Masseuse are also available on the Wiley website at www.wiley.com/go/extremetech).

If you build the following source code in the BlackBerry JDE, you wind up with a BlackBerry Masseuse program, shown in Figure 14-2, which can be installed to your BlackBerry through the BlackBerry Desktop Application Loader feature.

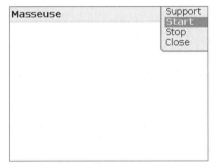

FIGURE 14-2: Masseuse running on my BlackBerry

```
/**
 * Masseuse
 */
import net.rim.device.api.ui.*;
import net.rim.device.api.ui.component.*;
import net.rim.device.api.ui.container.*;
import net.rim.device.api.system.*;
import java.util.*;

public class Masseuse extends UiApplication
{

    public static void main(String[] args)
    {
        Masseuse theApp = new Masseuse();
        theApp.enterEventDispatcher();
    }

    public Masseuse()
    {
        MasseuseScreen myScreen = new MasseuseScreen();
        pushScreen(myScreen);
        addAlertListener(myScreen);

    }

}
```

```java
class MasseuseScreen extends MainScreen implements ↵
TrackwheelListener, AlertListener
{
    // some menu items you will add to the menu
    private MenuItem _closeItem = new MenuItem("Close", 0, 0)
        {
            public void run()
            {
                onExit();
            }
        };

    private MenuItem supportItem = new MenuItem("Support", 0, 0)
        {
            public void run()
            {
                boolean bBuzzer = Alert.isBuzzerSupported();
                boolean bVibrate = Alert.isVibrateSupported();
                if (bBuzzer)
                {
                    Dialog.alert("Buzzer supported");
                }
                if (bVibrate)
                {
                    Dialog.alert("Vibrate supported");
                }

                // shows how to set the volume
                Alert.setVolume (100);
            }
        };

    private MenuItem startItem = new MenuItem("Start", 0, 0)
        {
            public void run()
            {
                Alert.startVibrate(1000);
            }
        };

    private MenuItem stopItem = new MenuItem("Stop", 1, 0)
        {
            public void run()
            {
                Alert.stopVibrate();
            }
        };

    public MasseuseScreen()
    {
        super();
        LabelField applicationTitle =
            new LabelField("Masseuse");
        setTitle(applicationTitle);
```

```
        }
    public boolean onClose()
    {
        Dialog.alert("What? Leaving so soon?");
        System.exit(0);
        return true;
    }

    // this overrides makeMenu in UIApplication, and gives ↵
you full control over the menu
    protected void makeMenu(Menu menu, int instance)
    {
        // this attempts to see if there are any context ↵
menus added, and makes sure that they are retained
        Field focus = UiApplication.getUiApplication()↵
.getActiveScreen().getLeafFieldWithFocus();
        if(focus != null) {
            ContextMenu contextMenu = focus.getContextMenu();
            if( !contextMenu.isEmpty()) {
                menu.add(contextMenu);
                menu.addSeparator();
            }
        }
        // here you add your own items
        menu.add(supportItem);
        menu.add(startItem);
        menu.add(stopItem);
        menu.add(_closeItem);
    }

    public boolean trackwheelClick( int status, int time )
    {
        Menu menu = new Menu();

        makeMenu(menu, 0);

        menu.show();

        return true;
    }

    public boolean trackwheelUnclick( int status, int time )
    {

        return true;
    }

    public boolean trackwheelRoll(int amount, int status, ↵
int time)
    {
        return false;
    }
    protected void onExit()
    {
```

```
            Dialog.alert("What? Leaving so soon?");
            System.exit(0);
    }
    public void vibrateDone(int reason)
    {
        // if the vibration ended because the duration was over
        // just restart it. Let it stop for all other reasons
        if (reason == AlertListener.REASON_COMPLETED)
        {
            Alert.startVibrate(1000);
        }
        return;
    }
    public void buzzerDone(int reason)
    {
        return;
    }
    public void audioDone(int reason)
    {
        return;
    }
}
```

Summary

In this chapter, you extended some of the same concepts covered in the previous PianoBerry chapter, but this time the end result is not a toy piano, but instead a personal vibrating massager! This is just another example of some of the creative things that you can pursue to make your BlackBerry do some pretty weird and unexpected things, if you are willing to get your hands dirty with a small amount of Java programming.

If you want to take Masseuse to the next level, here are some ideas to pursue:

- Provide onscreen controls.

- Provide visual feedback (via LED blink or other means) for when vibrate is on or off.

- Allow users to set a duration limit if they want (to ensure that the massage feature won't run down the battery if they forget to turn it off).

- Play a little nice background music by incorporating some of PianoBerry!

Printing Your
Notes Wirelessly

D espite the ongoing race to digitize everything from e-mail and documents to banking, commerce, books, music, and video, you will still find that there is still at least one printer in virtually every home, business, or office where there is a computer. Many predicted the demise of paper decades ago, yet here in the twenty-first century, printers continue to sell like hotcakes. Why? It turns out that the desire to print a hard copy, hold it in your hands, and read it comfortably continues to be more desirable than going blind squinting to read a two-inch square screen.

Most desktop and laptop users print something every day. With much of the same content being moved to handhelds and smartphones, the only reason people don't print from these mobile devices is because their handheld vendor did not include printing in the built-in feature set for their device. For me, if someone sends me a lengthy e-mail with a document attached to it and asks me to review and comment on it, the first thing I want to do is print it out on the nearest printer rather than going through the pain of reading it all on my tiny device.

In this chapter, I offer a remedy to the lack of printing capability on BlackBerry devices by showing you how to add Bluetooth printing. You will see how to open a Bluetooth connection, send data to a printer, and even add printing to the built-in MemoPad program.

Bluetooth Printers

Relative to other handheld devices, BlackBerry devices have a limited number of ways in which you can achieve a connection to a printer. Infrared is a built-in option for Palm, Windows Mobile, and most other device models, but no BlackBerry device to date includes an infrared port. The few commercial printing solutions that are out there employ a backend server host that requires you to route the data to the server where it is printed over the network to a target printer which must be registered for use with the specific service.

It is possible, however, to print directly from your BlackBerry device using the one local wireless option available to BlackBerry owners, namely Bluetooth. As you will see later, modern BlackBerry devices include Bluetooth radios, giving them the ability to wirelessly connect to other local Bluetooth-enabled devices, computers, and peripherals.

---

chapter 15

in this chapter

☑ Connecting to your printer

☑ Opening a serial port connection over Bluetooth

☑ Sending text to the printer

☑ Adding a custom menu to MemoPad

This begs the question, what printers support Bluetooth? While not widespread as a built-in printer feature, Bluetooth is available as a built-in option on many printers that are specifically aimed at the mobile user. Additionally, most desktop or network printers that do not include Bluetooth can be upgraded rather inexpensively by the addition of a Bluetooth "dongle," which plugs into the printer's parallel or USB port and upgrades the printer to support Bluetooth.

Printers with Built-In Bluetooth

Among business-oriented printers that support printing on normal letter-sized paper, the main choices are HP's Deskjet 450 or 460 models and Canon's i80 and i90 portable printers. These printers are inkjet printers that have been designed especially for mobile users in that they are portable, support battery power, and have built-in wireless connectivity. You also will find Bluetooth to be a common feature among specialty thermal printers, which generally print on roll paper and are used for printing receipts, labels, and barcodes in a retail or warehouse environment.

Bluetooth Printer Adapters

Although printer manufacturers have not seen sufficient demand to make them embed Bluetooth radios in their mass-market printers, as a result of continued rising interest in Bluetooth, a number of Bluetooth printer adapters have appeared on the market. HP's BT1300, as well as adapters from Belkin, Epson, IOGear, and others all allow you to add Bluetooth to your printer by plugging a *dongle* into the back of your printer. These adapters then act as the missing Bluetooth radio for your printer and route any print requests to it.

About Printer Drivers and Specific Printer Languages

This chapter gives you an overview of the basic techniques involved in wirelessly sending BlackBerry data to a "generic" HP-compatible printer, using either a Bluetooth or direct TCP connection. However, this demonstration blissfully ignores many issues you would face in creating a real-world printer driver for any given printer. Many printers, including a good number of HP models, will let you simply send unformatted text to the printer and will print it in a very generic fashion. But to get a printer to do much more than spew out some text, you need to learn to speak its command language. A command language is defined as the protocol for how to communicate with a target printer. For example, to tell an HP printer to switch from portrait to landscape, you need to send it the special command `ESC&l1O`. There are hundreds of special commands like this one that control all aspects of the printer's operation, from paper trays to image formats to font control and more. Although many printers from HP and other vendors have come to support HP's PCL command language, many other printers support PostScript or Epson languages. Still others, especially low-end ink-jet or photo printers, support sending data only in the form of an image of the page.

In this chapter, I ignore the issue of printer command languages other than the very basic commands needed to create a print job on an HP printer. In the real world, creating a commercial-quality printer driver involves understanding and implementing the native printer language of the printer to lay out a print job (for example, PCL or Postscript). It would also include support for fonts, image formats, sophisticated layouts, page sizes, margins, error conditions, and more. Although these matters are beyond the scope of this chapter, it still manages to demonstrate how to hack together a basic printing capability into your BlackBerry.

BlackBerry-Controlled Functions

In an effort to provide a measure of security on BlackBerry devices for users and wireless carriers, Research In Motion controls access to functions available to developers in the BlackBerry SDK. Any function can be called from a program within the BlackBerry Simulator, but when it comes to running a program on an actual BlackBerry device, certain families of functions are controlled for security purposes. This means that any application program that uses a protected function must be digitally signed before being loaded onto a device.

Now, as luck would have it if you are anxious to print, among the functions protected by RIM are those that enable direct Bluetooth communications. Accordingly, because you will be using these functions in this chapter, it is necessary to talk briefly about the signing process and how you go about obtaining a digital signature for your program.

Why Require a Digital Signature?

Of course, any obstacle that gets in the way of writing code results in a predictable chorus of groans, whining, and complaining from developers who simply don't want to be bothered. While a part of me is happy to add my own whiny voice to this chorus, the rest of me recognizes that the idea of keeping BlackBerry devices and the wireless networks they operate on safe is a pretty good one. It is also important to note that code signing isn't necessarily about having Big Brother look over your shoulder as your write your BlackBerry program. Rather, it's about assuring BlackBerry customers who download your program onto their device that they are really downloading what they think they are downloading. Without code signing, a malicious person could, in theory, take your program and patch it to do something horribly destructive with the connection that you allowed your program to open. Signing gives your users the knowledge that the program they are installing onto their BlackBerry is the exact same program you published, unmodified.

How to Sign Your Application

Before going to the trouble of obtaining a digital signature, make sure that you really need one. If you are just curious about network and Bluetooth functionality and have no intention of creating an application that runs on a real device, you do not need a digital signature. Simply take the code in this chapter and run it in the Simulator. As long as you run your program only in the Simulator, you do not need to sign it.

If you are sure you want to run your application on a real device, you first must register for a signature by completing the form at www.blackberry.com/developers. (A small fee is charged by RIM in order to obtain the signature.) When your registration is approved, you will receive an e-mail from Research In Motion that contains one or more .csi files as attachments. These files are then run on your desktop in order to complete the registration process by creating a private key and password.

This registration process has to be completed only once. After you have completed the registration process on your desktop, you can then sign your application from within the BlackBerry JDE by choosing the Build ⇨ Request Signatures menu item. This displays all of the program components that need to be signed and prompts you to submit a request for code signing. At this point you are prompted for the password you specified when you registered for code signing, and the JDE then goes out to the Internet, obtains the proper signatures, and signs your .cod file for your application.

Because every time you make changes to your code it changes its signature, you will need to reapply your digital signature to your application's .cod file every time you rebuild it and want to run it on your device. While this is bothersome to remember to do every time you build your program, the signing process takes less than a minute to complete so it is not too painful.

About Bluetooth on BlackBerry

Bluetooth is a wireless technology that allows mobile devices to communicate wirelessly with other Bluetooth-enabled computers, devices, and peripherals. As opposed to your phone's wireless GPRS connection, which lets you connect to the Internet via a cell tower that can be miles away, a Bluetooth connection is very short-range and is intended to allow connections between computers, devices, and peripherals that are within a range of 1 to 300 feet. (Your distance may vary depending on many factors including the device, the Bluetooth radio, and the presence of interference sources.) Intended as a replacement for cables between devices, Bluetooth is great for connecting multiple devices that are on your person, in your car, or in your room or office.

What You Can Do with Bluetooth on Your BlackBerry

When Bluetooth was first introduced years ago, industry pundits went a little bit (okay, a lot) off the deep end, imagining all kinds of ways that Bluetooth technology would change our lives for the better. One of the more amusing (but disturbingly common) predictions was that you would be walking through the shopping mall or an airport and your handheld would receive wireless transmissions of special ads and coupons, which were beamed at you from the merchants and shops all around you. I for one am thankful this particular scenario has not come to pass, and as it turns out, most of the more fanciful predictions about Bluetooth have been grounded more in fantasy than in fact.

Bluetooth also experienced some problems in the marketplace because it was confused with Wi-Fi. Often compared with Wi-Fi, it is true that there is a small amount of overlap in functionality between the two technologies. For example, although not nearly as popular as the Wi-Fi version, there are Bluetooth network access points you can buy and use as a wireless gateway to the Internet. Similarly, Wi-Fi can provide a way for two computers to connect with each other. But in general the two technologies do not really compete head to head. Wi-Fi is more powerful, supports a wider range, and is faster, making it more suitable for heavy-duty applications such as networking a group of computers together, downloading e-mail, or doing a large file transfer. Bluetooth, on the other hand, draws less power (and thus is friendlier for battery-powered devices), offers an easier way to make quick connections between multiple devices, and is installed as a feature on a considerable number of cell phones, PDAs, computers, and peripherals.

Despite the fact that it has yet to solve world hunger or put a man on Mars, Bluetooth has in the past five years carved out a useful niche in the world, focusing on the problem of *cable replacement*. Cable replacement is a term applied to Bluetooth that means that where two devices are connected by a communications cable, Bluetooth can replace that connection with a wireless one instead. A perfect example of cable replacement is a Bluetooth phone headset. Have you noticed an increase in the number of people walking around talking to themselves lately? No, the world's population is not losing its mind. If you look at these people more closely, what is usually happening is that they have a Bluetooth-enabled earpiece and a tiny microphone that lets them talk on their cell phones without having to hold the phone up to their head. In the old days, this same arrangement was possible, except that there would be a wire that ran up to the earpiece from the phone. Bluetooth replaces that wire so that the phone and headset are no longer tethered by a bothersome cable.

Bluetooth headsets have become very popular recently, no doubt in part because of new "hands-free" safety laws requiring that a headset be used if you are driving a car and talking on the phone at the same time. In addition to headsets, Bluetooth has found its way into other products of interest to BlackBerry users, including GPS headsets, car kits, and wireless adapters such as print adapters.

Which BlackBerry Devices Have a Bluetooth Radio

More recent BlackBerry devices such as the models 7130 and the 8700 come with Bluetooth radios as a built-in feature. Older devices that come with Bluetooth radios are the 7290 and the 7100 series, as well as the 7250 and the 7520 models. Given the growing popularity of hands-free phone headsets and other gadgets that employ Bluetooth, it seems a good bet that most devices moving forward will also come with Bluetooth.

Owners of models older than these are out of luck as they do not support Bluetooth, nor am I aware of any add-on adapters that add Bluetooth to these older device models.

Pairing with Bluetooth Devices

You connect two Bluetooth devices together (such as a BlackBerry and a printer) by first creating a *pairing*. A pairing is made when you identify another Bluetooth device and authorize your BlackBerry to allow a connection between your BlackBerry and the target device. Pairing is important because in an increasing world of Bluetooth devices, it allows you to designate which Bluetooth devices you are really interested in communicating with. Only after a pairing is successfully made can an application program make use of a communications channel between the two devices.

To pair your BlackBerry with a Bluetooth device, follow these steps:

1. Assuming that your BlackBerry device supports Bluetooth, a Bluetooth Settings screen is available in the BlackBerry Options program. When you select Bluetooth Settings, you are presented with a screen like the one pictured in Figure 15-1.

2. The first thing you need to do is to make sure your Bluetooth radio is enabled. By default, the Bluetooth radio is disabled because it can contribute to shorter battery life if it is constantly on. The Bluetooth radio is enabled by clicking the trackwheel menu and choosing the first option Enable Bluetooth.

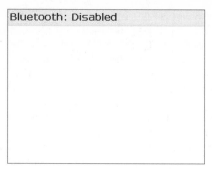

FIGURE 15-1: The Bluetooth Settings screen

3. After Bluetooth is enabled, you are able to add one or more device "pairings" to your Paired Device list. To add a paired device, click the trackwheel menu and choose Add Device. This initiates a search ("discovery" in Bluetooth parlance) for other Bluetooth devices that are in range of your BlackBerry, as shown in Figure 15-2.

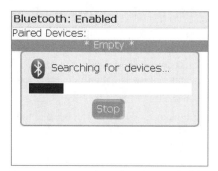

FIGURE 15-2: Searching for Bluetooth devices to pair with

If any available devices are found, your BlackBerry presents you with a screen showing a list of all of the devices it was able to identify. The names in the list can appear a bit strange. Depending on the device type, the name can be either manually assigned by a person, or an obscure product code or serial number. I will never forget the trade show I was at one year where I was demonstrating a phone solution involving Bluetooth, along with about 60 other vendors in the same pavilion. When I initiated a discovery, literally hundreds of Bluetooth devices were found. It took minutes for the phone to stop listing the devices it found, and the list was filled with so many obscure device names I had no idea which device I was trying to pair with! Let's hope your device's search will turn up only one or two devices, as shown in Figure 15-3, in which my BlackBerry found both my laptop as well as my Bluetooth-enabled printer.

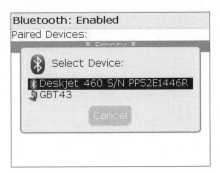

FIGURE 15-3: My BlackBerry discovers two Bluetooth devices nearby!

4. To complete a pairing with a selected Bluetooth device, you need to supply a passkey that authenticates you as a legitimate pairing partner for that device. For instance, if your laptop has a Bluetooth radio, you would configure your laptop to allow different kinds of connections from other Bluetooth computers and devices. Naturally you would want to establish some kind of security to prevent unauthorized access, so you would assign a passkey to protect your laptop. Any other computer or device would need to know your passkey in order to successfully connect to your laptop.

When trying to pair with a Bluetooth printer, you normally do not have an opportunity to assign a passkey to the printer, so what happens is that the manufacturer assigns a default passkey to its printer (for example "0000"). Some vendors give you a software utility that lets you change your printer passkey from your laptop with a USB cable, but because printers are not usually thought of as a high risk for security intrusions, generally the passkey remains the default. You will need to consult your printer's documentation in order to find your printer's default Bluetooth passkey.

Figure 15-4 shows the BlackBerry passkey screen.

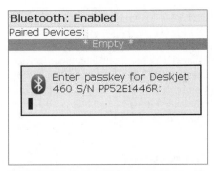

FIGURE 15-4: Connecting to my Bluetooth printer with my passkey

Once you've entered the correct passkey, you have established a successful pairing! As shown in Figure 15-5, your pairing appears in the Paired Devices list, and the pairing is remembered until you delete it. You do not need to re-establish the pairing each time you print.

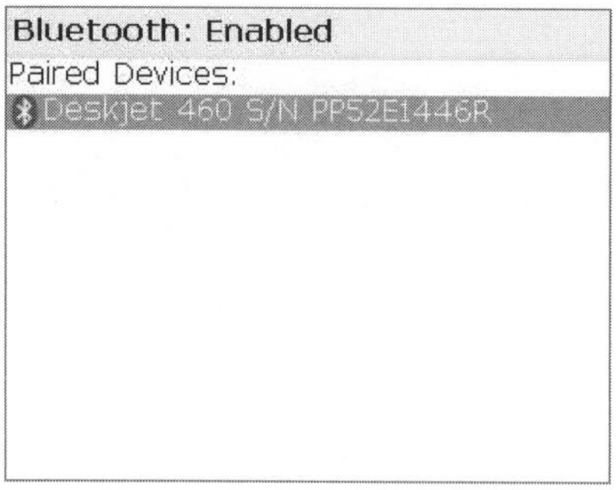

```
Bluetooth: Enabled
Paired Devices:
 Deskjet 460 S/N PP52E1446R
```

FIGURE 15-5: My BlackBerry is now paired with my printer.

Now that you have successfully created a pairing, you can look at information about the device pairing by selecting your pairing from the Paired Devices list and choosing the Properties menu item, as shown in Figure 15-5. The most interesting piece of information here is under Services, indicating that the one and only Bluetooth service available from my target Bluetooth printer is the Serial Port service. This probably doesn't sound too promising to you at this point, but as a matter of fact it's perfect. You will make excellent use of the Serial Port service in the next section!

Using a Bluetooth Connection from an Application

This section explores how to create a simple BlackBerry program, written in Java, that can make use of a Bluetooth pairing between your BlackBerry device and your Bluetooth printer by connecting to the printer and printing some text over that connection.

Although the program code you write will not be very complicated or lengthy, I will assume that you have at least a very basic knowledge of Java programming and an interest in working with the BlackBerry Java Development Environment (JDE) to write your own programs. For an introduction to the BlackBerry JDE and BlackBerry programming, please refer to Chapter 11, as this chapter builds on the basic concepts presented there. For the sake of space and clarity, only the most relevant portions of code are presented here on the printed page, but please note that complete source code for the program described in this chapter is available for download on the Wiley website at www.wiley.com/go/extremetech.

Bluetooth as a Serial Port Connection

From the perspective of a software application running on a BlackBerry device, a Bluetooth connection to a printer looks like an old-fashioned serial port. This concept is in line with Bluetooth's "cable replacement" goal, and it explains why the Serial Port Service displays when you pair your BlackBerry with a Bluetooth printer. Accordingly, in order to print, your program should logically have to perform the following steps:

1. Determine if there is an available serial port.

2. If available, open the port.

3. Send print commands and printable data to the printer via the open port.

4. Close the port.

Determining If a Serial Port Is Available

In the BlackBerry Software Development Kit, (SDK) a Bluetooth Serial Port is modeled in a Java class called (amazingly enough) `BluetoothSerialPort`. This class has a number of useful member functions, two of which you will use in your Bluetooth printing program.

The first member function is called `IsSupported`, and it returns TRUE if the host device supports a Bluetooth serial port connection. Although not required, it's a good idea to call this function before you attempt to open a serial port on the device.

The second function is called `getSerialPortInfo`, and it returns an array of `BluetoothSerialPortInfo` objects if it finds an available `BluetoothSerialPort` on your device. A `BluetoothSerialPort` would be available if you had one or more Bluetooth-paired devices on your BlackBerry. Although multiple pairings are possible, for simplicity's sake this little printing example will make a shortcut assumption that if at least one `BluetoothSerialPortInfo` object is returned, there is at least one available pairing and the program will simply use the first one.

Here is a short piece of code that shows how your program detects the presence of an available Bluetooth serial port:

```
// Call getSerialPortInfo to determine if any
// Bluetooth serial ports are available for you to use
BluetoothSerialPortInfo[] info = ↵
BluetoothSerialPort.getSerialPortInfo();
if( info == null || info.length == 0 )
{
    // no Bluetooth ports were found, give the user the bad
    // news
    Dialog.alert("No Bluetooth serial ports are available");
}
else
{
    // Great - a Bluetooth serial port is available!
}
```

If at least one `BluetoothSerialPortInfo` object was returned, you know that there is at least one available Bluetooth serial port from a pairing that exists on the device. Note that this does not imply anything about the ability to connect to the target Bluetooth printer other than the fact that a pairing was made at some point in the past and the paired device supports the Serial Port Service. At this moment in time, the actual target Bluetooth printer may not be in range, may be busy, or may even be turned off, but at least you know there is a valid pairing for it, so you can proceed and try to connect to it.

Opening a Bluetooth Serial Port Connection

The next step is to try to open a serial port connection using the first BluetoothSerialPort device that was returned from the call to getSerialPortInfo(). To accomplish this, you use the Connector class. The Connector class manages all kinds of BlackBerry connections, including those related to Bluetooth. You call the Connector class's static function open() and pass it the name of the target device and the mode in which you want to open the connection. For the name of the device, you pass the value returned by the BluetoothSerialPortInfo object's toString() method, and for the mode you will pass the Connector mode flag READ_WRITE, as follows:

```
bluetoothConnection =
    (StreamConnection)Connector.open( info[0].toString(),
    Connector.READ_WRITE );
```

If successful, Connector.open() returns an object of type StreamConnection that can then be used for managing both inbound and outbound data communications. If unsuccessful, Connector.open() typically throws a Java ConnectionNotFound exception or an IOException.

You are almost there. The last step in opening the connection for printing is to actually open an outgoing data stream that you can use to write bytes to the printer. A StreamConnection in and of itself does not have useful methods, but it is derived from an OutputConnection, and as such it inherits the method openDataOutputStream(), which is exactly what you are looking for. Opening a Bluetooth output stream is done like this:

```
outputStream = bluetoothConnection.openDataOutputStream();
```

If successful, openDataOutputStream returns a DataOutputStream object, which in this example means you are now ready to write data to the printer.

Writing Data to the Printer

Once you have a DataOutputStream object in your hands, writing text data to the printer is easy: Simply create strings containing the text you wish to print and pass the text to the printer using the DataOutputStream's writeChars() member function. For example, if I want to print a page that contains the text "Hello World," I use code such as the following:

```
// Create a string object with the text value I want to print
String value = "Hello World";
// write the string using DataOutputStream's writeChars() method
outputStream.writeChars(value);
```

Printer-Specific Commands

As mentioned earlier, this example ignores several real-world printing problems, and one of them is dealing with the many different kinds of printers that are out there. For many printers, it is perfectly valid to simply spew out text to them and they will print that text in a generic fashion. However, many printers require special codes for proper initialization. For example, to properly initialize an HP LaserJet printer, a program must begin the print job by sending the special code sequence ESC E. For other printer makes and models, different initialization codes may be required.

The `writeChars()` function will copy the value you provide to the `outputStream` variable, but this in and of itself does not guarantee that it will be immediately sent to the printer. This is because the `DataOutputStream` class buffers output for efficiency. Buffering means that `DataOutputStream` sends data out over a connection only when it has filled up its memory block with a specific count of bytes — kind of like waiting for a bucket to be completely filled with water before you dump it out. If you need your data to be sent immediately, you need to use the `flush()` member function, which forces `DataOutputStream` to send whatever it has in its memory buffer, regardless of whether it is full, like so:

```
outputStream.flush();
```

Putting It All Together

Pause here and take a look at what you have so far:

```
// Call getSerialPortInfo to determine if any
// Bluetooth serial ports are available for you to use
BluetoothSerialPortInfo[] info = ↵
BluetoothSerialPort.getSerialPortInfo();
if( info == null || info.length == 0 )
{
    // no Bluetooth ports were found, give the user the bad
    // news
    Dialog.alert("Sorry! No Bluetooth serial ports ↵
are available!");
}
else
{
    // Great - a Bluetooth serial port is available!
    bluetoothConnection =
        (StreamConnection)Connector.open(
        info[0].toString(), Connector.READ_WRITE );
    outputStream = bluetoothConnection.openDataOutputStream();
    // Create a string object with the text value I want to print
```

```
    String value = "Hello World";
    // write the string using DataOutputStream's writeChars()
    // method
    outputStream.writeChars(value);
    // flush the data out
    outputStream.flush();
    // close up shop, you are done!
    bluetoothConnection.close();
    outputStream.close();
}
```

Although you print only a trivial "Hello World" character string in the example, this is pretty much a ready-made printing function that will work for larger and more complex print jobs.

However, you need to take care of one more final detail before you are done, and that is to put the printing code inside of a thread. Now, if you are not an experienced programmer, topics such as threads and multitasking may sound complicated and scary, but for the purposes of this program, it's really not all that bad. To give a very brief and simple background, a thread can be thought of as a job or task that you do while you are also simultaneously doing another job. For example, at the same time as you read this page you are also breathing, your heart is beating, and maybe you are even listening to background music. Your brain is somehow able to do all of these tasks at once, without them interfering with one another. This is called multitasking, and computers multitask in the same way. A computer program can accept user input, perform calculations, display information, and wirelessly communicate with other computers and peripherals, all at the same time.

In order to multitask safely so that each of these tasks can work independently and does not interfere with any other task, a BlackBerry program uses a Thread class. A BlackBerry program always has at least one thread running, which is the main program thread. Your program can also create additional threads if it needs to initiate tasks that should not interfere with the main application thread. Here is a simple code snippet that illustrates how a thread is created in a BlackBerry program:

```
public MyApp()
{
    // other initialization code goes here
    // . . .
    // Start a new thread by creating an instance of the thread
    // class
    new MyThread().start();
}


// The thread class, derived from the basic Java Thread class
private class MyThread extends Thread
{
    public void run()
    {
        // Do stuff here
    }
}
```

In the preceding code example, any work that you wish done in the thread is performed inside the run() method of MyThread, and this work is done independently from any other tasks the program needs to take care of, such as writing to the display or accepting keyboard input.

Because the Bluetooth printing task is dependent on other factors, such as wireless connections as well as availability and responsiveness of the target printer, it is a great illustration of the threading technique. All you need to do is to take the code you previously developed to open, print, and close, and put that code inside of the thread's run() function, like so:

```
public BluetoothPrint()
{
    // other initialization code goes here
    // . . .
    // Start a new thread by creating an instance of the thread
    // class
    new PrintThread().start();
}


// The thread class, derived from the basic Java Thread class
private class PrintThread extends Thread
{
    public void run()
    {
            // Call getSerialPortInfo to determine if any
            // Bluetooth serial ports are available for you to use
            BluetoothSerialPortInfo[] info =
            BluetoothSerialPort.getSerialPortInfo();
            if( info == null || info.length == 0 )
            {
                // no Bluetooth ports were found, give the user
                // the bad news
                Dialog.alert("Sorry! No Bluetooth serial ↵
ports are available!");
            }
        else
        {
                // Great - a Bluetooth serial port is available!
                bluetoothConnection =
                (StreamConnection)Connector.open(
                info[0].toString(),
                Connector.READ_WRITE );
                outputStream = ↵
bluetoothConnection.openDataOutputStream();
                // Create a string object with the text value
                // I want to print
                String value = "Hello World";
                // write the string using DataOutputStream's
                // writeChars() method
                outputStream.writeChars(value);
                // flush the data out
                outputStream.flush();
```

```
                    // close up shop, you are done!
                    bluetoothConnection.close();
                    OutputStream.close();
                }
            }
    }
```

The complete program BluetoothPrint has a simple trackwheel menu that creates the `PrintThread` instance and then goes about connecting and printing.

Debugging BluetoothPrint

Unfortunately, Bluetooth communications are not supported at all within the BlackBerry simulator, so developers need to test and debug their programs on an actual device. This is an inconvenience and definitely makes for a slower edit-compile-test cycle during code development, but that's the way it is, at least for the currently available simulators from RIM.

To debug on the device, you can either sprinkle your program liberally with message boxes that will tell you what is happening inside the code, or you can actually conduct a complete debugging session with your device over USB from within the JDE debugger. In order to use this feature of the JDE, follow these steps:

1. Make sure your BlackBerry device is attached to your computer via the standard USB cable.

2. Make sure you have installed your program to the device. (The debugger will not do this for you!)

3. In the JDE choose Attach To ➪ Handheld from the Debug menu. If all goes well you will see a Debugger attaching screen on your device.

4. Set a breakpoint in your source code.

5. Go to the device and run your program. The JDE debugger follows your program's execution, just as it would if your program were running in the simulator.

Adding a Print Menu to the MemoPad Application

The printing demonstration program demonstrates how to connect to a printer, but it isn't terribly useful unless you like printing lots of paper with the words "Hello World" on it. Given a printing capability, what would be a useful thing to print from your BlackBerry? What if you were able to somehow gain access to some of the built-in application data that resides on the device, such as the notes stored in the MemoPad program? Even better yet, how about adding a Print menu to MemoPad itself so that the user could print right from within his or her memo? In this section I show you how to add your own menu to the MemoPad application that comes with every BlackBerry device and how to hook that menu to the printing code that you have already written.

Using the ApplicationMenuItemRepository Class

The BlackBerry SDK offers support for registering your own menu items, which will be added to the BlackBerry built-in applications. The `ApplicationMenuItemRepository` is a system service that tracks menu items registered for this purpose and the applications they belong to. Registering a menu item with the Repository involves the following steps:

1. Create an instance of your menu item object.

2. Obtain an instance object from the `ApplicationMenuItemRepository`.

3. Pass your menu item object to the `Repository` by calling `addMenuItem` along with the identifier for the built-in application view you wish to add your menu to.

Instantiating your menu item object is a little bit different than creating a standard menu item for your own program. The main difference is that your menu item class needs to be derived from an `ApplicationMenuItem` class, which is a special class that provides the functionality to extend application menus with custom menu items. The other difference is that your menu item's `run()` member function obtains the text of the memo item currently being viewed.

The following source code implements a menu item class that acts as the handler for a new Print Memo menu item that appears in the MemoPad's View screen when you choose the trackwheel menu:

```
// The MemoPadMenuItem class
private static class MemoPadMenuItem extends ApplicationMenuItem
{
    // Just call the default ApplicationMenuItem constructor.
    MemoPadMenuItem(int order)
    {
        super(order);
    }

    // The Run method is called when the menuItem is invoked by
    // the user, and passes a Memo
    public Object run(Object context)
    {
        // the Memo object is undefined by the BlackBerry SDK
        // so instead you will grab the text directly
        // from the MemoPad's input field onscreen.
        UiApplication uiApp =
        UiApplication.getUiApplication();
        Screen myScreen = uiApp.getActiveScreen();
        String theMemo = "The Memo is: " +
        myScreen.getFieldWithFocus();
        // prove that you got the text by displaying it in a
        // message box
        Dialog.alert(theMemo);

        // here is where you would print!
```

```
        return context;
    }

    // The toString method returns the name of the menu item
    // as it should appear in the MemoPad menu.
    public String toString()
    {
        return "Print Memo";
    }
}
```

All of the real action happens in the run() method, which gets kicked off any time your custom menu gets selected by the user. When this method gets called, your code is really in the context of the MemoPad View screen. Unfortunately RIM has not seen fit to document a Memo object; otherwise you would simply be able to reference the contents of the memo via the passed-in Object variable. Not to worry, however. You are able to hack around this problem by simply obtaining the onscreen field that has the focus and grabbing its text. Although not the most elegant solution, because the MemoPad's View screen just has the one input field, this technique will suffice, and indeed it works just fine.

The other interesting thing about the menu item class is the toString() method, which offers you the opportunity to give your custom menu item a name. This name will be the label for the custom menu item that appears within the MemoPad View menu. You can choose any label you like, but in this example, name the menu "Print Memo."

Now that you have a menu item class to handle the Print Memo menu from MemoPad, you need to register the menu with the ApplicationMenuItemRepository. (As with the Bluetooth SDK functionality described earlier, the ability to add custom menu items is understandably also a protected piece of functionality, and because of this you will need to register with RIM to obtain the ability to sign your code.) The following source code is called from the constructor of the BluetoothPrint application class. After it instantiates the Print Memo menu item class, it goes on to register the menu item with the ApplicationMenuItemRepository such that it is injected into the MemoPad View menu.

```
public BluetoothPrint()
{
    // Other program initialization code goes here . . .
    // Now create a menu item that will insert itself into
    // the BlackBerry MemoPad application
    MyMenuItem myMemoPadMenuitem = new MemoPadMenuItem(0);
    ApplicationMenuItemRepository instance = ↵
ApplicationMenuItemRepository.getInstance();
    instance.addMenuItem (ApplicationMenuItemRepository. ↵
MENUITEM_MEMO_VIEW,myMemoPadMenuitem);
}
```

Figure 15-6 shows the menu item appearing on the MemoPad menu for the View Memo screen. Figure 15-7 offers proof that you were able to successfully obtain the text for the currently selected memo item.

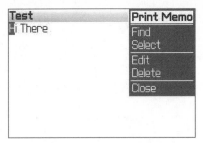

FIGURE 15-6: The custom Print Memo menu item appears in MemoPad's menu

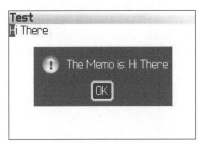

FIGURE 15-7: Successfully hacking into the MemoPad screen to obtain the memo text!

Adding the Print Function

The only thing left to do at this point is to add a call to the print function from within the Print Memo `run()` method. You do this by first retaining the memo text in a class variable where the threaded print function can access it.

Then you initiate printing the way you did earlier in the chapter by calling the following:

```
// copy the memo text into a class static variable
_theMemo = theMemo;
// start the print job
new PrintThread().start();
```

Now, inside of the `PrintThread` code, instead of printing the boring old "Hello World" text like this:

```
String value = "Hello World";
outputStream.writeChars(value);
```

you now print the memo as follows:

```
outputStream.writeChars(_theMemo);
```

More Uses for ApplicationMenuItems

The capability to add your own custom menu item to a built-in BlackBerry program is very powerful. In addition to the printing functionality covered in this chapter, I'm sure you can imagine all sorts of other useful things you could do if you had the ability to extend the built-in applications with your own menus. For example, imagine launching a map from within the Address Book given a contact's zip code!

Summary

This chapter covered quite a variety of topics, including Bluetooth communications, wireless printing, using digital signatures for protected areas of BlackBerry functionality, and even how to hack your own menu into a built-in BlackBerry application. Obviously each one of these topics is rich enough to fill a chapter by itself, if not more, and this chapter only scratches the surface on each of them in order to put together the BluetoothPrint demonstration printing program. Whether you decide to pursue more information on Bluetooth, printing, or application integration, the BlackBerry JDE and SDK documentation is a great place to go to learn more.

Index

How to take it to the Extreme.

If you enjoyed this book, there are many others like it for you. From *Podcasting* to *Hacking Firefox*, ExtremeTech books can fulfill your urge to hack, tweak and modify, providing the tech tips and tricks readers need to get the most out of their hi-tech lives.